ROCK LEGENDS
AT ROCKFIELD

ROCK LEGENDS AT ROCKFIELD

JEFF COLLINS

2022

www.uwp.co.uk

British Library Cataloguing-in-Publication Data
A catalogue record for this book is available from the British Library.

ISBN: 978-1-91527-904-0

Cover artwork by Andy Ward
Typeset by Agnes Graves
Printed by CPI Antony Rowe, Melksham, United Kingdom

The publisher acknowledges the financial support of the Books Council of Wales

CONTENTS

INTRODUCTION

This is the tale of a small farm in south Wales with big ideas.

Big ideas that turned into big success and put the studio's name at the forefront of rock legend.

I first visited Rockfield Studios in 2006 for a guided tour of the place where the great, the good and the bad of rock had spent time writing, recording and creating music that would make its mark on the world.

As a presenter of a rock show on FM radio, I had spoken to, and interviewed, numerous musicians, who had either recorded at Rockfield or dreamed of doing so. That was – and is – Rockfield's lure.

Any artist, or band, who has dreams of being part of rock folklore wants to record at this studio in Monmouth.

When I first wrote this book in the mid 00s, bands and musicians delighted in telling their stories of Rockfield. What they experienced there was always a highlight of their career.

Legends such as Rush, Motörhead and Robert Plant regaled me with their experiences there. Whether it was backstage at a gig chatting to Lemmy ahead of one of Motörhead's thunderous gigs or reuniting Robert Plant with his solo band for a catch-up on days gone by, all looked back fondly on their time together here in the studio.

As well as the rock legends, newer bands like the Tokyo Dragons would breathlessly try to explain to me how they could almost physically feel and absorb the heritage of the place.

Acts such as Coldplay would find inspiration in the studio's surroundings that would help them write the lyrics for worldwide hit singles. Sometimes, bands who found themselves at the studio at the same time would bond, either spending time drinking together or playing football matches on nearby fields against each other. At other times tensions between bands would spill over into physical altercations, whether it be Oasis ending up in a fist fight with another band or groups like Simple Minds and Judas Priest indulging in a food fight.

Occasionally the studio would hit the headlines for other reasons, such as when The Stone Roses were arrested there for taking revenge against a record company they felt had exploited them. Rockfield has seen it all.

Fifteen years after I first visited the studio to see where all this musical magic was made, I have spoken to bands and musicians who have recorded there in the last decade. In four new chapters, we hear from the likes of Thunder, Gun, The Damned, Opeth and Pixies, who share their reminiscences of life there. This time we'll also take a closer look at Rockfield's sister studio, Monnow Valley, which started out as its rehearsal studio before becoming famous in its own right, favoured by bands like Black Sabbath and Oasis.

We'll also see how Rockfield saw itself reaching new audiences, such as when it featured in a major Hollywood biopic about Queen as well as in a TV documentary.

So let's start at the beginning of my journey with my first trip to Rockfield Studios back in 2006 ...

CHAPTER ONE:
FROM SMALL ACORNS ...

**It really was a working dairy farm. They'd get us
to help them round up the cows ... There was a bit
of haymaking in the summer and we'd drink cider.
You just mucked in like one big happy family.**

Ray Martinez, Rockfield session guitarist

It is like that scene from the cult movie *Wayne's World*. I'm driving
along the M4 motorway from Cardiff, cheerfully singing along to one
of music's best-known songs as Freddie Mercury and Co move into
overdrive. Brian May's guitar is blasting out of my car speakers at an
ear-splitting level as the band reaches their crescendo. Roger Taylor's
drums are pounding in sync with John Deacon's booming bass line as
'Bohemian Rhapsody' moves into its beautiful finale.

With 'Bohemian Rhapsody' drawing to a close, I turn off the M4
and onto the A449 to Monmouth, heading for the very place this legendary song was recorded: Rockfield Studios here in Wales. I continue
to drive past miles of wide open countryside. A gorgeous expanse of
trees rushes by as the bright sunshine lights up the lush green mead-
ows and fields, which stretch as far as the eye can see.

'That's Queen at their very best,' the DJ on the classic rock station
Planet Rock informs me as I make my solitary journey to the world's
first, and most famous, residential studio. 'We've a classic from Black
Sabbath in a moment, but first here's 'Closer to the Heart' by Rush.'

It is like listening to Rockfield FM as song after song pumping out of my car stereo seems to be yet another famous tune from that studio. Whether it is Queen, Judas Priest, Robert Plant, Oasis or The Stone Roses, some of the world's most famous artists have recorded at the farm converted into a recording studio in the sleepy countryside, just outside the Welsh market town of Monmouth. Some of the world's best-known songs and albums were brought to life at these studios, which are now just a few more miles down the road. The beautiful landscape continues to roll past as I leave Raglan Castle in my wake, and by the time Black Sabbath and Ozzy Osbourne have kicked up a storm on the radio, it is the turn of Motörhead and 'Ace of Spades'.

I smile to myself as another band forged at Rockfield commandeers the airwaves. As a teenager I had bought record after record bearing the legend 'Recorded at Rockfield Studios, Wales'. It is not the kind of place you'd expect a whole host of classic albums to be made. It lacks the glitz and glamour associated with the bigger, richer studios based in the more fashionable cities of the world. So what is it about this rural studio that has captured the imagination of so many major bands? How could a small Welsh farm compete against some of the major names such as Abbey Road in London, George Martin's Air Studios (which started life in Montserrat before relocating to London), The Record Plant in Los Angeles or The Hit Factory in New York? This was something I was determined to find out. Rockfield has locked horns with these giants of the recording industry and more than held its own. In doing so, Rockfield has carved itself a major place in rock history.

I drive through the town of Monmouth and out the other side, where the roads become small lanes, and just ahead, I see a turning. There in front of me is a huge green sign at the bottom of a big driveway. It reads: 'Rockfield Studios – Video surveillance systems operating at all times.' Any worries I had about getting lost evaporate with a sigh of relief and no little excitement. I am here. I have arrived at the spiritual home of rock music from my youth.

I carry on up to the top of the drive and park up alongside one of the outlying accommodation blocks. The anticipation is building as my thoughts turn to how many famous musicians have trodden this well-worn path down to the studios. Following in their footsteps, I turn right into a large courtyard, which is the hub of the studio complex, to be greeted by an incongruous sight: right in the middle of the yard is a horse box! It is not the kind of vehicle you expect to see at a major recording studio. But that's the charm of Rockfield. Things here are done differently. Very differently. I look around the courtyard, known as the Quadrangle, and find the reception. Inside, Rockfield's owner, Kingsley Ward, is waiting to greet me and I find myself shaking the hand of the man who has been and continues to be at the centre of all that Rockfield has achieved. He's a friend to all the stars who stay here. Kingsley always wins over his rich and famous clients with his warm hospitality and friendly, easy-going style. No one who has recorded here has a bad word to say about him. And legend has it that the huge-selling album by the Canadian rock band, Rush, *A Farewell to Kings*, was named affectionately after him. It is not true, but when have facts ever got in the way of a good rumour!

After a warm welcome and introductions to his wife and daughter, who also work at the studio, Kingsley invites me down into the farmhouse for a cup of coffee, where he outlines the beginnings of this venture.

He tells me that he founded the two-studio facility back in 1963 along with his brother Charles, who passed away in 2022. Back then, it had the most basic of beginnings:

> All I can say is my brother Charles and me started off as a group back in the early 60s called the Charles Kingsley combo. We used to go to London to record all the time. But that was very time-consuming and we thought we'd be better off making our own records at home. And that's how we started really. We began in the loft just above us here and put a studio together – and it just expanded from there.

Over the years they added the Quadrangle and the Coach House studios, building them from redundant farm buildings with ingenuity, and an eye for detail, that has given Rockfield an edge over most – if not all – of its competitors. But, from the way Kingsley talks, it's clear the brothers had no idea just how big it would become.

Having started in the loft in this house, by 1965 we went to a granary and then a stable block. The Coach House studios, as they are now, were horse stables. I could go on for hours about how we got going and why, but basically it was pretty much because we had our own group, and it was easier than going to London. So we did it out of necessity. That's how we became the world's first residential studio. We made history, but unknowingly.

Coffee time over, Kingsley takes me on a tour of the studios. We enter the Coach House where Pedro Ferreira, who produced the hit album by The Darkness *Permission to Land*, is setting up the studio ready to record with Liverpool band The Maybes?. Kingsley watches Pedro through the thick glass panel which separates the imposing studio desk from the main recording area. Either side of the mixer are two huge speakers built into the wall, which resemble giant aircraft engines. 'It's a bit of history isn't it?' reflects Rockfield's owner. 'It's all happened in here. Oasis recorded here. Ozzy Osbourne did his first record here. That's going back a bit.'

Creating that history is something Kingsley and his brother took in their stride as the fledging studio started up. 'People just came to record here,' Kingsley says in a very matter-of-fact way. But it was clear that by the end of the 1960s the studio had become more than just the Ward brothers' personal plaything.

> All kinds of different bands in the 60s and 70s seemed to end up here, and it all took off and developed from there. As for the accommodation, it wasn't part of any great master plan. It was simply just to give people a place to stay. We mainly drifted around, while the whole project just got bigger.

Many of the early groups in the 1960s started their recording careers at the studios, including Amen Corner with Andy Fairweather Low, and a band called The Silence, who eventually became Mott the Hoople.

During its construction, the brothers saw no need to bring in designers and engineers from the outside. Instead, their plans involved the studios relying on the natural acoustics of the farm buildings to help capture the raw energy and sound of those recording at

Rockfield. Pedro Ferreira strolls into the control room to join us and tells me that he loves the old-style feel the studio has. 'Working in this environment is a dream. I really like to mix the old equipment and the new. Sometimes when people say Rockfield has vintage equipment, they can make it sound like a bad thing – but it's not. It has loads of great-sounding gear from way back, including the old tape machine in here, which is still working. As a result, I always lay down the tracks on tape first and then use the digital modern technology that's here – such as Pro Tools editing – to finish it all off.'

That history – in terms of both the artists and the equipment – is what makes the place stand out. It's like the Holy Grail of recording studios for some people. Jeff Touzeau, author of the book *Making Tracks: Unique Recording Studio*, says that in America Rockfield is considered an institution in rock music. But he marvels at the studio's success, given Kingsley and Charles Ward's insistence on not involving 'outsiders'!

> It is startling to me that Rockfield has achieved the success that it has, despite having a minimal degree of 'proper' acoustic design. Though funnily enough, this is how the design of Woodstock's famous Bearsville studio (used by The Band, The Rolling Stones, REM and Muddy Waters among others) evolved as well – through hanging and moving blankets by trial and error. This directly corresponds to Kingsley Ward's intuition, ingenuity and inventiveness. He is strictly non-conformist, and this is one example of his rebellious approach towards otherwise universally accepted studio design protocol. For him, none of the rules seemed to count ... even physical laws.

The name Rockfield is also hugely appropriate. It literally is rock music made in a field. The name, though, has a simple origin. Local rock star Dave Edmunds suggested that the studio adopt the name of the nearby village of Rockfield. It's often the simplest ideas that work best! Edmunds also became one of the first artists to be promoted by the studios, and was the musician who gave the studio its first hit record.

At that time in the late 1960s, Edmunds had started a band called

Love Sculpture, who had a tremendous influence on many groups starting in the early 1970s. They had a massive hit single with the song 'Sabre Dance'. This frenzied instrumental would turn out to be a favourite of many bands, who were later to choose to record at Rockfield. Love Sculpture and Dave Edmunds would become almost synonymous with the studio. To get their story, and the part they played in bringing a blossoming young Rockfield to the attention of a wider audience in the music world, I had to travel just a few miles away to another, smaller studio called Berry Hill.

The studio, on the edges of the Forest of Dean, was started by John David, who was with Edmunds in Love Sculpture, and later stayed on at Rockfield to produce many bands and write numerous hit records. When I catch up with him a few days later, he's sitting in a chair in the main studio at Berry Hill in a dark shirt, blue fleece, jeans and brown trainers. The studio walls are covered with gold and silver records from the bands he's produced and written for over the years, including the likes of Status Quo, Cliff Richard and Sam Fox. There are also signed photographs from Ozzy Osbourne and Catatonia, among others, proudly on display. John explains how he fell in with Dave Edmunds and Love Sculpture.

> I was a drummer and I really wanted to be in a rock band – like a Shadows type band – so I bluffed my way into Dave Edmunds' group. He was looking for a bass player, so I went out and bought myself a bass guitar, learnt it real quick and then I went to see him at a gig he was doing at Cardiff Castle. Back then, I used to dress like a highwayman – which was a bit stupid – but that's the look I went for. There was another guy called John McFadden, who was a proper bass player, and he was up for the audition as well. But I could see Edmunds looking across the dance floor at me. The way I was dressed he must have thought 'What a twat. I've got to have him.' So he came across and asked me to join on the spot.

The band was essentially a showpiece for Edmunds' considerable technical ability on the guitar and they played, mainly, highly revved-up blues covers. 'Sabre Dance' was to become their signature tune and would be the band's finest hour. The song, a reworking of a classical melody by Russian composer Aram Ilyich Khachaturian, was a six-minute guitar maelstrom. It was broken by legendary BBC Radio One DJ John Peel, whose support turned it into a big hit.

John David recalls,

> John Peel didn't always get to hear what he was going to play before he played it. So, on a busy show, he'd sometimes rely on a producer to check stuff for him. At that time, on this particular live show, John hadn't heard 'Sabre Dance', but when he put it on he was just blown away! He told his audience, 'Wow. That's Love Sculpture. And believe it or not, there are only three of them making all that sound. I'm so amazed I'm going to see if I can play that again.' And he had to get permission, because it was six minutes long. But he comes back at the end of the show and says on-air, 'I've got the OK. So I am going to play it once more. This is Love Sculpture and 'Sabre Dance' and I advise you all to go out and buy this.'
>
> Well, EMI phoned us up the next day and asked us to get up to London quickly so they could put it out as a single. We went to Advision studios in London at 9 o'clock on a Monday morning, green as grass, and whacked this single down. It was out in a week. It was selling – within 48 hours – 40,000 copies a day and went to number 2. And I don't think John Peel ever liked the fact he had that much power. He only had to say the word and people would go out and buy stuff.

It was after the success of 'Sabre Dance' that Edmunds and John David would become almost permanent fixtures at Rockfield for the next few years.

> I think, first of all, we did try to record 'Sabre Dance' in Rockfield [John recalls]. But we did other stuff there as well. We were trying to find out what would make a single. We did a few more things at Rockfield, but Love Sculpture were a one-hit wonder really. The band did a tour of America, but it was the

end of the road for Love Sculpture.

Overall though, John David enjoyed his time with them. It was a period in his career, which set both him and Edmunds on course for Rockfield and even more success. It was now that the studio was to score its first big hit, thanks to Edmunds' first solo record. He and John David travelled to Rockfield to put together their next project. But, back in the late 1960s, even travelling to the studios from nearby Cardiff was no easy thing. John David remembers that he and Edmunds later bought houses in Monmouth to be nearer to the studios.

> Back then there was no motorway link. So we'd drive up from Cardiff in this old van, which was pretty awful, and navigate these tiny, winding old roads through the pretty towns of Caerleon and Usk. It would take forever. I think the journey lasted more than an hour and a half, whereas now it is around half an hour. At the time, Dave knew Rockfield's owner, Kingsley, before I joined. When we went up to try out 'Sabre Dance' and some other material, it all looked very hi-tech to me, but it was just a potato loft with two tape machines in. By the time Love Sculpture had folded, though, they'd moved the studio down into what was an old granary or pig-shed, I can't remember which. They were moving up in the world. They did this next studio – called The Coach House – much better and it really looked like a proper studio. Instead of the two tape machines upstairs, they now had an eight-track tape machine. Kingsley also gave us downtime to record. He often does that if he believes in someone. He's very altruistic like that is Kingsley. He just told us to use the studio and see what we could come up with.

By then it was just John David and Dave Edmunds. They would take it in turns to produce and play the instruments. It was Dave, though, who came up with the idea of recording a version of 'I Hear You Knocking' after he picked up on the old Smiley Lewis blues version. John David leans across to pick up an acoustic guitar, which is resting up against the studio mixing desk, and starts strumming away. 'I don't know whether you've heard it, but it's like a Fats Domino/New Orleans type thing.' John gently plucks a standard blues beat and sings the opening lines of what became the Christmas Number One single in 1970.

He then pauses as he remembers the different musical components that would be welded together to make the hit single, and then starts playing once more.

> We crossed that with the tune from another song. We were driving around on the outskirts of Cardiff one day, when this song came on by a one-man band called Wilbert Harrison, who played bass with his toe, a washboard thing with his elbow, and also the guitar. It was a song called 'Let's Work Together', which loads of people have since covered. Bryan Ferry did a version, which he called 'Let's Stick Together'.

He smiles at the memory of putting the track together.

> We got all the guitars and drums down. Then Dave would overdub a steel guitar, and all kinds of other stuff. It was good, but nothing special.

So the duo drafted in local guitarist Mickey Gee to play lead guitar. There was only one problem. He'd never heard the track before! 'Dave simply told him "It's an E, but it starts in F-sharp," recalls John.

He pressed record on the tape machine, and as soon as the track started, Mickey started playing. But because he hadn't heard the song, he didn't know what he was supposed to play. He wasn't sure where it was going. That's why he played that distinctive long, drawn-out guitar twang you can hear. It was to give him time to figure out what was coming next. But as fortune had it, it turned out to be a classic guitar line. Dave was so excited he turned off the tape machine, without thinking, to tell Mickey how brilliant he thought it sounded. And Mickey said, 'If you want me to play the rest, hadn't you better turn the machine back on?' Dave hadn't realised what he'd done. Later I put some percussion on the track by improvising. I had an old microphone with an ordinary grill, but a flat top. So I just scrubbed a guitar plectrum across the top of it to make a percussive noise. We put that in.

With the song wrapped up at Rockfield and ready to be released, Dave Edmunds and John David had a stroke of luck that was to help propel the record to major success and put Rockfield's name at the top of the charts.

Gordon Mills, who was Tom Jones' manager, was starting a record label called MAM, which stood for Management, Agency and Music. He was looking for something special to be the label's first single. He had heard the early tapes of 'I Hear You Knocking' and decided that this was to be the one. Mills was a big player in the music business with a host of big names on his books. His backing was the break Dave Edmunds and John David needed to get the song maximum exposure. John David was delighted. 'There's so much luck involved. I always say in this business if you get anywhere it's 99 per cent luck. For us, we were lucky that Gordon came along and really pushed the song and the rest is history.'

'I Hear You Knocking' went to number one for six weeks in the UK and to number one for two weeks in America. But Dave Edmunds stalled on a follow-up to capitalise on the song's success. 'He didn't want to be seen to be jumping on the bandwagon and selling out,' recalls John David. 'It was a big thing in the early 70s not to be seen to be selling out, which was so naïve really. What we should have done was put something else out straight away. But we didn't.'

Edmunds stayed at Rockfield for a few years recording his own songs and producing other bands. He taught himself all the studio techniques he needed to create his own wall of sound, similar to that of his hero, the legendary American producer Phil Spector. John David also started producing records at Rockfield and started writing songs as well. More than 200 artists worldwide would record John's songs and he'd also go on to perform as a musician with the likes of Eric Clapton, Bruce Springsteen, Sting and George Harrison.

With the ball now rolling, another early band to make its mark at Rockfield was a group called Spring. Down the years members of the band would eventually become key components of the Rockfield story, and the way they found themselves involved with the blossoming Welsh studio is typical of the way much happens at Rockfield. The band's long love affair with the studio would develop after fate delivered them into the hands of Rockfield, following a concert in Cardiff in 1970. On the way back from the gig, the Spring touring van broke down, leaving the band stranded. Then, as luck would have it, the first car to stop and help them was one driven by Kingsley Ward! The Rockfield owner had, ironically, been on an unsuccessful scouting mission looking for local musical talent. With Spring handed to him on a plate, he invited the band back to the studio, where they ended up staying and recording an album with Elton John's long-time producer Gus Dudgeon. When the band split up some time later, various members remained at the studios to pursue careers there instead. Vocalist Pat Moran became one of Rockfield's engineers and producers. Ray Martinez also found the lure of Rockfield too strong to resist. He remembers clearly his first impressions of the place:

I had answered an advert in the *Melody Maker* – the music bible in those days – and it turned out to be from a band called Spring. Up to that point, I'd been working in Italy with Pick Withers, who'd later join Dire Straits. We both decided that we'd had enough of the Italian scene, as we'd been there a few years, and felt we should come back to the UK. By chance we both ended up joining Spring – but at different times. I'd not had a lot of experience in studios when I first came to Rockfield. I'd been in RCA's Italian studios in Rome to record, which was a massive modern studio. But when I got down to Monmouth it was a slightly different ball game. Here were these converted stables, and inside was the studio and control room. But you had things like home-made, makeshift screens and mattresses to dampen the sound down. It was wild really. Eventually when I parted company with Spring, I played with another band for 18 months. But I came back to Wales as I was really attracted to learning the recording side of things. So Kingsley eventually found a position for me as a house musician. I was a guitarist doing sessions and making records.

Ray returned to Rockfield in mid 1973 and did session work there for ten years, working with the likes of Iggy Pop, The Searchers, The Teardrop Explodes, Echo and the Bunnymen, and Michael Chapman. 'I loved working with Michael, who was a big folk guy,' says Ray.

> He was a real character from the north of England. He was from near Carlisle, and he said that if ever I wanted to go and visit him I should just walk up the M6 into Carlisle, then turn right and I'd find the key under the doormat.

By the early 1970s, Rockfield was really starting to develop. The brothers added to the one main studio, the Coach House, by developing the Quadrangle studio in 1973. The Quadrangle is a large courtyard surrounded by buildings on four sides. Today, as you enter from the driveway, the left-hand side consists of echo chambers and equipment stores. In front of you there is the residential accommodation and the dining room for the bands staying there, while to the right is the main studio, which is connected, via underground cables, to the echo chambers directly opposite. The last remaining side also contains accommodation, as well as horse stables and the studio's reception and office. The Quadrangle had been a series of run-down equestrian buildings and stables. Now it is the studio's showpiece.

By 1975, Rockfield had acquired a strong reputation. Bands were flocking to the two studios, which were being hired out at a premium rate. The groups and artists were paying for the best. Rockfield had three maintenance men on call 24 hours a day and its own cordon bleu chef. The food became the stuff of legend. One story has it that the Welsh indie-rock group the Super Furry Animals decided to write a song about their recording time at Rockfield in the 1990s and composed one about the meals at the studio. The song 'Guacamole' is allegedly about the studio cooks putting the Mexican delicacy on every plate of food served there. Throughout the 1970s, there was no expense spared as Rockfield was kitted out with state-of-the-art recording equipment. As a result, the studio attracted more and more famous artists, and its reputation spread worldwide. Big bands like Queen and Rush and artists like David Bowie, Iggy Pop and Phil Collins were all coming down to Rockfield to work. By the late 1970s well-known bands from America were also starting to arrive in Wales. Rockfield's growing musical heritage meant bands were desperate to come over and record in the same studio where Queen had created *A Night at the Opera*.

Producer Pedro Ferreira recognises that the legacy of Rockfield has many bands drooling at the prospect of recording there:

> It has a massive heritage, which I was very aware of when I arrived here for the first time. It's the same for a producer as it is for a musician. I think a lot of the people, who have been here, are big fans of the groups and music that was recorded here in the past. That's one of the reasons I like this studio. And the bands, as soon as they get here, get very excited. That's part of it really.

These bands would move heaven and earth to persuade their managers and record companies that Rockfield was the place to be. John David remembers working at the studio as it was becoming clear that it was probably the best-known residential studio in the world.

> Lots of residential studios sprang up in the late 70s and early 80s, like Ridge Farm in Sussex. But the problem for them was that they had to buy land and get mortgages. In 2002 Ridge Farm closed down after 28 years in business. It's very sad. But the advantage Kingsley and Charles had over most residential studios was that they owned Rockfield outright. So they didn't have the overheads. And they also later bought the Old Mill House at Monnow Valley, just down the road, originally as a rehearsal studio, so the bands could practise there and then record at Rockfield. And that's what they did for a long time. Everyone from Black Sabbath onwards, they would all rehearse down at the Old Mill House and then head up to Rockfield. Later when the place was split up between the two brothers, Kingsley ended up with the main house, the Rockfield studio blocks and a couple of fields. Charles had the rest of it, including the Old Mill House, which became Monnow Valley recording studio.

He built it, almost, on his own. It took him probably two to three years. In fact, it took him nine months just to build the con-servatory. The pillars are concrete posts, which have been carved to look like oak trees. By the 80s, even Monnow Valley had got a great name with bands like Catatonia and Oasis recording there. But I don't think Charles wanted to run a studio in the end. He was very artistic and just liked to paint. So about five years ago, he sold it to a guy in Cardiff and now I believe it's up for sale again.

The person who would go on to buy the Studios this time was the current owner Jo Riou, who we'll discover more about in chapter thirteen. By the early 1970s life at Rockfield was a ball. Despite the famous names, who were recording there non-stop, Rockfield had a relaxed, informal feel. There was no security and no video cameras, such as the studio has fitted today. Back then, there were no signs to say what Rockfield was, so people who worked there, or used the place, would walk in and out as they pleased. John David says the groups who came there seemed not to mind that much.

That was one of the joys of Rockfield. It had a very friendly atmosphere. And although the equipment was second to none, the place itself was just thrown together. It was a farm that had become a studio and it felt very homely. Charles built most of the stuff. But he wasn't really interested in the running of the studio. He just pottered about. If it was broke, he'd fix it, or paint it. From the outside, it didn't look like a proper recording studio that you'd see in a magazine, but on the inside, it was the bee's knees.

Far from being an ordinary studio, for much of the time Rockfield was also a working farm. John David recalls Kingsley was always mixing the farming and the recording:

> Having spent some time down at the farm, Kingsley used to come into the studio stinking of cow shit to watch people recording and to chat to the bands. Sometimes if it looked like rain, he'd come into the studio and ask for volunteers to help out on the farm. No matter how big the band was, they'd be asked to help. We'd all go out – the band, producer, everyone – and bring in the hay and load the bales.

Ray Martinez was one of those musicians who didn't mind being asked to help out.

> It really was a working dairy farm at the time. Both Kingsley and Charles were working hard doing the milking and whatever else was needed, while also running a studio at the same time. It was all very primitive really, but it worked. Occasionally they'd get us to help them round up the cows now and again. There was a bit of haymaking in the summer and we'd drink cider and all that. It was fun. You just mucked in like one big happy family.

There aren't many recording studios where rock stars get to become farmhands for the day. But Kingsley's way of running the studio is unique and John David is full of praise for the way he controls Rockfield. 'Kingsley is the arch motivator. His ambition is limitless and he's always really enthusiastic. He's one of the most eccentric people I know, though he's also such an infectious character.'

Ray Martinez was also taken by Kingsley's distinctive way of doing things:

> His attitude is very bold. He used to walk into any record company managing director's office with a Mickey Mouse T-shirt on, and tell them in no uncertain terms 'Here I am. This is what I've got.' He'd cut the bullshit. He didn't creep around people, but always went straight for the top guy and treated them the same way he'd treat anyone else. So he got through loads of doors that way. But it's not what you expect from the head of a major recording studio.

John David remembers a particular incident where Kingsley left the suits at a big record label with their jaws dropped in disbelief:

> We went up to a meeting at Phonogram Records in around 1977. Once inside, he did a handstand on a boardroom table! He just went through these double doors that he'd picked at random. Inside there was this high-powered meeting going on but,

unfazed, Kingsley just did a headstand on the table, looked at these guys, said 'sorry' three times and came out again. I mean you just don't do that. It was the board of Phonogram! But, yeah, he's funny and he hasn't changed a bit, he's still exactly the same. And the studio's doing well again. There was a dip when Napster was about and records weren't selling as downloads started to take off. That meant bands weren't spending much money at studios. But now it looks like it's turned a corner and people are using studios again. If you're a big band you need that kind of facility, particularly when you're on that higher level. I mean, on the lower levels of success, you can come here to Berry Hill Studio, which is a similar size, but we've nowhere near as much equipment as Rockfield. Overall, I think Kingsley wanted Rockfield to be a Motown kind of place, where you have lots of artists, producers and writers all working in the one place. He's full of ideas.

One of those ideas was to create a permanent landing strip at Rockfield to help the more famous American bands bring their equipment over by plane. Farm. Studio. And airport! Surely not? But nothing was too extreme for Kingsley and Rockfield. John David sits back in his chair for a moment, and smiles gently, as he recalls the chaos of Rockfield's foray into air travel. It all started with a guy called Jim Buckingham.

Commander Jim we used to call him. He managed a female singer, who recorded there. He used to come over from Bristol in his own plane and land it in the field at the side of the studio. He was a strange character. He was as nice as pie and always immac- ulately turned out with Brylcreem in his hair, wearing a sport jacket and grey flannels. He was very suave. As I say, he used to turn up in this rickety old plane, which he'd been restoring at his flying club in Bristol.

So he'd come over to Rockfield, land the plane, and this girl would record and then they'd both take off and fly home. I always thought that there was not enough room for this. But Kingsley had been talking to some guy in Los Angeles – some manager of a big American band – who was planning to fly stuff down from London in a plane called a de Havilland Twin Otter. This was a big Canadian-made plane, which could hold around twenty passengers, plus masses of equipment. To land at Rockfield though, they'd need twice the length of field we'd used before. So Kingsley had the Post Office move the telegraph poles and then he took out a hedge separating two fields, in order to make one long landing strip.

Now, it was always an event when Jim came over. People would always stop what they were doing and come out of the studios to watch. They'd just be waiting for something to happen. First of all, he came over in the little plane to check out the new landing area. Well, that day the wind was blowing fiercely up the drive. Now the drive from the main road to the studio is only about 100 yards long, if that. So he had us all pull the plane right up to the studio wall, so that the back wheel of the plane was touching the building.

He said 'I've got to take off that way, because the wind is blowing that way.'

And we thought 'Well hang on. There's only 100 yards to take off and then there's a tree and a hill on the other side of the road. There's no way he can make it!'

But he reassured us that he'd be fine and could manage it. We found it hilarious. I mean we shouldn't have, but we did. Anyway despite our laughter, and our fears I guess, he did make it, but how he took off in that space I'll never know, as the wind was so strong.

Anyway later he came back over in this big twin-engined plane and landed OK. We all went out to have a look and, to me, it seemed like a rather big plane to be landing in a couple of fields. But when it was time for him to go, he turned the plane around and started going down across the fields, and although Kingsley had mown the grass, it must have been slowing him down. You could see him trying to get off, but the plane bounced and went up, and came down again, bounced up once more and back down again. Now things were getting close, as all this time, the hedge at the end of the second field was looming, as was a road with cars going up and down it. You could see branches and stuff getting hit by the plane and you could hear them all snapping as he sunk down the dip at the other side. We were expecting a crashing sound, you know, but suddenly you could see him climbing up. There was the plane taking off with branches trailing from the wheels and you could see Jim in the cockpit shaking his head, with a thumbs down sign.

So that was the end of that. They never did fly stuff into Rockfield. But we did get raided by the police and Customs and Immigration. They thought we were bringing in illegal immigrants. It was hilarious. They had all these people staked out in the bushes and behind trees. I don't know why they thought people couldn't see them, because it's the country and we could see all around. And these Customs guys and police officers sitting in bushes stuck out like a sore thumb. That was the Jim Buckingham saga!

Another of Kingsley's ideas saw Rockfield accidentally create its own hit band, Airwaves. In 1976, Kingsley had the idea of making a video of the studio in action. The plan was to take the finished film to Los Angeles to try to attract American bands to the studio at a time when the exchange rate with the dollar was a good one for US groups, who could save money by coming to Wales. John David was producing at the studios and found himself caught up in the middle of Kingsley's plan:

He wanted to make this video and he said to a few of us, 'Can you pretend to be a band?' So there was me, Ray Martinez, engineer Dave Charles and producer Pat Moran, all playing instruments and pretending to be in a group recording one of my songs. All the while, they filmed us recording my song and mixing it. Much later when it was done and dusted, we were in the Coach House studio doing something at about 1 o'clock in the morning, when Kingsley phoned up from LA and said 'You'll never guess what? I haven't got anyone for the studio yet, but Joe Smith – who is head of Elektra Records – wants the band.'

My first reaction was 'Shit! There is no band. Not really.'

Then Kingsley said 'What's more, he's willing to pay three quarters of a million dollars and you only have to do one album a year and one tour a year of America.'

So I told him to take it. He said that he would and would call me later to let me know.

Anyway he called back two hours later, at 3 a.m. in the morning, and said 'You'll never believe this? Jerry Moss, who owns A&M records, has upped the bid. He'll give us one and quarter million dollars. You only have to put an album out every 18 months and you don't have to tour at all.' So we said 'Even better! Take it!' It was crazy. Total madness and looking back we should have taken the first deal, because A&M thought they could break America with just records. But we should have done what Elektra wanted and toured America. We'd have probably done better. We did two albums in the end, which did OK, though they were not hugely successful. But some of the songs have been covered by other people. One of my songs from those albums, *New Day*, has been cut by probably 80 or more artists, mainly choirs, as it sounds like a hymn. I remember Robert Palmer did one and Showaddywaddy covered another. So it was useful in getting my profile up as a songwriter.

Ray Martinez was equally as astonished by the turn of events surrounding Airwaves.

It was unbelievable. This record company in America sent us this massive cheque, but we hadn't done anything and we were definitely not going to go on tour. We didn't really want to leave the safety of the studio, because we weren't a proper band.

Of the Airwaves foursome, Dave Charles, just like John David, Ray Martinez and Pat Moran, would become an almost permanent fixture, over the years, at Rockfield. Dave first came across the studios when he was with the country rock outfit Help Yourself, who began recording there. Dave would slip away during sessions to help out producing other bands and it wasn't long before he drifted into the Rockfield way of life.

The story has it that when Dave arrived for his first proper day at work, he found the studios empty. Bemused, he searched the farm for his co-workers only to find them down by the Coach House, milling around an old shed. It was a picture of inactivity and Dave was told, in all seriousness, that this was an example of the traditional country pursuit of shed watching. Who knows what was happening there – if anything at all! It's a typical example of how life on a farm collides with life as a rock star in an almost surreal way at Rockfield.

Kingsley also wanted to capitalise on that country lifestyle for those artists who stayed there. He introduced fishing and pony-trekking, among other country pursuits. John David also recalls that he decided to set up trap shooting for the bands. 'It was just a lunatic idea. It was set up outside the back of the kitchen, where the patio doors are. The trap shooting was rigged up there and he gave the bands shotguns. I mean, drunken bands at one o'clock in the morning trying to hit clay pigeons in the dark. With guns! It was nutty, absolutely nutty.'

Also hugely popular at the studios were the regular football match-es. Top American producer Jack Endino was recording with the Irish rock band Kerbdog in the 1990s and remembers fondly the football contests held on the fields surrounding Rockfield. It was at the same time that Brazilian heavy metal band Sepultura were also staying there working on their *Chaos A.D.* album.

Well, there were two studios, the Coach House and the Quadrangle. We were mixing in the Coach House, while Sepultura were re-cording in Quadrangle with producer Andy Wallace. I had met the Sepultura guys before then, in Brazil, so it was cool to see them again. It was great watching the two bands playing football togeth-er. It was these pale Irish guys against these tough Brazilians. No contest really. But I was thinking, 'I'm a Seattle guy, and here I am in Wales, watching an Irish and a Brazilian band play football at the studio where Budgie recorded those great albums in the 70s. How did I get here?' It was a friendly place, very relaxing.

John David, though, remembers that not all the Americans got the hang of football – or soccer as they call it.

For the football, there'd be the Rockfield people, like me and Pat Moran, on one team. We were supposed to be recording and spending the record company's money, but we'd all stop for a kick-about, which was great fun. And then there were the groups – whoever they were – as the opposing team. I remember one team was Huey Lewis and the News – but I think back then they were called Clover. There was about six of them, plus roadies. But they were all American and kept catching the ball as if they were playing American football or gridiron. We just couldn't get it over to them that in soccer they couldn't touch the ball with their hands. America hadn't really seen much soccer at this stage. We kept trying to explain to them, 'You've got to kick it to the next person.' But – despite our detailed explanations – they always caught it! It was frustrating, but hilarious. Mutt Lange, the famous producer, was on this team as well. And Mutt, being Mutt, is such a perfectionist that he took everything so seriously. It wasn't just a game to him. If he lost he was devastated. It was very funny.

He chuckles at the memory before remembering another famous artist, who didn't really get the hang of 'the beautiful game'.

Ozzy Osbourne didn't have much of a clue really. He used to wear these black tights – like leotard tights – and Doc Marten boots with a gigantic white T-shirt. And that was his kit! He nearly broke my bloody ankle one day, when the Rockfield crew were playing Black Sabbath – minus drummer Bill Ward, who was on the sidelines drinking cider! It wasn't really a tackle from Ozzy, but a mistimed kick. He knocked me flying. He was the worst football player you've ever seen in your life!

It wasn't just the football that could lead the musicians astray. Just like being on the road, drugs and booze also played an integral part of studio life. When asked about the experience of working at Rockfield, one of the most common opening statements I've encountered from the artists and staff alike is: 'It's all a bit hazy as we did a lot of drugs back then.' It's not unheard of, of course, for groups to turn to drink and drugs to ease the monotony of life on tour, or in the studio, or simply to cope with the pressure of recording a hit song or album. And life at Rockfield was no different. Ray Martinez recalls that sessions were frequently helped along with a drop of alcohol or three!

There was a lot of drugs and boozing going on. I did one session for Iggy Pop in the 80s. He came into the studio carrying a bag crammed full of wine for the afternoon session. He really was a regular guy, though, despite his wild man image on stage. And I remember in the 70s, Shakin' Stevens came down very early in his career, when it was still Shakin' Stevens and the Sunsets. Dave Edmunds was producing them and they were due to start at 9 o'clock in the night. I remember their van pulling up dead on time. The group poured out of it and started to carry crates of ale into the studio. They were taking through crate after crate after crate for their recording session. I rubbed my hands together and thought, 'Here we go! This session's going to be a real humdinger!'

It all helped to oil the wheels and encourage friendships, as bands recording at Rockfield mingled and shared stories – such as the time when Black Sabbath and Hawkwind smoked a few joints together in the Coach House accommodation in the early 1970s. And Lee Slater, a guitarist with the band put together by former Iron Maiden singer Paul Di'Anno, was gobsmacked to meet one of his heroes when rehearsing there in 1982.

We were there for a few weeks doing a demo for what was to become Di'Anno's first album after leaving Maiden. We were relaxing one night when in walks Robert Plant! He came in to say hello, and at the same time he dropped us a case of twenty-four lagers for us to enjoy. We had a chat about our band, the studio, Led Zeppelin (of course!!) and what he was doing at the time. To be honest, most of the time my chin was on the floor in amazement that Robert Plant had walked in with a case of beer and said, 'Hi guys, how's it going?'

But it wasn't always fun and games. Every studio has its ups and downs, and John David, who's worked there longer than most, remembers his worst Rockfield experience. He was working with Pat Moran, recording the second album for the band The Barracudas. They were with the group in the Quadrangle during the last night of mixing. As the project was over budget, the album had to be finished that night. The pressure was on. But then all hell broke loose when punk rock band The Damned arrived. 'The Damned were due to record in the Coach House studio the next day. But they turned up that night at about 11 o'clock,' remembers John David with a shudder.

> All of a sudden, we heard the sound of screams from the girlfriends and wives of The Barracudas, who'd been in the lounge watching the TV. The Damned had gone over to the stables and filled up this wheelbarrow full of horse shit, raced it across the courtyard, through the patio doors and tipped it all over them. It was everywhere! All over the girls, the coffee tables, the carpet. It was a right mess. I couldn't get hold of Kingsley as he'd gone to bed. So I rang Charles and he said 'Well, what do you want me to do?' And I told him that he had to come over and sort this mess out. The Damned had done all this damage at 11 at night and we still had a couple of mixes to do. But Charles was very casual: 'Well,' he said, 'boys will be boys. There's not much we can do now. I'll see you in the morning.' And I thought, 'Bloody hell! Thanks a lot!'.

John David assumed The Damned had disappeared to go to bed ahead of their recording the next morning. The girls were cleaning up the lounge, while John and Pat went back to mixing. But then work in the Coach House stopped once more as a loud banging noise reverberated through the studio. 'It was Rat Scabies, The Damned's drummer,' remembers John.

> He was in the corridor outside our studio bashing the wall with a fire extinguisher. So I went out to speak to him. Now he didn't

look like he was drunk, or on drugs, but he was just smashing the wall with this fire extinguisher. So I grabbed hold of it and told him to – quite bluntly – 'Fuck off and not be such an arsehole!' But he wouldn't let go of it and it was pointing right at me. He pushed in the nozzle and sprayed it right into my face. It was very painful as it froze my face with the carbon dioxide. But he finally let go of it, so I went back into the control room. But that still wasn't the end of it. He started kicking the studio door. So The Barracudas were holding the door shut, while Pat and I were desperately mixing this record. Our reputation was on the line.

Anyway it suddenly all went quiet and I thought to myself, 'Great. He's finally gone to bed.' But all of a sudden the door burst open and I'm just pulling the fader down on a mix, when Rat starts effing and blinding at the back of my head. And I'm saying, 'Yeah yeah, I'll be with you in a minute,' in reply to whatever he was saying. But he just kept on shouting insults at me: 'You effing twat! Call yourself a producer? You couldn't produce a rabbit out of a bloody hat!' He had this really snarling cockney accent. Well, I'd just got the fader down and turned round to speak to him, when he whacked me right in the chops and sent me flying right over the mixer. Of course The Barracudas leapt on him and gave him a right pummelling. Anyway we finally finished about 5 o'clock in the morning. I had a thick lip and I was toying with the idea of suing him, but the moment was past and I thought, 'Sod it. I can't be bothered.' But, the next day when I was picking up some of my stuff from the studio, I heard someone talking in the control room. And it was him, Rat Scabies. But he was talking in a fairly upper class accent. And I heard him say to whoever the producer was (puts on a posh accent), 'Oh, don't let that get out. It would ruin my street cred!'

Then about 18 months later, Dave Edmunds phoned us all up as he wanted to do a tour and wanted to know if we were interested. Well, me, Dave Charles, Mickey Gee and Geraint Watkins all agreed, because Dave Edmunds being Dave

Edmunds, he won't slum it. The hotels will be great and we'll fly everywhere. The money may not be fantastic, but it would be like a holiday for the boys.

So we did it and we were rehearsing in London, when after one session, we went to the pub and The Damned were there as well. Rat Scabies, when he was told that I'd been in Love Sculpture, came over and said 'Oh I love what you did on "Sabre Dance". It was bloody brilliant. Brilliant that.' And he asked me what I'd been doing since. He had no idea that it was me he'd carried on with at Rockfield. He didn't recognise me at all. He was as nice as pie. I thought about reminding him, but decided not to open that whole can of worms.

Scrapes with angry punk rock bands aside, for the most part, recording at Rockfield is fun, relaxing and exciting all at the same time. The surrounding scenery is beautiful. The atmosphere is chilled and the living quarters and equipment are of the highest quality. Producer Jack Endino revelled in the studio's unique setting.

> The surrounding countryside was the best part. I'm really big on walking, it's my main exercise, and in the mornings I took some very long walks up on the hills above the studio, through fields and deep into the woods. I saw deer and foxes and even a very old parish boundary stone. What's left of Offa's Dyke [an ancient earthwork, which roughly follows the border between England and Wales] is right nearby, and Kingsley explained some of that ancient history to me. The atmosphere was so friendly. I remember the *Rockfield Review*. It was a mock newspaper they used to print up every now and again.
>
> It was full of pictures and interviews with clients, but always had some goofy spoof stuff in it too. I recall one where Kingsley and his staff were dressed as Star Trek characters.

More than forty years at the heart of rock music has left an indelible mark on the farm buildings that serve as Rockfield's two main studios. There's the stone wall of the Coach House, which allegedly played a part in inspiring the Oasis hit single *Wonderwall*. And, of course, there's the converted feed store that now serves as the studio office. It's said the far wall is where Freddie Mercury wrote 'Bohemian Rhapsody' surrounded by food bags and saddles. But that's just part of the Rockfield story. It's a story that will take me on a journey to speak to those who were involved with, or witnessed, Rock Legends at Rockfield.

RECOMMENDED LISTENING

Forms and Feelings, Love Sculpture 1970

'I Hear You Knocking', Dave Edmunds 1971

Spring, Spring 1971

New Day, Airwaves 1978

CHAPTER TWO:
SABBATH BLOODY SABBATH

OZZY'S CAUSING MAYHEM AT ROCKFIELD

He'd get up early in the morning before everyone else and then you'd hear this 'BOOM! BOOM!' and it was Ozzy firing his shotgun into the air to wake everyone up, especially outside Bill's room. He always enjoyed standing outside Bill's room and firing off a few cartridges to get him up.

Les Martin, roadie, Black Sabbath

On the bank of the river Monnow, Ozzy Osbourne has taken a break from rehearsals for what will become his last album with Black Sabbath: *Never Say Die!* The band are staying at the Old Mill House. In 1976 this was Rockfield's newly refurbished rehearsal studio. Fishing on the river was a favourite pastime of some of the band and Ozzy has settled on the riverbank, preparing to chill out and catch fish. One of Sabbath's long-time roadies, Graham Wright, has also left the Mill House and is heading out for some air, when he spots Ozzy running back up the riverbank looking terrified. The

self-proclaimed Prince of Darkness has been spooked. He's screaming repeatedly at the top of his voice: 'He's trying to bloody kill me!'
Graham looks around for the source of this terror and there chasing
Ozzy, as fast as he can go, is a swan! The bird has leapt out of the
river and taken an instant dislike to Ozzy, who hares past Graham
toward his car where he keeps a shotgun. Despite warnings from
Graham that 'You can't shoot swans!' Ozzy – now unsurprisingly
feeling somewhat braver – runs back to the riverbank blasting away
at his attacker – who has luckily sensed the singer's wrath and pad-
dled back down the river to safety.

Thirty years on from this incident and I'm waiting outside the main
gate of the Millennium Stadium in Cardiff to meet Graham Wright.
Tomorrow night, on 29 August, 74,000 people will fill the stadium to
watch the latest leg of The Rolling Stones on their A Bigger Bang tour.

Graham is currently working as one of the drivers hauling the
Stones' massive generators around Europe. The band have three stages
in use at all times so while they were performing in Glasgow at
Hampden Park, three days ago, crews were hard at work setting up
stages at the Don Valley Stadium in Sheffield and here in Cardiff. Each
stage needs forty trucks to transport it from venue to venue so it's like a
minor city descending on each gig.

Graham strolls up the ramp leading to the security point at the
stadium entrance and introduces himself. 'Hi. You must be Jeff.' He's
dressed in a 2003 Rolling Stones Licks tour T-shirt with a cluster of
backstage and access-all-area passes hanging around his neck. He has
a big smile on his friendly looking face, which is partly covered by a
huge white handlebar moustache. Graham was assistant to Sabbath
drummer Bill Ward throughout the 1970s and spent a large propor-
tion of that decade in the studio and on the road with the band. He
and another of the band's crew, David Tangye, wrote a very humorous
account of their time with the band in a book called How Black Was
Our Sabbath: An Unauthorized View From The Crew.

Graham takes me inside the stadium for a quick behind-the-
scenes look at the Stones operation. I've been inside the bowels of
this stadium many times before during my eight-year stint as a sports
reporter for BBC Wales. But I've never seen it like this. There are

BLACK SABBATH

Cited by many to be *the* original heavy metal band,
Black Sabbath have had a massive influence on
the genre and have sold countless millions of albums
worldwide. The group's ominous sound, apocalyptic
lyrics and satanic imagery stirred up much controversy
over the years. Ozzy Osbourne fronted the band
until 1979 and was replaced by Ronnie James Dio,
Ian Gillan and Tony Martin, among others, before the
original line-up got back together in 1997.

hundreds of people, dressed mainly in black, bustling around, moving equipment into the main arena. The corridors inside the top half of the stadium are lined with fridges, freezers, washing machines and vending machines. A huge canteen, which has been set up to cater for the crew, is constantly busy as people drop in for a coffee break or to be fed. It's like a small tribe of nomads has decided to spend a day or two at the stadium before moving on to pastures new.

Inside the arena, a giant steel structure – four storeys high – is being installed. This is the stage where Mick Jagger and the rest of the Stones will blast out four decades' worth of hits tomorrow night. It's an impressive operation, working like clockwork, with the crew moving in total harmony to get the job finished before the band arrive for rehearsals tomorrow. The sightseeing done, we decide to head across from the stadium, which is situated right in the heart of Cardiff city centre, to one of the nearby pubs to talk about Graham's time at Rockfield with Sabbath. 'First though,' says Graham, 'do you mind if we wait for my friend Les Martin? He's due to arrive soon and he was at Rockfield with us as well.' Les is due to start work from tomorrow on the Stones tour for the next few weeks. He's arriving here by train from West Wales and, after a ten-minute wait, we spot him walking just outside the stadium.

'Oi! Over here, you old bastard!' shouts Graham affectionately by way of a greeting. Les and Graham hug and shake hands, and then the three of us head into the pub. 'I guess the first time Sabbath used Rockfield would have been at the end of 1971 or early 72. At first they practised at Rockfield in the studios before the owners bought the Old Mill House, which eventually became Rockfield's rehearsal studio,' says Les after a large sip from a pint of real ale. It was Les's father who made the huge wooden cross which Sabbath used to suspend over the stage during concerts in the US in 1975. It was carried on tour in a purpose-built coffin!

Back in 1971, Black Sabbath had hired Rockfield to prepare for their second album: *Paranoid*.

The band's first album had been recorded at Regent Sound studios in London. Sabbath basically laid down their live set and the record was released in February 1970, making number 8 in the UK and number 23 in the US.

For the follow-up, producer Rodger Bain brought the foursome to south Wales and the still developing Rockfield Studios.

In the evening the band and crew all slept in the same room in the main farmhouse, while by day they spent most of their time in the rehearsal room. It was an old barn with great acoustics, but wasn't prepared for its first onslaught from the West Midlands heavy metal quartet. Sabbath played at such volume that the whole barn shook and the Welsh slates were rocked off the roof, sending them hurtling to the courtyard below where they all smashed.

The band would spend the day jamming and then listen back to the tapes of each session to select ideas and riffs they liked and then try to craft them into finished songs. 'We used to record them playing live at Rockfield,' says Graham.

> Some of the time it was just riffs: the guitar hooks that Tony Iommi came up with. We'd tape them so he didn't forget them, because occasionally he might accidentally come up with a terrific riff and you wouldn't want to lose it. That's how they rehearsed mainly. It was the guitar riff first and then that developed into the tune. The words always came later. So when

rehearsing, Ozzy would make the lyrics up as he sang. He'd ad lib these nonsensical, but often funny, lyrics to the tune. Geezer Butler, the bass player, wrote most of the lyrics. So Ozzy would come up with the tune of the vocal line, but needed Geezer to write the words afterwards.

Graham looks across at Les for confirmation. Les nods in agreement and adds, 'I used to record the rehearsals on a Revox tape machine. I've got loads of recordings still in my loft!'

Sabbath's road crew remember Rockfield as idyllic and peaceful, a place to relax away from pressures of hectic city life in London. Ozzy was especially keen on it, recalls Graham.

He loved it, because it was secluded and off the beaten track. The whole band enjoyed being there. They could really concentrate on being themselves, rehearse and write. It was a great atmosphere, especially later at the Old Mill House. I remember Kingsley Ward, the owner. He was a little eccentric, wasn't he? But he was such a nice bloke. In the mornings he used to go out, milk the cows and bring the band fresh milk.

As we talk, I notice that virtually every table around us appears to be taken up with Rolling Stones crew members. Slowly but surely, they have taken over this pub, which is now a sea of black tour T-shirts or tour jackets.

'Sabbath used to love fishing,' continues Graham. 'Ozzy also enjoyed shooting in the country. He always had a shotgun in the boot of his car.'

'It was one of his great pleasures,' chips in Les.

He'd get up early in the morning before everyone else and then you'd hear this 'BOOM! BOOM!' and it was Ozzy firing his shotgun into the air to wake everyone up, especially outside Bill's room. He always enjoyed standing outside Bill's room and firing off a few cartridges to get him up.

It seems that, in those days , the poor Sabbath drummer tended to be the victim of many of the band's practical jokes.

'They were great at winding each other up by playing pranks,' explains Graham, 'and Bill was usually the victim. We'd often sneak into his room and pretend to be ghosts.' Les bursts into laughter and puts down his pint.

> I remember, we put a mirror over his face one night and woke him up. He opened his eyes, let out a massive scream and then seemed to pass out. The next morning he came down stairs all pale and shaking and told us, 'I woke up and there was something horrible staring at me!' He was terrified. He'd been spooked by his own face! They also had a big thing about Ouija boards. They used to scare each other to death. You'd hear one of the band members saying 'I'm not sleeping in that room anymore. There's somebody in there!'

The practical jokes often spilt over into meal times. It seems it was never safe to eat at the Sabbath table.

'Food times were hysterical,' says Graham.

> Ozzy loved curries. He'd make one and give himself a plate first. Then he'd doctor it, usually with one of Bill Ward's socks. Bill would be sitting eating and would suddenly pull this long horrible thing from his food and shout 'Errghh! What's this?!' It would be one of his own socks. Or Ozzy would get a jar of vindaloo paste, put the whole lot in and dish it up to the unsuspecting band. It wasn't just Ozzy. Tony Iommi would get some meat pies from the fish and chip shop in Monmouth. He'd bring them back, take the tops off, take the filling out and put cat food inside instead. Then he'd offer them round to the rest of the band: 'Anyone want a meat pie?'

Even the road crew were fair game. Les looks me straight in the eye as his mind flicks back to when the Prince of Darkness singled him out for the old 'switch-a-rooney'.

I used to like tuna fish sandwiches and Ozzy would take the label off a tin of tuna and put it on the cat food. It took days to get rid of the taste of those sandwiches.

The band had so much fun at Rockfield that the spectre of drinks and drugs didn't really rear its ugly head for a change, according to Graham.

We didn't really drink all that much when we were rehearsing. It's like this rock 'n' roll myth that you drink and take drugs 24 hours a day, but it wasn't like that! They were very serious about writing and working out their songs. They respected being musicians in a band and wanted success. We'd go out and have a few pints in the town or smoke the odd joint or two, but I'd say the drink and drugs weren't that prevalent at Rockfield.

But, on one of their visits to Rockfield, the band suffered their first major crisis. Singer Ozzy Osbourne quit mid-rehearsal in November 1977. Ozzy had threatened to leave before, but this time he left both the studios and the band.

Les recalls that 'he just disappeared. He got into his car and he was off. He normally didn't drive, but got someone to drive for him as he hadn't passed his test. He tried about six times, but just couldn't do it.'

The three remaining members – guitarist Tony Iommi, bassist Geezer Butler and drummer Bill Ward – remained convinced Ozzy would return. But days passed and the singer was still somewhere other than Monmouth. Eventually the band decided to call Ozzy's bluff and hire a replacement. They recruited Dave Walker, a former member of the blues band Savoy Brown.

'That just died a death,' frowns Graham. 'He turned up at Rockfield with this strict American wife, who demanded he had to go to bed at 11 o'clock every night.'

'He made Black Sabbath sound like a cross between a West Coast US band and The Allman Brothers,' bemoans Les. 'He was an old mate of Bill's from Birmingham.'

For the next three weeks the band started work on their next album with Walker. They even appeared on a BBC TV show in the Midlands called *Look! Hear!*, presented by Toyah Wilcox, to play some of their new songs. Songs which would never see the light of day.

The experiment with Walker was a failure and eventually ended in January 1978. A few weeks later, back at Rockfield, the familiar sound of a shotgun being fired outside Bill's room signalled that Ozzy was back.

Graham remembers that it seemed like Ozzy was gone for a long time, but it was just a few weeks.

> It was when the band were rehearsing. We did the album with Dave, but when that didn't work they had to redo the whole thing. Ironically that was to be the last album with Ozzy called *Never Say Die!* I think deep down the guys knew Ozzy would come back. Overall, everyone was unhappy. They wanted to try someone else to see what it would be like with a different singer, while Ozzy was always hellbent on forming his own band. He used to go on about it all the time during the mid 70s. He had even named the band: The Blizzard of Ozz. He also had a T-shirt printed up, which he used to wear. So he left and started rehearsing with some members of the band Necromandus, who'd toured with Sabbath in the early 70s. But eventually he came back to Rockfield and Sabbath.

Ozzy was back in the fold and the ribbing and mickey-taking soon restarted as Sabbath got back down to rehearsing.

Graham borrows a lighter from a roadie sitting on the table next to us and lights up a cigarette before telling me, 'I remember Ozzy was trying to grow a beard. Tony Iommi just looked at him, smiled and said, "What are you doing? Auditioning for a folk tour with the Dubliners!" and that was the end of that!'

'He was more concerned about his expanding waistline though,' adds Les.

One day at Rockfield, Ozzy was sitting on the floor in front of me watching the television when Meatloaf came on. Ozzy shouted, 'Look their singer's fat!' and everyone fell about laughing. He was very touchy about his weight. He would always claim he was going to get fitter and used to go on long walks at Rockfield.

BLACK SABBATH

The name was thought of by bassist Geezer Butler.
It was taken from a 1963 film – a trilogy of horror
stories, which featured the legendary Boris Karloff.
As a 15-year-old, Geezer had wanted to call his first
band Black Sabbath, but as he was living at home,
his mum and dad wouldn't let him. So he called them
Rare Breed instead and had to wait until he left home
before he could use the name Black Sabbath.

The band used to have a dartboard hanging up in the main room
at the Old Mill House. Graham tells us 'Sabbath loved to play darts.
We dubbed Bill Ward "The Jocky Wilson of the Band". Not because
he could play as well as the famous former World Champion, but
because, like Jocky, he enjoyed a drink or two while throwing!' We're
on our third pint now and the pub is starting to empty as many of
the Stones crew return to work. The stage is almost built, with just
the final touches to be added before the band can play the final UK
performance of their 2006 European Tour.

Graham has worked with the likes of UFO and U2 as well as
the Stones, among others, down the years, but his favourites remain
Sabbath.

They were the best band I've worked for, because they were so
down to earth and a pleasure to work with. They were so ordinary, despite being rock stars. I was Bill Ward's drum tech for
years and he was the nicest, most ordinary bloke I've met. Ozzy
was fine. He just loved being out in the country, going shooting
and fishing. Rockfield really did suit them. They loved it and it
was close enough to Birmingham for them to nip home. And
they had the cars to do it! Tony always had a Ferrari, or a souped-

up sports car, while Geezer would drive around in a Mercedes convertible. And Sabbath would spend a lot of time at Rockfield, rehearsing for six weeks or so – sometimes a couple of months. For a major studio, it was very unusual.

You could easily think that you had the wrong place when you first went there. I remember driving the seven-and-a-half tonne truck. We went to the farm first as we couldn't find the Old Mill House. They told us to go up the road, but it was a really tight turning and we barely got the truck in there. The people there were great as well. Kingsley and the Rockfield staff would leave us be. So we didn't get disturbed by anyone. It was one of the few places where the group wasn't mobbed by autograph hunters. Tony and Ozzy could walk up Monmouth High Street and nobody would bother them. That's what they liked about it. A lot of the bands appreciated that. Rockfield was just miles away from anywhere and was so unusual that, when you think about it, it's amazing what came out of Rockfield.

As we drink up and prepare to leave, having reflected on the vast musical legacy of Rockfield, Les tells us how the studio affected his life. 'It's why I ended up living here in Wales, because I was looking for a farmhouse myself to buy and to convert into a rehearsal studio. Those types of studios are so in demand and always booked up, so I thought it would be a good thing to retire to.' He laughs. 'I'm still looking!'

Later, having bid farewell to Graham and Les, I leave the pub and, on my way home, I realise that despite the huge amount of time spent writing and rehearsing at Rockfield, the line-up regarded by many as the classic Sabbath – with Ozzy on vocals, Tony Iommi on guitars, Geezer Butler on bass and Bill Ward behind the drums – never actually recorded there. When that line-up dissolved in 1979 it would be more than a decade before the band – minus Ozzy – would record tracks in Wales. Ozzy himself would return in the late 1980s to rehearse his solo material in preparation for his *Blizzard of Ozz* album. In the meantime, Geezer Butler went back to Rockfield in 1986 to record solo material. House engineer Paul Cobbold remembers being impressed by the fledgling Geezer Butler Band.

I didn't work with Sabbath, though I did work with Tony Iommi on occasion and with Geezer. He came down to Rockfield with his band, which included former Sabbath keyboard player Jezz Woodroffe, Geezer's nephew Pedro Howse on guitar and Gary Ferguson, who'd played with the Gary Moore band, on drums. He was quite a loud brash American and a loud brash player.

Jezz was recruited by Geezer ten years after he'd played keyboards on Sabbath's 1976 album *Technical Ecstasy*, which the band recorded in America in the May of that year. 'We did that album in Miami and it was a fantastic experience for me – a 24-year-old kid,' says Jezz.

Being in the famous Criteria studios in Florida was unbelievable. Fleetwood Mac were recording in one studio and Mick Fleetwood kept coming to get me, and would drag me into their control room to listen to what they doing, which was amazing. And the Eagles were in studio 3 finishing off *Hotel California*! And that's how I did my first professional recording session. It was an amazing time. Before recording *Technical Ecstasy* we had toured for a year and had written the songs for the album at Glaspant mansion, which was this run-down rehearsal studio in Wales. They've renovated it now I believe, but it was a ruin when we were there. Half of its roof was missing, which was probably a good thing, because we had Ozzy with us!

Geezer Butler bumped into his old Sabbath bandmate at a Robert Plant concert at the Birmingham NEC nearly a decade on from their time together in the band.

In those 10 years, I hadn't spoken to anyone from the band in that whole time. It was weird, because when the Sabbath thing ended, nobody really told me: none of the band anyway. I had a letter from their accountant saying, 'Here's your pay-off cheque. Goodbye!' I never heard from any of them, until I saw Geezer that day when I was playing with Robert at the NEC. He simply said, 'Oh well, these things happen. How do you fancy doing this solo project with me?' Geezer is a nice guy, but he's very shy and doesn't face up to problems too well. He lets others do that. So he didn't talk to me about the way things ended with Sabbath. It wasn't a thing between him and me, it's just the way he is. We became good mates and we still are.

So the Geezer Butler Band arrived in Wales in 1986 and started to write and rehearse at the Old Mill House. Studio engineer Paul Cobbold remembers:

> They came to do some demos at Rockfield for their management company. The idea was to get a band together to do a showcase gig at some stage in the future. But the initial step was to come to our studio and do some tracks. They had three written to start. I didn't know Geezer at all then. I just knew the stuff written about Sabbath in the press. But I was very impressed by how nice they were, especially Geezer. He was a major piss-taker, but lovely fellow. So I engineered these three tracks and later I had a call saying they wanted to come back to the studio, and would I be interested in producing them from that point on. So I agreed. The three initial tracks turned into thirteen in the end. It finished with a showcase gig, which was a great evening. But what happened afterwards was that the record company said, 'Yeah, very good! We're impressed' and that was it. But I think the whole idea was they had to go: 'Fucking fantastic!' or Geezer felt there was no point in carrying on. So it ground to a halt. It's a shame because I felt the songs were brilliant – really solid stuff with excellent playing. But I think, if anything, they were too good. They were a little ahead of their time.

Jezz Woodroffe, though, saw it differently and was not as happy with the band's sound. He feels they suffered from trying too hard to achieve commercial success.

> We were at Rockfield for weeks and weeks, and then we had a big showcase gig in Kent in the rehearsal studios by Leeds Castle,

which Paul McCartney always used to use. We did that gig, and it was all filmed on videotape, so somewhere there's a recording of that show. Overall, I enjoyed the experience, but I think we were a little average as a band. It was all sort of 'middle of the road' and trying to sound like REO Speedwagon. We were trying too hard to get that commercial rock hit sound. It didn't really have a cutting edge.

One track did surface nine years later. Geezer placed an MP3 track of one of the songs from those Rockfield sessions on his website in December 2005 for fans to download as a Christmas present. The track was 'Computer God' (no relation to the Sabbath song from 1992's *Dehumanizer* album).

But four years later Geezer would be missing from the Sabbath line-up when they recorded their first album at Rockfield. In 1990 the band were in Monmouth to put together an album entitled *Tyr*. Tony Iommi was the only original surviving member. Birmingham-born singer Tony Martin was now the vocalist. Bill Ward, who had departed in 1984, was replaced on drums by Cozy Powell. Geezer Butler had left at the same time and Powell's Whitesnake bandmate Neil Murray stepped in on bass. 'With Whitesnake, I had already recorded two albums near Monmouth, at Clearwell Castle,' says Neil.

So I was familiar with that part of Wales. Rockfield had a legendary reputation as the archetypal residential studio for bands to get away from the pressures and distractions of most normal studios, and from the list of famous bands that had recorded there such as Queen, Rush and Robert Plant. The personality of Rockfield was very much a product of Kingsley Ward's own personality, plus that of his family. I think I expected the main recording room to be larger, but that's often the case with places that one has heard a lot about.

And Neil told me how the new line-up enjoyed recording and living together at Rockfield.

I joined the band in April 1989 and we did quite a bit of touring that year before getting together for the recording of what became *Tyr* in February 1990. So the band was a strong unit. We had done extensive writing and rehearsing in Birmingham, but in the studio, we tended to record our parts separately, with Cozy putting down drum parts, Tony supplying guide guitar parts, then bass, vocals, keyboards and guitar overdubs being added at different times later. Tony Iommi and Cozy Powell were very amusing company, and quite fond of practical jokes, and we all had an amusing and stress-free time there. We could withdraw to our own rooms and get some privacy if required, but the band members got on well. Most of us would go for walks in the surrounding countryside, and go into Monmouth for the occasional drink or three.

The album *Tyr* made number 24 in the UK, but didn't chart in America. Neil is quite proud of the album, but admits it may not have been Sabbath's best work.

I think the *Tyr* album suffers a little from lyrically being too tied into a Norse legend theme, and I was disappointed that the bass wasn't louder in the mix, as it should be on a Black Sabbath album. However, there are some good tracks, such as 'Valhalla', 'Anno Mundi' and 'The Sabbath Stones'. As usual, the songs from the album sounded a lot more powerful after we played them on tour, but it's hardly ever possible to try new songs out live as the audience prefers to hear songs that they know. Eventually, I left Sabbath at the end of 1990, but the same line-up reformed in late 1994 for the *Forbidden* album and tour, which took up most of 1995. I continued to play with Cozy in the Peter Green Splinter Group for most of the next two years, playing much quieter blues music. Sadly Cozy died in a car accident on 5 April 1998. Vocalist Tony Martin joined me in M3 Classic Whitesnake for a year in 2003, and I did a little bit of recording with Tony Iommi for a non-Sabbath project in 2005.

Two years later, in 1992, when Sabbath returned to Rockfield for their next album, it was all change again. Tony Iommi reunited the line-up which had recorded the successful album *Mob Rules*. It brought former Rainbow frontman Ronnie James Dio back into the fold. He'd replaced Ozzy as singer back in 1981 for the albums *Heaven and Hell* and *Mob Rules*, followed by the live LP *Live Evil*. Also back in the band was Geezer Butler on bass, with Vinny Appice returning on drums and Geoff Nicholls providing the keyboards. With Black Sabbath and Ronnie's own band Dio suffering from falling record sales, *Dehumanizer* was a return to form that suited both the singer and Sabbath's driving force, guitarist Tony Iommi.

New York-born Vinny – the younger brother of Vanilla Fudge and Cactus drummer Carmine – enjoyed his time at Rockfield with Black Sabbath, growing in confidence as they once again hit top form.

I think we were there for two months. It was cool waking up late every morning and being right there ready to make music with the band. We actually had a good time and it shows in the music we created there. It was the second time I had recorded that way. The first was with Dio for *The Last In Line* album. We lived and recorded at Caribou Ranch outside Denver, Colorado. The elevation there was over 6,500 feet and it took a few days to get used to. But being at a residential studio is a very cool way to make music. It keeps you focused on the music, and not the everyday headaches, so the band spends more time hanging out together sharing ideas and thoughts.

Despite being almost twenty years on from the first time Sabbath were at Rockfield, one constant remained: the boyish japes and practical jokes. Vinny recalls the day when he and Ronnie played a joke on Tony Iommi.

Tony had just bought a new Range Rover, which he was proudly showing us outside the studio. Well, I decided to screw around a bit and poured a bit of motor oil under the car. I told Ronnie to tell Tony that he'd noticed some oil leaking from under the car, because if I'd told Tony he wouldn't have believed me. So Ronnie ran into the studio and told Tony he thought his new car had a leak. Tony came out and asked me to look under the car for him as I knew a bit about motors. I said to Tony, 'It looks like a very bad leak.' I was under the car trying to stifle my laughter while Tony's face dropped. He was very upset and called the car breakdown people, the RAC. They had to drive quite a distance to get to the studio and charged Tony about £100 to have a look and maybe tow it elsewhere. I then told Tony it was all a joke! He was so angry I thought he was going to kill me, but I hadn't finished the drum tracks yet, so I survived! Later on though, he was laughing about it. But he hadn't forgotten! The next day I opened the door to my room and there was a loud explosion. Tony had gotten a load of fireworks and rigged the door. When I got in the room it was an absolute mess! All my things were upside down and all over the place. Yeah Tony, very funny!

During recording Tony and the band also played tricks on trainee engineer Nick Byng.

I ended up in the studio with Black Sabbath for a while. After being labelled a 'space cadet', Tony Iommi asked me to go into the rehearsal room to check if his amp was working. The band, engineer and producer were looking at me through the glass and I could hear them over the intercom speakers saying, 'Can you hear a buzz in the amp Nick?' 'Naa! nothing,' I said. 'Are you sure?' they replied. So I knelt down, and cocked my ear to the amp at which point Tony struck his guitar as hard as he could, and much to everyone's amusement my eardrum suffered a full volume Black Sabbath chord twang.

Black Sabbath would later return to Rockfield during their 1997 reunion. For the first time in nearly twenty years, the original line-up got back together again. Ozzy Osbourne, Tony Iommi, Geezer Butler and Bill Ward reconvened in their home town of Birmingham for two performances at the NEC Arena, which were recorded for a live album called *Reunion*. Preliminary mixes were done at Rockfield before being completed at A&M Studios in LA by Bob Marlette. The band also recorded two new studio songs, 'Psycho Man' and 'Selling My Soul', for the album – the first new material by this line-up for two decades. Sadly, while rehearsing for the reunion tour on 19 May 1998, drummer Bill Ward suffered a mild heart attack at Rockfield during a break from one of the sessions. He was replaced temporarily on tour by Vinny Appice.

Ward underwent an angioplasty procedure and was discharged from Cardiff University Hospital on Friday 5 June. The drummer then spent the next few months relaxing and exercising in a rehabilitation programme proposed by Nevill Hall Hospital in nearby Abergavenny. Two weeks later, as Ward was making good progress, he visited his bandmates at the Milton Keynes Ozzfest concert on Saturday 20 June to watch the gig from the side of the stage. He was introduced by Ozzy in the middle of the set. The lead singer then pulled down Bill's trousers in front of 60,000 fans. Some things never change! Long live rock 'n' roll! Long live schoolboy humour!

RECOMMENDED LISTENING

Paranoid, Black Sabbath 1970

Never Say Die!, Black Sabbath 1978

Blizzard of Ozz, Ozzy Osbourne 1980

'Computer God', The Geezer Butler Band 1986

Tyr, Black Sabbath 1990

Dehumanizer, Black Sabbath 1992

Reunion, Black Sabbath 1998

CHAPTER THREE:

WELSH ROCKERS BUDGIE INFLUENCE METAL GREATS

**I was a big fan of Budgie.
I used to see them at places
such as the Roundhouse in
London back in the early 70s.**

Steve Harris, Iron Maiden

It's fitting that one of the first bands to use Rockfield extensively was a Welsh one. Cardiff rockers Budgie recorded their first seven albums, as well as a few of their later ones, at the rural studio, laying down some of the most influential rock sounds of the early 1970s. Their songs would inspire, and be covered by, many top acts emerging in the 1980s and 1990s. Their classic anthem 'Breadfan' was covered by Metallica. Iron Maiden reinterpreted 'I Can't See My Feelings', Soundgarden put out their version of 'Homicidal Suicidal', while a live favourite of Van Halen in their early days was 'In For The Kill'. While most of Budgie's albums sold well in Britain, and eventually in Europe, with the early ones attaining gold disc status, the band had more of a cult status and to this day they still have a dedicated following.

Budgie also had a delicious sense of fun as captured in their quirky song titles, such as 'Napoleon Bona Parts I and II', 'Hot as a Docker's

Armpit' and 'Nude Disintegrating Parachutist Woman', not forgetting the album title, *If I Were Britannia I'd Waive The Rules*. But more importantly their classic songwriting with its catchy, heavy guitar riffs made them one of the most influential bands of the late twentieth and early twenty-first century.

The Budgie story started back in 1967, when bass player and lead singer Burke Shelley formed the group in Cardiff. What follows is from my interview with him in 2006 as sadly he died in January 2022.

As with many who ended up at Rockfield, the young music fan had been inspired by Dave Edmunds' band, Love Sculpture. 'They were the best band you'd ever seen in your life and they were only a three-piece,' he says as he leads me into the kitchen of his flat, just outside the centre of Cardiff. We pass through a living room, which is surprisingly free of rock memorabilia, apart from two guitars, one at either end of the room. Burke Shelley looks remarkably sprightly, and much younger than his 58 years. Dressed in fashionably torn jeans and a brown woollen jumper, he recalls the beginnings of Budgie over a cup of tea.

> Love Sculpture was rehearsing just around the corner from here, near St Peter's Church, in Bedford Street. There was a youth club there back in 1967 and my friend's brother in school told me, 'You've got to come down. There's a band rehearsing and they are fantastic.' The priest was letting them practise there, and in return they would do a free gig on the Sunday. 'They must be from London,' my friend said, 'they're so good!'

So Burke went along and was blown away by what he saw.

> They were simply amazing. They were doing some Beatles *Sgt Pepper* stuff and it sounded phenomenal. I walked out of there knowing that I had to form a band of my own. I'd wanted to do something like that for ages, but now I was determined. So I found somebody to play the guitar – a guy called Tony Bourge – and then I got a drummer, Ray Phillips, by answering his advert in the local music store.

BUDGIE

Hailing from Cardiff, Budgie spent most of the 1970s building a loyal cult following with their killer guitar riffs and infectious sense of humour. They headlined the Reading Festival in 1982 and influenced a huge number of bands, including Iron Maiden and Metallica.

So Budgie were up and running and they started making big noises on the south Wales college and club circuit. Drummer Ray Phillips remembers them being a particularly close outfit. 'If ever you wanted to get in touch with Tony, Burke or me, you simply had to look for one of us. That way you'd always find the other two in tow.'

After two years of gigging and writing songs, the band's big break was just around the corner. One day when they visited their agent to pay her, she told them about an audition taking place at Rockfield Studios down the road from Cardiff in Monmouth. A producer there, Rodger Bain, was looking to sign a rock band and was auditioning a few acts from across the UK. Burke laughs, though, when he remembers the agent's warning to them as they left her office that day.

Our agent, Mrs England, I think her name was, took on a very stern face and told us, 'Don't you dare play any of your own stuff!' [He giggles at the memory.] You've got to laugh, haven't you? We were playing a few well-known tunes by other bands to get gigs, but half our set was our own material and although she warned us not to play that stuff – and I'd reassured her that we wouldn't – as soon as we got outside I said to the guys, 'Forget that. We're doing our own songs,' and it worked.

Before they went to Rockfield to play for Rodger Bain, Budgie found themselves a wealthy backer. The band had done a gig at the Top Rank club in Cardiff with the hit 1960s band The Tremeloes, who'd enjoyed two UK number ones with 'Do You Love Me' and 'Silence is Golden'. The concert, though, was a disaster and the promoter lost a lot of money that night. But drummer Ray Phillips was determined to make amends and tracked down the promoter through the band's agent.

> His name was Windsor Wallby, and his dad owned a civil engineering company. This Windsor was only a young chap, but he was very rich. I rang him and told him that I was the drummer from Budgie and I was going to help him get back the money he'd lost on our gig. We got together and he became our would-be manager for a short while, though it was really more like a hobby for him.

Windsor invested money in the band to allow them to buy new equipment and Budgie headed to Rockfield to play their audition.

The band, armed with songs like 'All Night Petrol', 'Guts' and 'The Rape of The Locks', impressed the veteran music producer. Rodger Bain told them he was keen to sign them, despite the fact he had already given a contract to one other budding young band. The group in question was Black Sabbath, a band that Budgie would frequently be compared to over the coming years. Before that deal could happen, the band had to play another audition in London for representatives from some of the major record companies. Ray Phillips was baffled that they didn't hold the second audition at Rockfield, but instead at a small recording studio in London.

> As we set up our equipment, we noticed two guys there. One was from a company called Bell Records and the other was called David Howells, from MCA Records. I'd always thought that if a record company heard us play, then they'd sign us straight away. Dave Howells was Welsh as well. He was Merthyr born and bred, so we had an affinity with each other. Anyway he loved us and we signed a major deal with MCA Records just a few weeks later. I was quite proud of the fact that Budgie had only been playing for four or five years, before we signed a major worldwide deal.

That was fast work, because most guys had been in bands for ten years before they got a deal. But we'd practised and rehearsed non-stop. We wanted to be the best.

The man who signed them that day now runs Darah Music in London. A few years after the deal with Budgie, David Howells left MCA to form his own successful label, Gull Records, signing bands like Judas Priest, Wishbone Ash and the Average White Band, before joining Stock, Aitken and Waterman's label PWL in the 1980s as managing director. He helped oversee the label's phenomenal success during that decade with acts such as Bananarama, Mel & Kim, Rick Astley and Kylie Minogue.

A few days after meeting Burke at his Cardiff home, I travelled down to David Howells' offices and studios at Darah Music in London to find out, first-hand, what it was he liked about these young Welsh rockers back in 1971.

The walls of the offices of Darah Music are kitted out with album covers – many designed by David himself – and pictures from his career in the music business, including a framed American flag used by Sly and the Family Stone to promote their influential 1971 album *There's A Riot Goin' On*. It caused outrage in the US, because the band had embroidered their name over the flag. Americans don't like people – especially scruffy rock stars – defacing the Stars and Stripes. The product was hastily recalled, though David managed to hang on to his one. Sitting in the boardroom, David casts his mind back to Budgie's audition and tells me how he'd been bowled over by the band and knew straight away he had to sign them to MCA.

They knocked me out. Budgie had this huge energy level. Ray, in particular, had more energy than most drummers I've ever met. He also had an impish charm. They were great guys and I thought their song titles were so funny and off the wall, like 'Hot as a Docker's Armpit'. Just everything about them was great. You're always looking for something different, possibly unique and out of step with what's going out around you. In Budgie I'd found it.

So in 1971, with a record deal secured, the band packed their bags and made the short trip up the road from Cardiff to Rockfield Studios to start work on their debut album. Back in singer Burke Shelley's Cardiff home, he told me that he clearly recalled his first impression of the place the band were to call home for the next few weeks.

> Countryside. Cows and countryside! Monmouth's a small town and Rockfield's just outside it. And the studio had this real hippie thing going on. It's the flower power period we're talking about and it was all love and peace. The people who started working there had that hippie feel. They sort of drifted in and never left. There was a band, for example, called Spring, who Rockfield's owner Kingsley Ward had stumbled across. Stranded after a concert, he rescued them in typical Kingsley style and said to them, 'Come back and have a cup of tea at my place, at the farm, and I'll show you around.' And they did. They all crashed out there and never left! As it turns out, most of those guys would become the house producers and engineers there. The whole thing was just taking off, and Kingsley was full of enthusiasm, so these guys were saying, 'What a great place! Let me work here.' Well, why not? It was all very loose. Pat Moran, who was the singer with Spring, was there doing production. Dave Charles came from a band called Help Yourself. All these people were doing production all through the years at Rockfield.

Budgie's drummer was also taken with the studio's unique charms. After life gigging around the clubs of south Wales, it was the band's first real experience of a recording studio. Ray Phillips felt at home straight away, despite Rockfield's dilapidated look.

> Looking back now it was just a shack. They had these bed mattresses stuck up on the walls to help with the sound. It was very basic. Compared to what we'd seen in London, it was the pits. But it was our pit! It was the way we liked it: rough and ready. We were very economical. I'll always remember we recorded the first album on an 8-track machine. It cost £450 to record. The second

cost us just £900 and the third album, *Never Turn Your Back On A Friend*, cost £1200. It was nothing money – even back in those days, but for today … well just forget it. It's peanuts!

The farm-cum-studio was still quite small and basic at this point, but recording novices Budgie were still overawed. Burke remembers the layout.

You had this manor house and this giant barn. There was also a courtyard in front of the house, while over on the other side of the farm there was a quadrangle, which is now the main studio area. It was a typical stables, which back in the 18th or 19th century would have been used for horses and the farm implements. At the time of our first album, the Quadrangle area wasn't used for recording. That happened some years later, when it was redeveloped once the studio took off, and they had all the money coming in. It was a big thing when they redid the Quadrangle. They put this beautiful recording desk in there and they had some fantastic recording equipment as well. There'd be banks of limiters and condensers, with these flashing red lights. It was quite impressive.

Due to the huge amount of space available at the farm, the two Ward brothers could put their imagination to use. They could create anything to help improve the sound in their studio. Some of their ideas were quite striking and incredibly innovative: 'One of the brothers, Charles, tiled this entire thirty-foot room,' recalls Burke.

I doubt there was anything like it in the world. The floors, ceiling, everything was tiled. On the ceiling, they had these runners, and hanging from them were plates of glass. You could slide these glass panels up and down or sideways – whichever way you wanted – in order to alter the reflection of the sound in there. And so that's what they used for any reverb effect. That would have been on 'Bohemian Rhapsody' I can tell you! It was a great idea to make this cavernous room into one huge sound chamber.

They had the space to do it – unlike most studios. It was fantastic. Mad, but fantastic. They used a whole building just to create a special sound. I thought that was amazing.

With all these facilities to hand, Budgie set to work on their debut album with Rodger Bain, who would eventually disappear from the music business altogether in the mid 1970s having produced Black Sabbath and Judas Priest. At the time Budgie, with three years' experience of playing live, had no knowledge of recording or studio techniques.

Ray Phillips was fascinated by the skills used by the studio staff to put together a record.

When I look back at the first album, we were learning the tricks of the trade. People like Kingsley, Charles and Rodger Bain would use their talent to help us get to where we wanted to be. We had to have an open mind to let people help us get the best out of our songs. I loved it. Our first album was recorded on an eight-track machine. Now, you might have eight tracks on which to record a song, but for some songs you might have twelve pieces of music to lay down. As a result, you'd have to fit those extra four pieces in to wherever there were gaps in the eight tracks. So, say if you recorded a guitar piece that only lasted thirty seconds on track 5, you could also put in a short drum sound later on, putting both pieces on the one track. So you had to squeeze the music you wanted into the eight tracks like that. As a result, it was an excellent learning curve. I also remember we always used to record at night. Sometimes we'd get into a rut, where nothing was happening. So we'd jump in a car with Rodger Bain, or Kingsley Ward, and head into Monmouth to have a couple of pints. Afterwards we'd go back into the studio and start again. And we'd finish recording at around 6 or 7 o'clock in the morning.

But the start of work in the studio was a bad time for Budgie's drummer. He'd been involved in a car accident while taking home lead singer Burke Shelley, after seeing a band play live in nearby Penarth.

It was terrible. I was driving home when I ran a child over. The police came around, checked my van and spoke to these three women, who'd witnessed the accident. They told the police that the injured child had been playing chicken with his friend. Every time a car came along the two of them would run out into the middle of the road. It was an awful time. The following week we were at Rockfield to start our first album. I remember going to the studio and we were playing this one track, when all of a sudden I was back at this road accident. This flashback just completely took over. It wasn't a nice time at all, but thankfully I had plenty of support from Burke and Tony.

As they started to record their early material, Budgie's inexperience meant they found themselves in the hands of the studio staff. Burke Shelley, in particular, watched closely, picking up whatever he could from those early sessions.

Rodger Bain had his hands on the controls. Rodger was the producer, the guiding force. He was there in the booth, fiddling around with all the knobs and faders and trying to give us the sound we wanted. We also had help from the engineer, Pat Moran. Our debut album was done quite roughly, in the sense that we had a lack of understanding of writing and recording. So we did it quite quickly, in about five days I think. We rushed in, did it virtually live and recorded everything we had written. But you know, I listen to it now and I think, 'Well it could have been done better.'

Although pleased with the quality of the songs he'd written, Budgie's singer/songwriter was not a fan of the way studios back in the 1970s recorded albums.

Things were done differently back then. If you listen to modern recordings they are so huge, ambient and powerful. But when you listen back – and not just to Budgie – but all that stuff written and recorded by other bands back in the early 70s, it's got this dry quality. That was the sound of the time and I hated it. Back then, the idea was to dry the sound out. Once it was recorded, as live, the producers basically took almost everything off it, until all that was left was the bare bones of a signal. Then they tagged everything back on: the reverb and the ambience, everything. It was all restored until the song was finished. But it meant that they sometimes lost that live feel, which you get from a band – sometimes it just wouldn't translate in the studio.

The band's self-titled debut was released in 1971. The sleeve notes at the time were written in a special form of English known as '70s-speak'. The notes went like this:

> Rock and Roll, it all comes down to Rock and Roll, funky, loud, live and gutsy ... Budgie are a three-piece from Cardiff, probably the first British rock band to get to grips with the heavy American giants ... they're a rock band, a freaking good rock band.

Freaking good rock band or not, while Burke Shelley was happy, overall, with the finished product, he didn't get the heavy sound he had hoped for. He thought the album failed to capture the essence of the band's live performances. But another band coming through at the time had managed to put down on record the magic formula that Budgie were chasing.

> Led Zeppelin had just come out, and I was heavily into that. Their second album had just been released and they had this huge sound, which was mainly to do with John Bonham and his powerful drumming, and not so much the guitars, believe it or not. Nowadays we seem to be going back to that live feel. Most records seem to sound live, and all the drummers sound like John Bonham, but in reality it's all down to machines. It's this huge drum sound that you can get today, but couldn't get back then. I kept looking for it, though. It's a shame that it took so long for us to be able to simply press a button and get it. But, at the time, I was green, so I never really got off on our early sound down there at Rockfield. And that's not their fault. It's just the

way things were done thirty years ago. For example, I think Dave
Edmunds was pretty good down there. When he did 'I Hear You
Knocking' and all those radio hits at Rockfield, he wasn't after
our sort of sound. He had his eye on singles, which sounded
fine on the radio. Whereas we were looking for something else.
We wanted a sound that felt like an uppercut in the stomach.
Something with real punch to it. And I had no idea how to get it.

'I know now though,' he says with a massive smile on his face.

On the playing side, drummer Ray Phillips felt he was developing
as the recording of their debut album went along.

I listened to our first record the other day. I enjoyed the way that
I played the drums in line with whichever bit of music I thought
was most noticeable. So if it was Tony's guitar riff, I'd copy what
he was playing. If it was Burke's bass line which stood out, then
I play the drums along those lines. So a lot of imagination went
into those early albums. I just did it – not thinking about it too
much. We had a lot of problems and a lot of worries during those
first sessions at Rockfield, but we learnt so much. I remember on
the final track 'Homicidal Suicidal', I thought I'd got my drum
line wrong. So one of the guys played it back for me to check,
but when I heard it, it fitted in really well. So I learnt from that
experience that some mistakes often become an integral part of
making a song successful.

But it wasn't just about life in the studio learning the art of recording.
The Rockfield experience was a complete one and the band enjoyed
their time living on site. 'When we stayed at Rockfield, behind
the studio, there was a kind of 1930s bungalow where we lived,'
explains Burke.

It had four bedrooms, so we were in there sleeping, cooking and
chilling out – it was just fantastic. Right outside the door of this
building, there were these beautiful horses in the fields. On the
back of the cover of that first album, we're there, running away

from these horses. That photograph was taken just behind the bungalow, where the horses used to graze. I mean, if you think of what it's like now in the world, it was all so different back then in the late 60s and early 70s. It was idyllic. It was absolutely idyllic. To be around that part of the world in the summer and recording music was so good for the soul. My drummer always was a bit of a natural history buff. He was into his plants and animals. He'd be up there with his net catching butterflies. Every time there was a break, you'd step out of the studio and there was countryside.

Ray Phillips remembers the chaos of living together in that bungalow during that early period in the band's history:

It was like a madhouse most of the time. Once, we had two roadies: one was nicknamed Snowy, while the other was called Alan. And in this bungalow we had a really big fireplace. I remember Snowy had his washing hanging up in front of the fire – his socks, vests and shirts. He was going off for a bath and asked Alan to run it for him. Well, Snowy went up to the bath, jumped in and you heard him scream, because Alan hadn't put any cold water in. Back by the fire, his clothes had all melted in the heat. It just wasn't his day. He had bad burns on his legs and had lost most of his clothes.

The self-titled first album was released to critical acclaim and more than 51 years on, the band's first record still sounds fresh and inspiring. One year after Deep Purple and Black Sabbath had made their debuts, Budgie added their rock styling to a growing genre of music. Burke remembers when he first heard the band's music described as 'heavy metal'.

That term had just started to be used. At first, we were just described as being 'heavy'. The 'metal' bit got tagged on later. This is a heavy sound! That's a great description. That's what we were after. We wanted this heavy sound. We didn't want to sound like a pop band.

A year later the band returned to Rockfield to record the follow-up.

1972's *Squawk* was again produced by Rodger Bain, but at first the recording didn't go as smoothly as the band's debut. Ray Phillips says the band had doubts about changes made to the studio staff.

> Rodger Bain decided to bring in an engineer, Tom Allen, to help us record *Squawk*. But it didn't work as well for some reason. Tom was great, but maybe it was a case of too many cooks spoiling the broth. We worked superbly with just Rodger as producer, but not so well with an engineer added to the mix. When the album was finished, we sent a copy to the record company and had a telegram straight back. They were not happy with the sound of the album and told us so in no uncertain terms. So we went back into the studio, without Tom, and remixed it. We sent it to the record company once again. This time the telegram came back reading, 'Brilliant. Job done.'

Squawk followed the same formula as their debut with plenty of riff-laden rockers interspersed with acoustic numbers. But it was the third album that provided a benchmark for Budgie. In 1973, the band's self-produced album *Never Turn Your Back On A Friend* was their most accessible album to date. It included the band's most famous song – the heavy rocker 'Breadfan', which set the tone along with the manic up-tempo 'In the Grip Of A Tyrefitter's Hand'. The album ended with the Led Zeppelin-sounding, ten minute epic 'Parents' – a powerful mix of progressive rock and metal. Ray Phillips believes it was this album that saw Budgie finally grow up as a band.

> By the time we got round to the third album, we had some fantastic tracks like 'Breadfan' and 'Baby Please Don't Go'. By now, Tony Bourge had been dubbed 'The King of Riffs' in music circles, because of these killer guitar lines he could produce from nothing. Burke was becoming renowned for his great song titles such as for the song *You're the Biggest Thing since Powdered Milk*. So the sessions for the third album were where we started to mature as a band and musicians. We recorded everything as live.

We rarely had to go back and redo stuff. But I did a drum solo on that album, which, now I look back, is dreadful. Really dreadful. It took me a while to get to grips with doing a proper drum solo.

The album also featured a wonderful gatefold sleeve designed by Roger Dean – as had the previous album *Squawk*. The legendary album cover designer had been brought in by MCA's David Howells.

Roger and I first came together when I was at CBS in the 60s and we had a band called Gun, who had a hit with 'Race With The Devil'. We got Roger involved to do the sleeve. It was his first one. At the time, he'd been working decorating the upstairs of Ronnie Scott's famous jazz club in London. So we persuaded him to do the Gun cover for us. Funnily enough, he recently had a exhibition in London and right in the middle was that Gun cover. I also got him to do the Budgie covers – though the first one was done by David Sparling. In terms of his record and poster sales, there was a period when Roger Dean was the most famous art sleeve designer in the world.

Dean's designs were much loved by rock fans of groups such as Yes and Asia, but Burke Shelley had his reservations:

I think the first album cover – which he didn't do – was our best. I always liked it, because it was the only time our band emblem 'The Budgieman' actually looked like a budgie. Everyone thought 'Ah, heavy music! He can't be a budgie'. So they kept trying to change him into a hawk or something more like a bird of prey. So you'd have a budgie's body with a hawk's head and beak. They just didn't get the irony. We were big and heavy and not at all like the kind of budgie you'd find in a cage in the front room of a little old grandmother's house. So the name gave the impression that we were this twee little band – but when you saw us live we were the opposite: we were very in your face and bloody loud. That was the joke! Mind you, the first album cover was actually originally designed for Hawkwind, but when they saw it they didn't want it. So I came across it one day at the record company and I said 'Can you change the hawk's head to a budgie's head?' And the artist went away and did it. So we got it simply because Hawkwind's founder Dave Brock didn't want it.

The band was now getting used to the way Rockfield operated. Burke Shelley would make sure most of the songs were in reasonable shape before heading out to the studios.

> We used to go up there with most of the album written. But you'd often get up to Rockfield and something wouldn't work out, or would sound weak, so you'd have to rewrite it. Luckily the atmosphere at Rockfield is extremely conducive to writing. I found that was especially true with acoustic numbers. It would be great sitting outside in the summer, with a bit of straw in your mouth, laying back watching the birds fly by and trying to think of something. I did actually write a few of the tracks up there. I remember one, 'Black Velvet Stallion', was written at Rockfield as you can imagine.

Budgie were now in the groove. They were successfully balancing playing live against the pressures of recording. Though, occasionally, it didn't always go as smoothly as hoped, and Budgie's frontman would find himself up against it when mixing the band's very next release.

> I remember being there on one album. It was one of our most popular ones called *In For The Kill*. We were always on a tight schedule, but I remember being in the studio finishing the mix on this particular record, when right outside the Coach House studio was the tour bus, revving up and waiting to take us to the ferry. We had to be in Germany to tour, but I was still trying to mix the album. The rest of the band were calling out, 'Burkey, hurry up. Come on, man!' and I was shouting back at them that I was going as quickly as I could. In a panic and short of time, I'd turn to the studio engineer and ask him, 'Can you bring the guitar up a little bit?' Then I['d] start to leave the control room, but I'd get to the

door when suddenly, I'd remember something else. 'Hang on a minute,' I'd say, 'can you adjust the bass a little?' So I was trying to hand over the track to the engineer while the band was in a frenzy and screaming for me to leave. It was that tight! It was night and I can remember driving in the pitch-black to head off for Germany and Holland. We were really tight on time sometimes.

Despite those pressures, *In For The Kill* was eventually finished and was released in 1974. By then Budgie had secured a bigger following, and the album was well-received both critically and by the music-buying public.

The group also set off on tour with a new band, which was starting to make waves of their own: Judas Priest. Burke Shelley remembers they took Priest on tour as their support act as a favour to their Midlands-based agent, who looked after both bands. 'We toured with Judas Priest to give them a break. The Birmingham connection was via our agent at the time. He was doing Judas Priest.' Burke now mimics his former agent's thick Brummie accent as he continues with the story, 'I want to give them some work, like. I'll get you the work, right, but you've got to have them on the bill with you, like.'

He laughs.

It was a top time though. We did a load of great tours with Priest. We used to crash on the floor at their flat in Birmingham. Bands didn't stay in hotels in those days. If you stayed in a hotel, you were rich. It was usually 'Can I crash at your pad, man?' And there'd be three or four people crammed on the floor in sleeping bags.

During that tour in 1974, Judas Priest often joined Budgie on stage for the Welsh band's encore with both bands jamming a version of 'Running From My Soul' from that year's release *In For The Kill*.

Ray Phillips also enjoyed the band's time with the future metal gods.

When Judas Priest was supporting us, we'd all go on stage for the final song. There'd be two drummers, two guitarists, two bass players and Priest's lead singer, Rob Halford, on vocals. After the gigs, we'd all sleep in the tour vans together. If we were in Birmingham, we'd stay at their place and if we were in Wales, they'd crash with us. One night at my house, Judas Priest were staying for the night after a gig at Barry Memorial Hall. That night a neighbour of mine – who was a young woman – was staying with us. Now, for some reason, Judas Priest didn't meet my wife that night, and so they assumed I was married to this lass from next door. Years later when they finally did meet my wife, they thought she was some woman who I was cheating on my wife with. So they were very quiet and discreet about the meeting, even though they had no reason to be. It was quite funny.

1975 was to be another turning point for the band. Arguably Budgie's best album was to come out of their latest sessions in south Wales. It all seemed to come together on *Bandolier*. Burke Shelley agrees it's their best work as a group.

> Things changed around about the time we were doing *Bandolier*. By then the studio at Rockfield was more sophisticated. They'd had the Quadrangle developed for a year or so and had turned it into their main studio. Their clientele was not just us, Dave Edmunds and a few others. They were also getting some of the bigger names coming to Rockfield and, as a result, it was also getting better equipment. It was 24-track recording by then compared to the eight tracks we'd had available for our debut album four years earlier. Everything had upped and the place was being run as a real business. A reverb and echo room was built, as were more chalets for artists and bands to stay in. It was a lot more luxurious.

One of the main changing points for the band with *Bandolier* was the recruitment of a new member. Original drummer Ray Phillips had decided to leave. His departure, though, was an amicable one: 'Things started going wrong for me. It was no big deal. I decided to leave. Overall though my time with Budgie was one I still really cherish.' Budgie had to temporarily draft in Pete Boot to get them through the year, finish off *In For The Kill* and go on the road. Then the band persuaded Steve Williams to come aboard. Burke had been after Williams for some time, but now he was finally able to join the trio. Budgie's singer was delighted.

> When Steve arrived we just took it up a notch. He was such a good drummer. In my opinion he was above our standard. Me and Tony could bash out a few chords and attempt to write a few songs, but you can tell the difference listening to the album, because *Bandolier* is more sophisticated. I'm not sure if that's a good idea in the eyes of the fans, mind you, because they always like albums like *In For The Kill* and I'd think, 'What? That flipping dirge! What do you like that for?' It's funny with fans, you can never tell. So that's what happened there. We got better and we were now getting national, and even international, exposure and success. We were no longer a little Cardiff band. We had gone up a notch or five.

Steve Williams remembers joining the band at Rockfield and knowing he'd made the right move straight away.

> It felt like home. Everyone is so down to earth at those studios. So you felt comfortable there, shut away from the outside world, with very little distraction. Not only could you get on with doing the album, but it was also a very relaxed atmosphere being with a band there.

The new drummer was also adjusting to life in the recording studio for the first time, which is a task that takes some doing given Rockfield's unique look.

> My first impression of the place was that it looked like a farm, and not a major recording studio. The place consisted of a couple of cowsheds with recording equipment inside. It was my first time in a professional studio, so I think I was a little bit overawed by it all – the banks of equipment and being in a studio to make my first record with a band.

By now the band were producing themselves. All the tricks and tips Burke Shelley had picked up over the years were finally being put to the test. As the new boy, Steve Williams took a bit of a back seat, but remembers that on the whole the new record *Bandolier* was a group effort.

> We had a little bit of help producing the album from the likes of Pat Moran and Dave Charles, who were the main producers at Rockfield, but, basically, we worked on it as a three-piece band. Burke would do most of the writing, but we were all arranging the pieces, as and when they came along. A lot of the songs were already written, but we'd work on them in the studio, and change them. So it was very much a group effort. Of the songs on *Bandolier*, I love 'Napoleon Bona Parts 1 and 2.' That's one of the strongest songs and we still do that live now. I also like the slow song called 'Slipaway', which, funnily enough, we've never done live. But it's a nice song, very different. At the time we didn't realise just how good this album was. And for me, it was all happening very fast, being my first time in the studio. It was all brand new to me. It took me about a year to get used to being in the band. The album did chart just after it was released and we went on tour straight away, so there was an awful lot going on. Plus it was the end of our days with MCA and we were about to sign a new record deal. It was a very exciting time.

As the studio started to gain a name for itself, a whole social scene built up in the Monmouth area around Rockfield and the bands who'd come there to record. Burke remembers how it created an exciting buzz in the area.

> I was aware of this whole scene starting up, because we'd all go into the pub in town that was always used by Rockfield people. The Nag's Head in Monmouth became a kind of celebrity haunt. We used to go down there and you'd see Robert Plant, and no end of famous rock stars and their crews, standing there with a pint. Basically it was used by anybody who'd been working in the

studio. At the end of the day, they'd want a drink and they'd all end up in the Nag's Head. The whole town sort of cottoned on to what was happening and Rockfield became part of Monmouth. My girlfriend from that period, who lived in the town, used to tell me what everyone else was saying. What her mum had heard, you know. They knew all the gossip before we did! It was quite a big thing. But it was a nice atmosphere.

By the time the band returned in 1976 things were still changing at Rockfield. Steve Williams was impressed with the growing confidence of the studio and its owners.

When we turned up to record *If I Were Britannia I'd Waive The Rules*, they'd improved the studio equipment once again. We were again recording in the main Quadrangle studio. When we first went to Rockfield, there was just one eight-track studio in one of the old converted cowsheds. But by 76 it was more professional and a lot more impressive. Once again they'd put in better equipment and they'd improved the rooms where the bands stayed.

The band released just one more album in that decade, 1978's *Impeckable*, which was their first album not to be put together at Rockfield. It was recorded in Toronto as Budgie spent a year in North America touring from a base in Canada. The music scene back in the UK, though, was changing at a rapid rate while Budgie were away. Punk was now all the rage. By the time Budgie returned to Britain, they found themselves labelled as dinosaurs, out of step with the new trends in music. But Budgie's time out in the cold was short-lived. By the start of the 1980s, it was all change again and Budgie found themselves enjoying renewed success. As the grand old men of rock, the band discovered they had had an important influence on the rise of major new groups. The emergence of the new wave of British heavy metal, including bands like Iron Maiden, Def Leppard, Saxon and Girlschool, was rekindling interest in the Welsh power trio. As a result, Budgie played the Reading Festival in 1980 and 1981 and they returned for a third year in 1982 as headliners. Reading was one of the major festivals and carried much kudos. 'We did it three years running,' recalls Steve Williams proudly.

> And we were top of the bill in 1982, when *Deliver Us From Evil* came out. It was a fantastic experience to play in front of all those people. We played alongside bands like Def Leppard, who had just started to break. I think they were canned off by the crowd in 81. There were also bands like Slade, Whitesnake, Iron Maiden and Motörhead. I remember the way Slade went down in 1981. They were awesome and just pulled the place apart. Overall, I really enjoyed the first two appearances there, when we were the support act, more than the time we headlined, because there was less pressure. The headline band always feels the weight of expectation to perform. And even though it was a success from our point of view as a band, from a drummer's point of view, I enjoyed it more on the first two occasions.

By the late 1980s, though, Budgie had split up. Ironically, as soon as they decided to call it a day, several big name groups began covering Budgie classics, once again raising the profile of the Welsh band.

Iron Maiden laid down a version of 'I Can't See My Feelings' from *Bandolier* and the song was released on the bonus disc of Maiden's 1992 album *Fear Of The Dark*, which reached number 2 in Britain and number 12 in the US. It was the idea of Maiden's bass player Steve Harris to persuade the group to reinterpret this Budgie song and he explained to me why he picked this track:

> I chose the song 'I Can't See My Feelings' for Maiden to cover as a B-side, because I was a big fan of Budgie way back. I used to see them at places such as the Roundhouse in London back in the early 70s. My favourite album, at the time, being *Bandolier* and my favourite songs from their repertoire included 'I Can't See My Feelings', 'Napoleon Bona Parte' and, of course, 'Breadfan'.

Six years later, 'Breadfan' would also receive its own high-profile cover. Metallica recorded the track, along with another Budgie classic, 'Crash Course In Brain Surgery', for their 1998 CD *Garage Inc.* – a double album of covers. Burke is full of praise for Metallica's versions of their songs.

> They were into our music. In their teens, we were one of the bands they listened to. So when their music developed and took off, they decided to cover those two songs. They sound good [he laughs]. Probably because they copied us. They didn't change the songs. They just did what we did. But I remember I also heard a Japanese girl band version of our song 'Guts'. There's some funny stuff around. That was a good one.

He pauses and takes another sip of tea and then places the cup on the kitchen table.

> People look up to us, just as we used to look up to our heroes. You know, when we were at Rockfield, Robert Plant would tell us who he was into. Eric Clapton will praise Muddy Waters for example. I'd loved to have seen The Beatles live, but I never did. I thought, and still do think, they are great. Everyone enjoys their roots. I listen to a lot of young kids today and they are into bands from the 60s and 70s. When you think of Franz Ferdinand, they've got the look of the 60s about them, haven't they? They've got the tight trousers, the Cuban heels, and the floppy hair across the front. And they say they love that sound. So it all comes around in cycles.

Van Halen also covered Budgie's 'In For The Kill' when performing live, in their early shows, just two years or so before securing a record deal. The song was never officially recorded by the band, but does crop up on a number of bootlegs traded amongst Van Halen fans. These include a rare live recording of the band at Pasadena High School in 1975 called *School's Out*.

Budgie's original drummer Ray Phillips only realised how much influence the band had many years later.

I always remember I was watching some TV music channels and there was Metallica talking about Budgie and how they really thought we were a great band. And just a few months ago, I was driving down the motorway to London and I was listening to the Jonathan Ross show on BBC Radio Two. His guest was the former tennis star Pat Cash. Jonathan asked Pat what he'd been doing in the country since arriving here. And Pat said he'd gone to see a few bands. He'd seen Judas Priest a few nights earlier and he was hoping to catch Budgie doing a gig. And Jonathan Ross interrupted him by saying 'Budgie! I couldn't stand them.' But Pat Cash disagreed and insisted that we were a brilliant band. So I'm listening to this heated discussion on BBC Radio with a famous tennis player and one of the BBC's top presenters arguing about the merits of Budgie. So I think it's fair to say we played a big part in many people's lives.

In their 1970s heyday, the band had based themselves at a small Welsh farm, which was starting to make a name for itself. Budgie's influential sound played a major part in putting the studio on the map. And, as many bands would later discover, the residential experience of staying at Rockfield would also prove a bonding experience. For Budgie's lead singer it was also a great place to have fun and try to forget about the strains of studio work:

We just larked about all the time. Like the producer, Pat Moran. He had this high-pitched giggle, which would burst out at anytime, anywhere. It was mad. It was like Billy Bunter or Just William. There'd be flour fights at the barns. The band and the crew, they'd all be giggling and messing about. I remember Steve Williams in the bungalow, after a few pints following one session. He was supposed to be sleeping. But Pat Moran had put a big old vacuum cleaner in one of the wardrobes in the bedroom. The plug and socket, though, were outside in the hallway, and when we were all asleep he'd go down the corridor and switch it on. The vacuum cleaner would come on in Steve's room, as if a ghost had turned it on, and wake him up. Pat thought that was hysterical! Steve would be screaming, because he wanted sleep, but we'd all be laughing. That was going on all the time. There'd also be water fights in the summer. We'd all be running round with water bombs, when we were supposed to be recording. The record companies were paying for this, and if they'd come up, they'd have seen all these people in the barn, giggling and throwing water bombs, and they'd probably wonder why we weren't in the studio, instead of wasting their money. Sadly, I was usually stuck in the studio, because I was writing most of the songs and it was my band. I just remember getting cheesed off, because I'd look through the window and there'd be the road crew going past with fishing rods or tennis rackets while I was stuck inside.

The band also enjoyed mixing with other musicians, who were recording at Rockfield while they were there. 'The camaraderie was great,' says Steve Williams.

The three musicians in Budgie and our road crew, production team, engineers and producers all gelled. But it was cool to hang out with other bands as well. When we were there recording *Nightflight* in 1981, Robert Plant was there across in the other studio with Phil Collins in his band. So it was almost like being in boarding school. You had all these musicians staying in this one place with the same kind of attitude and the same love of music. Everyone also had a great sense of fun and we were all always playing jokes on each other.

Burke also enjoyed socialising with his peers from other bands.

It was fun to come across the likes of Hawkwind, Dave Edmunds, Robert Plant and I remember meeting Free down there and watching Simon Kirke on drums. They were part of the weaving of the time. I simply loved Rockfield. It was great. I'm just a town boy, so it was the first time I'd really stayed in the country. When we went to stay at Rockfield, the countryside was just beautiful and the river there is superb. It's a salmon river, as well, so you've got the poachers' pub on the way into Monmouth. It had that whole country atmosphere and the accents had a slight soft 'R' sound like you get with a West Country accent, which surprised me. It was just beautiful.

Though Budgie never reached the dizzying heights of success like Deep Purple, Black Sabbath or Rush, they did leave behind more than a dozen classic, hard rocking albums, which inspired a number of young people to start their own bands and forge their own piece of musical history. That legacy was hammered out in the studios at Rockfield during the 1970s and 1980s, and it wouldn't be the last time that a band decided to make Rockfield their second home.

RECOMMENDED LISTENING

Never Turn Your Back on a Friend, Budgie 1973

In For The Kill, Budgie 1974

Bandolier, Budgie 1975

Nightflight, Budgie 1981

CHAPTER FOUR:

HAWKWIND INVENT SPACE ROCK IN WALES

My girlfriend sold one of the members of the group Bad Manners her car. But what they didn't know was that it was stuck in reverse gear! So the poor guy picked it up in Monmouth and had to drive it, in reverse, all the way back to the studios.

Dave Brock, Hawkwind

It's a bright sunny day on the river Monnow in Monmouth in 1973. Just down the road from a busy Rockfield Studios, a group of girls are enjoying the summer sun. After a boozy picnic on the riverbank, they turn their attention to a big tree overhanging the water. Suspended from one branch is a giant tractor tyre's inner tube. Earlier in the day, the gang had taken turns swinging over the water in it. Now, though, a new plan unfolds. Skirts, tops, knickers and shoes are all playfully discarded on the grass as the girls decide to get naked and take a trip down the river in the tyre.

The girls are revelling in their afternoon in the sun in the middle of this beautiful countryside and their laughter and infectious giggling goes almost unnoticed, as they career down the river clinging on to the huge tyre. But some way down, both the tyre and the girls get stuck as the water narrows and heads into a weir. The girls are left thrashing about, naked in the water, desperately trying to get back to the riverbank. When they do, it's a mad dash up the grass back to their clothes. A few minutes later, a farmer pops into the Nag's Head pub just down the road in Monmouth. Crossing a bridge above where the girls had been stranded, he'd witnessed their struggle to get to dry land. 'I've just seen a group of naked girls in the river,' he announces to the bar full of locals relaxing after a day's work.

'Ahh', replies one of them, without batting an eye, 'That must have been Hawkwind's girlfriends then!' And the bar descends into fits of laughter. The conversation is overheard by some of the band's road crew who are also enjoying a refreshing post-work drink. Hawkwind are well known by the locals of Monmouth. Rockfield Studios has become the band's second home. Hawkwind were one of a number of high-profile groups to 'adopt' the studio. Since the early 1970s, the band has made more than twenty albums there. 'I've got many very happy memories from Rockfield,' says Hawkwind's founder Dave Brock.

> We spent so much time there it was like a home from home. It was wonderful being out in the countryside. We've been there for about three months nearly every year since. It's a great place to hang out while recording. All sorts of people and bands record there. During one session, we bumped into Black Sabbath and Robert Plant. Everyone knew each other. People would hang around with us and smoke a bit of dope.

Singer and guitarist Huw Lloyd Langton had two spells with the band. He recalls his time at Rockfield with immense fondness.

> I always enjoyed staying there. You could chill whenever you wanted. I'd be in the television room, or the pool room, while others would decide to go fishing. It was as much of a holiday as a work situation. But then, when you were working it was great, because it was so remote you could actually make a racket any time day or night when rehearsing. As far as I know most bands that use the place feel the same about it.

What appealed about Rockfield was its simplicity. It was a case of city life versus life in the country. In the city, bands have to learn to deal with the frustration and hassle of traffic jams, or the urban warfare involved in finding a parking space. That's not to forget the stress (and very funny smells) of public transport and the routine, petty problems caused by the daily grind of urban life. But out in the country, those recording at Rockfield were often faced with a different set of issues. Dave Brock remembers taking pride in tackling the most unusual predicament.

> We saved a tree once! It was a lovely tree out by the river, but it was dying. So we called out a tree surgeon to save it. That was pretty cool.

If there is one band which lives up to the phrase 'rock institution', it has to be Hawkwind. And, as with a number of other legendary bands, they are probably best known for one particular anthem. In the same way that Deep Purple has the classic 'Smoke On The Water' and Led Zeppelin have been immortalised by their epic 'Stairway To Heaven', Hawkwind are best remembered for 'Silver Machine'.

Much of their legacy was recorded in Wales at Rockfield. But the Hawkwind story began in Notting Hill in London back in 1968. A group of avant-garde musicians began gigging in earnest

---

HAWKWIND

Credited with inventing space rock, one of Britain's longest surviving bands have released more than thirty CDs, but remain best known for the hit single 'Silver Machine'. In 2002, The Sex Pistols opened their comeback tour with that song.

The band famously played a festival at ancient monument Stonehenge on summer solstice every year from 1973 until it was banned in 1985.

---

as Hawkwind Zoo. After gaining a record deal, they shortened the name to simply Hawkwind. If touring were an Olympic sport, then Hawkwind would have every chance of winning a gold medal. The band also acquired a reputation of doing concerts for free, providing the cause was the right one.

In the early days, Hawkwind were often compared to Pink Floyd, due to the band's trippy, psychedelic rock, coupled with its cosmic obsession. The band sang about travelling through time and space, inter-galactic wars and astral bodies backed by hypnotic rhythms, loud guitars and swirling, eerie synthesisers, all topped off with their own brand of weird special effects. At Hawkwind's spiritual heart were poet Robert Calvert and science fiction and fantasy writer Michael Moorcock, who developed many of Hawkwind's lyrical themes. Another factor was Rockfield. The laid-back approach to recording at the studio heavily influenced the band's sound. Put all these together and space rock was born.

The constant factor in the Hawkwind story is Dave Brock. While other musicians have come and gone, Brock has remained throughout the band's long, and sometimes turbulent, history. Another major figure is singer and guitarist Huw Lloyd Langton. He joined the band as it was evolving in its early days:

> I was working in a music shop in the West End of London, and Dave Brock used to come in after a day of busking to exchange his money for strings and harmonicas. That was how I first got to know him. Sometime later, I was in the underpass at Tottenham Court Road when I saw Dave busking and he offered me a job as a guitarist for a gig he had lined up.

As the band gathered momentum, Hawkwind recorded their debut album in London. The band headed to Wales for the first time in May 1972 to record a handful of tracks for their follow-up LP called *In Search of Space*.

> In the 70s, the studios were a lot different to the way they are today [says Brock]. Rockfield's owners, Charles and Kingsley,

had bought this old mill house, a few miles away by the river Monnow and used it as a rehearsal studio. It had a weird vibe. It used to be an angling club, so it was very ornate and oldey-worldey. I've got a booklet from the time when it was an angling club. It's amazing the things you keep!

The band returned four months later, to record the whole of their third album, *Doremi Fasol Latido*. By then they were hooked on the friendly atmosphere of the farm-cum-studio. The vibe at Rockfield was unlike any other recording studio at the time. Brock remembers:

Part of the Quadrangle was still being used for cows, as Kingsley's father was a farmer. Well, he was a farmer *and* a philosopher. I remember one time being at the studios with Arthur Brown, who was there with his band. We sat around one day with Kingsley's dad philosophising. It was very weird, but very enjoyable. It's a very family-orientated place. We got on well with Kingsley and Charles and their wives and in fact all of the people who worked there. Producers like Dave Charles and Pat Moran are still good friends. Being in the countryside was an attractive proposition for us. We started to go there, because our record company, United Artists, had a deal with Rockfield and would send most of their artists there. That was the way things were done in the 70s. I think RCA had a similar deal with Rockfield. But we really enjoyed it there. So it was our decision to keep going back. It was such a wonderful place. We'd wander amongst the trees, chilling out. There were lots of drugs and lots of freaking out and tantrums. I remember Black Sabbath were in the other studio, when we were there. But I must admit I don't remember a huge amount about them. They used to pop across to our accommodation and sit on the sofa smoking dope with us. It was all very amiable.

Joining the band for his first album with them, and his first experience of Rockfield, was Lemmy. Back in 1967, Lemmy had worked for eight months as a roadie to Jimi Hendrix, though due to the amount of drugs being taken at the time, he doesn't remember a whole lot about working for one of the greatest guitar players in rock music history. As a guitarist himself, Lemmy failed to find success with a number of bands, including the mod group The Rocking Vicars and the trippy raga ensemble Sam Gopal. But Lemmy had seen his future, and had his mind, and heart, set on joining Hawkwind.

> Originally I'd been hoping to join the band as a guitarist. I'd seen them play live and loved the whole thing surrounding them; the sound, their fans, everything. Their lead guitarist had just left. Huw Lloyd Langton simply vanished after one of their gigs. He'd been sitting round a campfire doing acid when he told the others 'I'm going for a walk.' He disappeared over a hill and I don't think anyone saw him again for about four or five years! But I still didn't get the guitar slot.

Langton himself blames the band's drug culture for his sudden departure.

> I spent a while, especially at the very start, taking any sort of illegal substance I could get my hands on. It had to stop and the result was a breakdown that forced me to put an end to the drug taking. I had to leave the band then. You can't live the Hawkwind way all the time!

Lemmy spent time mooching around in a few bands before realising that a change was needed and the solution, it seems, was a change of instrument. 'I was the worst guitarist ever. I was mediocrity squared. So I switched to bass.' Whether it was destiny or dumb luck, his fortunes were about to change as Hawkwind would soon need a bass player. Lemmy remembers,

> I wound up on bass for the band through the most fortunate of circumstances. Well for me anyway. In 1971, in the summer it was, the band had an open-air gig in London. Their bassist, Dave Anderson, I seem to remember, failed to show up. But like an idiot he'd left his bass in the back of Hawkwind's van. Well what

was I to do? He was asking for it. So with the band wondering who was going to play bass, I stepped in. I'd only just started playing bass though. But it must have gone alright because I was with them for the next four years.

As Dave Brock recalls, Lemmy was definitely in the right place at the right time. 'We had trouble with our bass player. Someone said they knew a guy who could do the job. Along came Lemmy and he stole the gig.' The switch proved a success all around. Lemmy brought a different sound to the group. As a guitarist who'd switched to bass, he didn't play the instrument in the conventional way. Lemmy played bass as if it were a rhythm guitar, resulting in a much more solid sound.

One of the first recordings Lemmy did with Hawkwind was the band's first, and only, hit single, 'Silver Machine' in 1972. It was written by Dave Brock and Robert Calvert, who originally did the lead vocals. But it was Lemmy's voice which ended up on the track. It was recorded live at a benefit concert at the Roundhouse in London. Afterwards, the band disappeared into the nearby Morgan Studios to mix it and add overdubs. They also decided to record Lemmy's voice to replace Calvert's live vocals. The single spent 15 weeks in the chart, reaching number 3 and gave Hawkwind a rare appearance on the BBC TV music show *Top of the Pops*. Typically though, the band refused to turn up at the TV studios and mime to the song. Instead they demanded that the BBC film a concert of the band playing live and show that on their programme. That performance of 'Silver Machine' turned Hawkwind into a household name. It was – and still is in some quarters – a radio airplay regular.

With Lemmy now firmly installed, the band finished gigging and headed off to south Wales again. 'The first album I made with the band,' recalls Lemmy, 'was *Doremi Fasol Latido*. It was their third one. And it was a revelation making it at Rockfield. The place was a blast!' The band spent September and October 1972 there and initially found the beauty of the surrounding Welsh countryside a distraction. Dave Brock remembers some of the early difficulties they had simply trying to get everyone in the group into the studio to record at the same time.

It was a great place. A place where time would stand still. It was all very tranquil. As a result people would just wander off. They'd be in the middle of recording and simply disappear. The producers would go nuts. They'd be yelling, 'Where's that idiot musician gone now? For Christ's sake, just go and get him.' It was very disruptive and would hamper recording, but we had plenty of time. We were staying there and we weren't going anywhere. Well, apart from the odd wander.

But eventually Brock marshalled the band together and soon the momentum of recording was almost unstoppable. 'At that time, we got enough down for two albums,' says Brock.

All the basic stuff was done very early on. We recorded bass, guitar, drums and vocals together, so it was as live as it could be. We'd just let the tapes run and play live. Then we put the other things on afterwards. It was heavily improvised, but the music was so together in the first place that it worked. That's why we did things that way.

One of the tracks on that album that the band were having problems with was called 'Brainstorm'. Dave Brock shakes his head as he remembers the difficulties the band's sax player Nik Turner was having with the piece.

He just wasn't getting it. So to help him out, we decided to spike his drink with LSD in the hope that it would sort out the problem. But somehow Nik got wise to our plans. He kept avoiding any food or drink we put his way. 'I'm not touching that,' he'd shout and then storm out. In the end, we had to get some of the road crew to help. One of them spiked Nik's yoghurt with LSD. And you know what? It worked. Nik played the piece really well and 'Brainstorm' was completed. He played it much better under the influence of drugs.

Doremi was released in November 1972 and marked the beginning of what many fans believe was Hawkwind's 'golden era'. The band then undertook a mammoth UK tour to promote the album, complete with an impressive light show, featuring slides and films. The *Space Ritual* tour, and the success of 'Silver Machine', helped Hawkwind make their mark in the American market. Throughout the band's career, drugs would play a prominent role. The band was a part of the British drugs culture, in a similar way that the Grateful Dead were integral to the West Coast acid scene. LSD was the main drug of the time and a few of the band's albums recorded at Rockfield were mixed under the influence. It meant that the band would frequently arrive at concerts to find the local drug squad already there, waiting for them. One band member at the time remarked, 'The police were scared of us as they viewed us as dangerous insomniac crack addicts in urgent need of a fix.' 1973 brought Hawkwind more unwanted attention from the police. With political tension running high in Northern Ireland and an upsurge in terrorist activity from the IRA, the band chose to release a single called 'Urban Guerrilla'. Written by Bob Calvert, it included lines like 'I'm an urban guerrilla, I make bombs in my cellar'. Sax player Nik Turner received a call from the bomb squad, who turned over his flat looking for explosives. The BBC banned the record and United Artists promptly withdrew it, rather than risk further damaging their name through the bad publicity which the record was receiving.

This saga marked the end of the famous *Space Ritual* line-up, which had enjoyed huge success. It had lasted 18 months, from 1972 until late 1973, before two key members departed: DikMik, who specialised in generating unusual sound effects with a range of electronic instruments, and Robert Calvert. Lemmy's time with Hawkwind was also soon to come to an abrupt end. The bass player was to feature on just a few more Hawkwind records.

'I did four altogether. Apart from *Doremi*, I also played on *Space Ritual, Hall Of The Mountain Grill* and *Warrior On The Edge of Time*.' But in May 1974, while Hawkwind were once again touring North America, Lemmy found himself in major trouble. While crossing the American–Canadian border, he was found to be carrying a quantity of amphetamine sulphate and arrested. Fears about the success of the tour meant Lemmy was sacked and replaced by Paul Rudolph, to ensure that they had a bass player for the rest of the tour. Dave Brock maintains the band had little choice.

> Lemmy was always late, taking speed and missing planes. So after this incident with the drugs bust we had a vote. And the majority of us agreed that Lemmy had to go. But the band was like that. A year later they tried to sack me! But it got him to form Motörhead, so I guess it turned out OK in the end.

Lemmy flew straight back to England to form his new band but remained on good terms with Hawkwind and Dave Brock. In 1977, Motörhead supported Hawkwind on tour and Lemmy still joined the band for a song or two at the occasional gig up until his death. Dave Brock insists,

> There was a magic between us. Some of the best times I had were with Lemmy in the band. And if ever you were to pick the ultimate Hawkwind line-up, Lemmy would be in it for sure.

During the mid 1970s Hawkwind's line-up changed on an almost weekly basis. It is surprising the river Monnow wasn't dragged for bodies as musicians disappeared swiftly into the night. Often it must have seemed that the band only knew who was in the group once they'd assembled to begin rehearsals or recording. By February 1977, the band gathered at Rockfield to record the album *Quark, Strangeness and Charm*.

But things didn't run smoothly and it would be more than two years before another Hawkwind release. The band had, to all intents and purposes, broken up, though an offshoot called the Hawklords – led by Dave Brock – released one record called *25 Years On*.

By 1979, Hawkwind had settled their differences and were back. The new line-up also welcomed back an old friend: original member Huw Lloyd Langton returned to the fold. The band met up in Wales to rehearse for their next album, which was to be recorded live. It was a return to an old haunt for most of the band, but a new experience for the returning guitarist.

That was my first time at Rockfield. We met up at the studios and rehearsed there for our next album and my first one since rejoining the group. That was called *Live Seventy-Nine*. Later we used the studio for actual recording purposes for our 1981 album *Sonic Attack*. I was quite taken by the set-up. We rehearsed, more often than not, in the Old Mill House, which is a lovely old place. It was large enough for everyone to disappear into different parts of it. It was a big rehearsal room with a river running around the back of it, where certain members of the band went fishing regularly. It was great. And Monmouth, which is a lovely little town, is just a walk from Rockfield. The whole situation is totally enjoyable. All the albums we did there were good albums. Good quality stuff.

Live Seventy-Nine would see the band back into the top ten of the UK album charts. The next album *Levitation*, recorded in 1980 in London, is one of Huw Lloyd Langton's favourites with the band, but it would also be the spark of a major crisis, which would reach a climax when the band returned to Rockfield.

Former Cream legend Ginger Baker was recording in London with Atomic Rooster. The famous drummer would often drop into the nearby Roundhouse studios to watch the Hawkwind sessions. Eventually the band invited him to play on some tracks on their album. He finished his drum parts in just one day and was invited by an impressed Hawkwind to join them on a permanent basis. His arrival gained Hawkwind renewed publicity at a time when they were hitting form once again. But, a few months later at Rockfield, things would fall apart in dramatic fashion. Huw Lloyd Langton winces as he remembers the divisions within the band.

There was a bit of hoo-ha at one point. Our bass player Harvey Bainbridge and Ginger had fallen out. It was a discussion over a minor musical point that turned into a big argument at one of our concerts. It happened after the show in the dressing room. Basically you don't argue with someone as famous and long-in-the-tooth musically as Ginger. We all knew Ginger was right, but Harvey wouldn't step down and made a bit of a fool of himself.

Later when the band were back at Rockfield rehearsing in the Mill House with a big American tour in prospect, the argument between the new drummer and the band's bass player came to a head. Huw Lloyd Langton remembers tensions flaring up after a seemingly innocuous incident.

> I think David Brock had refused to go to the shops to buy Ginger a few supplies and Dave had the only car at the time, so Ginger had to hoof it into town on foot with another member of the band. I think they stopped at one of the pubs in Monmouth. Ginger and his pals had a few pints and then they walked back to the studio, which was quite a stroll. By then he was in a bit of a temper. The doors and walls of the Old Mill House were fairly flimsy and I could hear the doors being slammed. I was watching tennis on the television upstairs in my room. Dave Brock was playing table tennis in the back room. And you could hear Ginger shouting, 'Effing bass player this. Effing Harvey that. I can't work with that effing bass player! He's the worst in the world.' You could hear the shouting all over the house, and Harvey, who was upstairs in his room, heard it all. The whole thing hit the fan and it looked like poor old Harvey was going to be out. He was wandering round with his tail between his legs and walking in the fields at the studio feeling really down. It was a nightmarish situation.

Dave Brock recalls that Ginger had plans to replace Bainbridge with a famous old friend.

> During that row at Rockfield, Ginger decided he wanted to sack our bass player Harvey Bainbridge and bring in his old pal from Cream, Jack Bruce. Well, we disagreed. We'd known Harvey for a few years and really liked him. We were not going to let him be booted out of the band by Ginger. So we fired Ginger instead! I remember him shouting at his roadie to pack up his stuff. He was going to leave and head back for London. I'll never forget seeing Kingsley get out this horse and horsebox

and put all Ginger's drums and equipment in the back to take him from the rehearsal room to the main studio, so he could get a cab back to the railway station and on to London.

Despite it being the right decision for the band, Huw Lloyd Langton was saddened by Ginger's departure, because having him as drummer would have been good for Hawkwind musically.

It was a shame as Ginger's style really fitted the band. He was a very original drummer. He was very percussive and it was just a very unfortunate thing that this row with Harvey got out of control. We agreed to say goodbye to Ginger. Well, we told him to piss off basically. So he left and Harvey was kept on.

The incident would remain with the band for years as they tried to figure out exactly what had happened. How had a minor row backstage after a concert been allowed to spiral so far out of control that it fractured the harmony of the band? And Dave Brock also finds it hard to pin down why Ginger wanted to be reunited with his former Cream colleague:

It was really strange. I'm not sure why he wanted Jack Bruce to join the band. We did a TV show in Germany, where we met Jack. And at the time, Ginger and Jack had been suing and countersuing each another for years. Over what? Well I think even they'd both forgotten. But there was a huge amount of animosity between them. Everyone was expecting a big bust-up, some sort of big fight between the two. We were getting ready to steer clear of them and watch the fists fly, when they both bumped into each other at the bar at the TV studio. But surprisingly, they greeted each other like best buddies. They were hugging and slapping each other on the back. It was bizarre. Years later Ginger Baker would sum up the row by claiming that 'The world's best drummer has been sacked by the world's worst bass player'.

That summer, the band recorded the *Sonic Attack* and *Church of Hawkwind* albums at Rockfield. But given the recent upheavals with Ginger Baker in the run-up to recording, the experience wasn't as enjoyable as it had been in previous visits. Dave Brock recalls:

> We got everybody together at Rockfield to do the album and Martin Griffin, who was our drummer for that record, promptly caught German measles. So everything had to come to a halt. It was really awful and the band was a bit concerned about how things were going. So I went home and got all the 8-track tapes I'd recorded of the band rehearsing, and transferred the ones we wanted on to 24-track, and worked them up from there into finished songs.

Overall, Hawkwind's main man was pleased with what they'd finally achieved against all the odds in Wales:

> *Sonic Attack* has a lot of weird sound effects on it. There are some things that will make you jump out of your chair. At high volume, it will actually vibrate things off tables. We broke a lot of coffee cups in the studio with it.

Looking back, the experience of recording *Sonic Attack* and *Church of Hawkwind* didn't sour the band's affection for Rockfield. 'It was a good atmosphere to work in,' insists Huw.

> I'm very much a city person myself. Dave Brock, though, has lived in the countryside and is very much a country bumpkin. But nearby Monmouth is pretty lively. There's like a pub per street. And you had the peace and quiet of the countryside, where you could sit by the river and contemplate your navel.

The band returned to Rockfield at the beginning of 1982 with its most stable line-up for years. Dave Brock and Huw Lloyd Langton were again joined by Harvey Bainbridge on bass and Martin Griffin on drums. The songs were rehearsed, and tapes recorded and mixed in south Wales with Rockfield mainstay Pat Moran co-producing. Moran had also worked on *Sonic Attack*. The album was released as *Choose Your Masques* during what was becoming a prolific period for the band.

The band also re-recorded a tenth anniversary version of 'Silver Machine' at the studios in Wales. It was meant as a special commemorative souvenir for their fans. But the record company released it, against their wishes, as a single.

By June 1982 Huw Lloyd Langton was finding the recording process of Hawkwind a difficult one.

> The album *Choose Your Masques* was done in bits. Dave had done some backing tracks, I'd done some work in Martin's studio, and he'd dubbed on the drum machine bits. The last few albums had been done that way. It's one way of doing it, but I'd rather do it as a band unit.

As the band recorded album after album at Rockfield, they became part of the furniture. If you recorded at the famous studio, you'd more likely than not come across the space rockers at some time or another.

Of all the bands that have crossed their path at Rockfield, one group sticks in the minds of both Dave and Huw: the 1980s ska band, Bad Manners.

The band, and its larger-than-life lead singer Buster Bloodvessel, made a big impression on the Welsh studio in general. In 1981, they took advantage of the more surreal of Rockfield's recording options when laying down tracks for their album *Gosh It's ... Bad Manners*. The band decided to record the song 'Don't Be Angry' live in the courtyard of the studio with a large crowd of drunkards assembled from the local pubs to play the role of the audience, who were also invited to join in with the chorus. The crowd effects were authentic to say the least. Hawkwind guitarist Huw remembers getting on well with the group. 'Even though Buster Bloodvessel looks like a complete maniac – he's the most civilised person in that band and their whole crew.' It seems the maniacs were elsewhere.

I remember the keyboard player, and one of the others, came screeching up the drive early one morning in their car. It was almost dawn, though I was still up watching videos or something on the television. I heard these screeching tyres, and these two nutters from Bad Manners were outside. They started beeping their horns when they saw me looking through the window and shouted, 'Are you coming out for a ride then?' They were in a fairly manic state, but I thought I'd better go, or they'd wake everyone else up. And we'd been recording until the early hours of the morning, so I knew most of the band wouldn't be best pleased. Anyway I went on this drive with them, which was absolutely petrifying. They were flying down little country lanes at amazingly high speeds. It was quite scary. But somehow we made it back and, to my surprise and delight, they dropped me off still in one piece.

But Huw's bandmate Dave Brock got one up on Bad Manners just before both bands left Rockfield at the end of recording.

My girlfriend at the time sold one of the band her car. But what they didn't know was that it was stuck in reverse gear. So the poor guy picked it up in Monmouth and had to drive it, in reverse, all the way back to the studios. I got a call from Kingsley a few weeks later. 'Hey', he said, 'this car of yours is still here. Bad Manners have disappeared and dumped the car here.' I think it stayed there for a year before they finally got rid of it.

The band continued recording throughout the late 1980s and 1990s, establishing themselves as genuine rock icons and, nearly 50 years after they began, Hawkwind are still going strong. I caught up with Dave Brock in October 2006 on the first night of their autumn tour. The venue was the Deco Theatre in Northampton, where around 700 fans packed in to watch the band play in support of their CD *Take Me To Your Leader*. The band were in sublime form playing classics like 'Psychedelic Warlords' and 'Spirit of the Age' and they sounded as good as they've ever done. The interview was held in the tour bus outside the venue.

Dave Brock sits on the light brown leather seat, which fills the back of the bus in a semi-circle, and reflects on a successful gig (apart from one or two glitches with their impressive light show). With *The Da Vinci Code* playing quietly on the DVD player in front of us, the Hawkwind frontman also looks back at the many good times the band had at Rockfield. Bass player Alan Davey arrives in the middle of this, and agrees that the Welsh studio has a special place in the band's heart. Talk turns to the Old Mill House rehearsal rooms and the wonderful days spent fishing on the river Monnow outside. 'I caught a huge grayling once,' announces the proud bassist.

> This fish was big enough to feed the whole band. But that bastard Nik Turner snuck down in the night and ate it all. He even scoffed the head and the eyes. Everything! What a greedy bastard!

Dave Brock changes the subject from the bizarre eating habits of the band's former saxophone player and returns to the subject of recording at Rockfield. It seems there may be some hidden gems recorded at the Welsh studio buried in the Hawkwind vaults.

Dave believes there's a good album gathering dust.

> There's a lot of stuff that was recorded at Rockfield studios that was never released. I've been doing some archiving and looking at loads and loads of tapes: all these wonderful golden oldies recorded on 16-track and 8-track at Rockfield. It's interesting stuff.

These archive sessions were later released as *The Rockfield Studio Session Tapes* by Voiceprint Records in late 2007.

It's nearly midnight, so I say my farewells and leave the bus as the band prepares to set off for their next gig in Cambridge the following evening.

As that night demonstrated to me, Hawkwind have built up a loyal following down the years. Since the 1960s, the band has ignored prevailing fashions and stuck steadfastly to their own rules and their own set of sounds. They've made their mark as the inventors and pioneers of space rock: a sound moulded much of the time in the serene setting of the Welsh countryside. Months and months were spent at Rockfield Studios, chilling out and smoking spliffs with other big name musicians. All the while the band were recording improbable tales of black holes and space overlords, all with their own unique blend of psychedelic rock. Rockfield found itself at the heart of a rock success story. But the studio's links with Hawkwind didn't end there. Former member Lemmy would return to ensure Rockfield would once again be at the centre of a major piece of rock history.

RECOMMENDED LISTENING

Doremi Fasol Latido, Hawkwind 1972

Warrior on the Edge of Time, Hawkwind 1975

Quark, Strangeness and Charm, Hawkwind 1977

Sonic Attack, Hawkwind 1981

Choose Your Masques, Hawkwind 1982

Machine 10th Anniversary EP, Hawkwind 1982

Gosh it's ... Bad Manners, Bad Manners 1981

CHAPTER FIVE:
MOTÖRHEAD'S PAINFUL BIRTH AT ROCKFIELD

How would you like to join the most evil band that ever walked the earth?

Lemmy

A tall figure, dressed from head to toe in black, strolls across the stage. He strides slowly in front of a huge stack of Marshall amps and an impressive drum kit, both of which are overshadowed by a massive black backdrop, featuring his band's famous snaggletooth logo: a hybrid of a gorilla and dog skull with two wild boar tusks, wearing a biker's helmet and chains.

Lemmy is taking a long, hard puff on a cigarette. He exhales slowly, and deliberately, and looks around the venue. Tonight it will be filled with thousands of Motörhead fans. The band is thirty years old and this is their anniversary tour. It's three decades since the band cut its first album at Rockfield.

His reflections over, Lemmy casts a simple glance at his bandmates and the music starts up. The grizzled singer saunters up to the microphone at the front of the stage, pauses and then takes up *the* stance. It's become one of Lemmy's trademarks. His microphone is set up higher than his head with the mic angled down towards his mouth. When Lemmy leans back to sing, it looks uncomfortable, but he remarks coolly, 'It's easier for me to hit the high notes this way!'

Guitarist Phil Campbell and drummer Mikkey Dee start strumming away gently on acoustic guitars. Both are sat either side of their singer, perched on chairs, rocking slowly back and forth, intently focused on the notes they are playing. Phil Campbell has been with the band for twenty years now and the Treforest-born guitarist saw his fame spread beyond the band's fan base, when he finished twentieth in a poll to find the top 100 Welsh heroes.

Former King Diamond drummer Mikkey Dee joined in 1991 and the trio have been together ever since. Only Lemmy, though, remains from the band's first line-up, which made its recording debut at Rockfield. In 1975, two years before the arrival of punk and the Sex Pistols, Motörhead based themselves at the Welsh farmhouse, which was rapidly gaining a reputation as a recording studio of note. It was here that Lemmy would capture the band's groundbreaking loud and fast musical bombardment on to tape for the first time.

Back on stage, the bluesy sounds of the song 'Whorehouse Blues' continue to echo round Cardiff University's main hall. On a small balcony overlooking the stage, a few students have managed to sneak their way past the tour office to get a peek at what's happening down below.

'Is that Motörhead?' asks one of the students. 'It doesn't sound like them,' replies one of her friends, 'but isn't that Lemmy?' The group nod as one as they recognise one of the most iconic figures in rock music. If Motörhead are a seminal band in the history of rock, then Lemmy is one of its most unmistakable and captivating figures. The group nods in unison, once again, as they hear his growling voice rumble across the venue, singing about the how music helped the song's narrators turn life on the wrong side of the tracks around.

Lemmy could easily be singing about the band's journey from the days when they were slated by the music press, and ignored by the record-buying public, through to the good times brought about by a string of successful records and tours. For those watching the surprisingly mellow end to this soundcheck, it's a strange scene. It's not often Motörhead cruise through a slow, bluesy, acoustic number. More often than not the soundcheck would end with their usual trademark sonic assault on the senses. Maybe time does mellow the soul. But in Motörhead's case that's extremely doubtful!

The song they are running through is taken from the band's critically acclaimed 2004 album *Inferno*. It's also the song the trio will start their encore with at tonight's show before sending the audience home reeling with the thunderous classic 'Ace of Spades' and then the mesmeric 'Overkill'.

Motörhead are notorious. The band's snaggletooth, or war pig, logo is instantly recognisable. It's now a style icon and other bands know it's cool to flaunt their Motörhead influence by wearing the band's T-shirt whenever they play live, or even in their music videos. In the Foo Fighters' video for their single 'Resolve', band leader, and former Nirvana drummer, Dave Grohl wears a Motörhead tour shirt with pride throughout. Grohl is a Motörhead fan. In 2004, he persuaded Lemmy to star in his recording project, which was released under the name Probot. Grohl said that hooking up with Lemmy was one of the greatest days of his life. He famously described how the Motörhead singer recorded his vocal and bass tracks for the album in just two takes, and when he was done asked everyone in the studio, 'Alright! Now then, who wants to go look at some tits?'

With rock music back in vogue, Motörhead's 'couldn't care less' attitude – coupled with a hint of hard drinking, hard rocking danger – has seen a whole stream of pop stars and supermodels take to wearing the band's merchandise in public. It might, though, have been so different. After leaving Hawkwind, Lemmy wanted to call his new band Bastard. But he decided against the name and instead opted for Motörhead – the American slang for speed freak. It was also the last song Lemmy had written for Hawkwind. This was the time for Lemmy to take centre stage. 'I'd been fired by my last three bands so I figured I'd start my own and that way I'd be safe.' So he recruited guitarist Larry Wallis, who was with the Pink Fairies, and drummer Lucas Fox, who he met through his roommate. Wallis explained to me how he frequently crossed paths with Lemmy.

It was because of the hippy scene going on at the time that we ran into each other an awful lot and we used to do gigs together that were known as PinkWind gigs. Then Lemmy got chucked out of Hawkwind when they were crossing the border from Canada to America. I was sitting around at home not doing very much, when Lemmy phoned up and said, 'I've just been thrown out of Hawkwind. How would you like to join the most evil band that ever walked the earth?' So I said, 'Sure,' and jumped into a taxi, right there and then, and went over to the rehearsal room in Chelsea, where Lemmy and Lucas Fox were waiting and that was that. We made an awful racket, took a load of drugs and became Motörhead.

Lemmy set out the band's stall early on. His amps, which had been psychedelic colours with Hawkwind, were now painted black. Their first show was at the Roundhouse in London on Sunday 20 July 1975. They were supporting pomp-rockers Greenslade. Motörhead took to the stage to the recorded sounds of marching feet and people yelling 'Sieg Heil'. One of the band's dark black amps had a big silver-painted human skull on it – the forerunner to the now legendary Motörhead logo. That night the band played just seven songs, including 'Silver Machine' and 'Motorhead'. Wallis was enjoying life with his new band and thought the Roundhouse gig boded well for the future.

It was a great gig! We'd let people know it was going to be an awful, noisy, speedy monster of a concert. And so all of Lemmy's fans were there and a lot of Pink Fairies fans turned up. They loved it.

After a handful of gigs – including a disastrous experience supporting Blue Oyster Cult – Motörhead were voted 'worst band in the world' by *Melody Maker* magazine. Splashed over the front page, it was nevertheless good publicity for the embryonic band. Many audiences, though, were bemused. Lemmy and the band were often confronted by rows of people with blank faces and their mouths hanging wide open. Despite it being early days, the trio already prided themselves on being the fastest band in the world. Sometimes this desire would get the better of them at their early gigs, much to the annoyance of many a promoter. Larry Wallis remembers:

> We were doing a Sunday night gig in Croydon. We rushed on stage and off we went at 100 miles an hour. I remember Lemmy and I were shouting at Lucas, 'Faster, you bloody idiot, faster.' We went down well, and triumphantly strode off the stage. In the dressing room we were considering an encore, when a furious promoter burst in to the dressing room, demanding to know why we'd done 25 minutes instead of the agreed hour. We were astonished to find we'd played the entire set in half the usual time!

With the band slowly finding its feet playing live, Motörhead's reputation as hellraisers was further cemented when the music press printed the now infamous quote from Lemmy: 'It'll be the dirtiest rock 'n' roll band in the world. If we moved next door, your lawn would die!' No invite to appear on *Gardeners' World* then! Never mind, the fledging band had, at least, secured a record deal with United Artists – Hawkwind's label. UA had decided to stick with Lemmy and his new project. Little did they know what to expect. Did the company believe Lemmy's new band would be another space rock outfit like Hawkwind? Possibly. But whatever they thought, they weren't prepared for the reality of Motörhead. Their music was in a class of its own: fast, heavy and very loud.

MOTÖRHEAD

Formed by Lemmy in 1975, after he left Hawkwind. Motörhead's groundbreaking loud and fast style inspired the creation of speed metal and thrash metal.

The band's big breakthrough came with the 1980 smash hit album *Ace of Spades*.

Unaware of what they were about to unleash on the world, the record company started making plans for the group to record some material. As UA had a deal with Rockfield for their acts, the trio were dispatched to south Wales. The Rockfield experience was one that was to tear the group apart, and see it reform stronger and better. It was the birthplace of one of the world's best, and most enduring, metal acts.

Three decades on and Lemmy smiles as the band finish their rehearsal in Cardiff to the applause of the watching roadies and university bar staff. The soundcheck over, I make my way down the winding staircase to the main hall along with my friend and photographer Andrew Pritchard, who's here to record the interview on film for this book. As we make our way across the empty hall, the road crew start to test the dry ice machine and thick bursts of white smoke drift across the stage. We move around the mixing desk in the centre of the hall, and then follow the steel barriers at the front of the stage around to a gap at the left-hand side. Just behind this opening, to the left of the drum kit, is a dressing-room door. Inside, Lemmy is standing in front of a portable fruit machine. Its door is open and Lemmy is restacking pound coins inside.

'I'll be with you in a minute,' he says as he slots more money into the steel grooves.

'Are you winning?' I enquire.

'Not really. It's my money.'

It might seem like a pointless exercise to gamble for your own money, but any distraction is a welcome one to the monotony of life on the road. Plus, Lemmy is addicted to fruit machines.

> I can't help myself. The first time I went to Vegas, I won £9,000. The next time I put £4,000 of it back. You can't beat the fruit machine. But there'd be no point to them if you won all the time.

Lemmy's other major distraction is Jack Daniel's. The frontman of the world's loudest band now takes a seat in front of me and pours himself a big JD and coke, and another for me. With concerns over his health, Lemmy's concession is to put ice cubes in his bourbon these days.

As the leather-clad singer picks up his drink, and moves away from a pile of untouched sandwiches, I can't help but think that Jack Daniel's was today's breakfast, lunch and tea. His former Hawkwind bandmate Dave Brock believes Lemmy 'has got to take it easy. He'll conk out one day if he continues to blaze a trail with his hard drinking and that would be a shame.' Lemmy takes a seat, fixes me with a big smile, and dismisses worries over his health. His eyes flicker briefly down to the tattoo emblazoned on his left arm: 'Born to lose – live to win'. Lemmy now turns his mind back to the start of this world-famous band and declares: 'Motörhead were born at Rockfield.'

He pauses after this announcement and takes a massive swig of Jack Daniel's and coke before continuing.

I was first there with Hawkwind in the early 70s. The first album I did there was *Doremi Fasol Latido*. Later when I was there with Motörhead, we did rehearsals at the Old Mill House. It was very basic back then. I remember they had these huge mattresses stuck to the walls for sound-proofing. It was a weird sight, man. But the studio had this awesome ambient sound – even with the mattresses. But the place was not like it is today. The courtyard was derelict back then and there were no residential facilities available for us, for some reason or other. They were booked up I think. So we had to stay in a hotel in Monmouth. At least, I think it was Monmouth. Do they have hotels there?

Not that the band had much use for hotel rooms back in those early days. Larry Wallis remembers Motörhead's drug use had become a way of life.

We didn't really sleep very much. In those days we took a lot of speed and we stayed up for days on end.

Motörhead's record was to be produced at Rockfield by Dave Edmunds. This news was met with delight by Lemmy. Edmunds was one of his heroes, and to this day he quotes him as a major influence on his work. He'd first come across the Welshman when he heard one of his early bands, Love Sculpture, and their version of 'Sabre Dance'.

That song was like everyone was on pills [says Lemmy]. It was the fastest thing I'd ever heard. I was determined to better it. Dave, though, was a brilliant producer and a guitar wizard. I watched him put down thirty-five guitar tracks for one song. He's a genius as a producer. He's as good as Phil Spector.

Other band members, though, were not convinced that Edmunds was the right man for the job. Larry Wallis had his doubts:

Basically I never agreed to it. Edmunds is a fabulous producer. Absolutely incredible! But just because Lemmy was a fan of his, he wanted him to do our record, which I never thought was a great idea. I don't think Dave could cope with working with a group of maniacs, who had a mental entourage of drug-addled Hell's Angels and groupies.

Long-time Rockfield producer John David also felt that Edmunds and Motörhead were unusual bedfellows.

At that time Dave wanted to do more production and was willing to look at pretty much any band. Motörhead's manager even came up to us in the studio at Rockfield and said, 'Of course they're not really a band. They're just car thieves.' That's how he explained them! But I do remember one time, when the band were completely out of their heads on drugs. It was about 6 o'clock in the evening and Lemmy was trying to overdub this guitar solo. It wasn't difficult. It was a very simple riff and only about ten seconds long. But Lemmy was so out of it, on some drug or other, that he just could not play it. But he was trying over, and over again, without success. Every time I walked past the door, I could hear it, the same bloody guitar phrase. And Dave is sitting at the mixer desk with a dazed look on his face, while Lemmy was in the studio, sagging at his knees, still trying to play this solo. Anyway I was back there at about 10 o'clock the next morning. They were still there! They were still doing it. All night they'd been trying, so they hadn't gone to bed. And there was Lemmy still playing that same guitar line – and badly! I couldn't believe it. Then later that morning, the maintenance guy, Otto, went in to the studio just to tidy some stuff up and he saw this plate of beans on the floor with mildew growing on it. He thought that the way Lemmy was staggering all over the place, he was going to step in it. So he was going to take it away. But Lemmy saw him and slurred in a loud voice, 'Aww, don't take that. I was going to eat that!' So he left it for Lemmy to have for lunch! Motörhead used to get in a terrible state.

In the end, Edmunds would only record four songs with Motörhead. Two of them were tracks Lemmy had written with Hawkwind: 'Motorhead' and 'Lost Johnny'. The other two were 'City Kids' and 'Leaving Here'.

Lemmy remembers,

We did just those four songs with him. Then it all ended. I remember management from Led Zeppelin's new label Swansong came down to poach him. I watched them walking in the court-yard with Dave. They were persuading him to join their label. He did, and that was the end of our time with him. He was whisked away by Led Zep's minions.

Motörhead didn't have to look far for a replacement. Larry Wallis recalls,

Down at the studios, they had a house engineer at the time called Fritz Fryer, who was originally a member of The Four Pennies. If you remember they had a number one single in 1964 with the bal-lad 'Juliet'. It was quite a popular song at the time. And his wife was also at Rockfield doing the catering. So Fritz stepped in and took over from Dave and got the album finished, while his wife fed us.

Lemmy, though, wasn't so happy: 'Fritz Fryer finished our record, but I don't think it was as good overall as it would have been if Dave had completed the thing with us.' It was around the time that Edmunds left that Motörhead would make its first change in personnel. During the recording sessions in Wales, the band decided Lucas Fox had to go.

Both Lemmy and Larry liked Lucas personally. But professionally, they didn't think the drummer was cutting it. Larry remembers that both he and Lemmy had a tough choice to make.

> In all honesty, Lucas is a lovely chap and a great guy. But he wasn't the best drummer in the world for Motörhead. It was a very fast band. Everything was done at a thousand miles an hour. And Lucas, quite brutally, couldn't keep up. It was a bit of a drag really. Lemmy and I were going at it hammer and tongs and poor Lucas was struggling.

The other two members of the band also viewed Lucas as a bit of a jinx. He was bad luck. 'I realised Lucas just wasn't working out,' says Lemmy.

> He was getting very weird. It didn't help that he was trying to keep up with my speed habit. So he was on a loser with that one. Basically Lucas caused chaos at Rockfield. One day, for example, we were in the studio listening to a playback. He was leaning against a part of the console that had a hinge on it, so it could be opened and cleaned. But someone hadn't put the catches back right. Lucas leaned on it and all this stuff – half-filled ashtrays and drinks and all kinds of shit – fell right into the desk. There were sparks flying everywhere. The whole thing just blew up. He screamed and ran right out of the studio. Larry shouted out after him, 'Hey Lucas, don't you dare walk past my monitors – they'll burst into flames too.' Lucas was a good geezer really but he just didn't cut it.

Lemmy, though, had a replacement in mind even before Lucas was finally given the boot.

> I'd already met Phil Taylor. I'd left Rockfield during recording for the weekend and was back in London. Phil had a car, so I asked him if he could give me a lift to the studio. He mentioned he could play drums, so I thought we'd try him out. I told him to bring his drum kit just in case.

The first track Phil played on was 'Iron Horse'. As soon as he'd finished, Lemmy knew he had his man. The new drummer also made an immediate impression on the group's guitarist.

> I used to disappear from Rockfield occasionally for a day or so, to do a Fairies gig, while Lemmy would shoot back to London to do whatever it was Lemmy was doing. And when he came back, one day, he had this 'little monster' with him: Phil Taylor. He was just a kid. Lucas wasn't around, and so Phil listened to the playback of the album. And this cheeky kid said, 'Get rid of your drummer. I can do much better than that.' And we thought, 'Well, why not?'

So Lucas was out and Phil was in. The new drummer installed his kit in Rockfield's recording studio and got down to work, revelling in his role in the band. It was his first time in a recording studio, and he was having the time of his life. The Leeds-born drummer was a hyperactive tough nut, and fitted in perfectly, earning himself the nickname 'Animal'. The day after he arrived at Rockfield, having slept the night on the floor, he got up stark naked and decided to roam around looking for breakfast. As his bandmates walked in, he simply said to them in explanation: 'It's OK. I'm on drugs.'

'He was absolutely perfect,' admits Wallis.

> Lemmy seems to recall me saying something like, 'He's a horrible little bastard. He's perfect for the band.' And he was. He was a cheeky little Dennis the Menace, who could play drums like a lunatic. He was marvellous and his sense of humour was the same as ours.

Life with Motörhead in Wales was full-on in every sense. It was an over-the-top experience with the band enjoying a love-hate relationship. There would be frequent fights between the band members, some of them real knockabouts. Arguments in the studio could soon turn into fist fights. 'The band became a very insular unit. Every so often there would be some kind of flare-up as these things do, but the band would eventually make up and go for a drink in the local pub in

Monmouth, with all forgotten,' recalls Larry. 'On the whole, while at
Rockfield we were a great gang and we really enjoyed it.'

Work on the album continued with the new drummer comple-
menting the other two members perfectly. Phil's main job was re-
recording drums on the whole album apart from the track 'Lost Johnny'.

Newly installed producer Fritz Fryer remembers that the night
Motörhead returned to Rockfield from London to continue with
their debut album, they went straight into the studio, recorded a new
song, 'Iron Horse', which was Lemmy's ode to Hell's Angels, before
going to bed.

It seemed to me that this augured well for a smooth, straight-
forward job: a few overdubs, mix the tracks and deliver the tapes
to the record company. Wrong! Lemmy explained to me that
they weren't happy with some of the drum parts the previous
drummer had laid down and they'd like Phil to re-record these.
'Oh, and by the way,' he told me, 'We have four days to do this, as
Her Majesty wishes to detain Phil at her pleasure for some minor
rock 'n' roll related misdemeanour involving drugs.' Yeah. Phil was
off to jail, so we had to get cracking. So we began to replace the
drum sounds. In building terms, this is like underpinning walls
that have just been built. It's a long laborious process. As a result,
this had a knock-on effect. Re-arranging drum rhythm patterns
meant that Lemmy's bass parts were now out of kilter with what
the bass drum was doing. So, many of the tracks needed the
bass replacing. Having done this, the original guitar parts now
didn't mesh with the new order, so guess what? Yes, we redid
those as well! One of the songs actually ended up with twenty-
three of the twenty-four tracks available re-recorded, the only the
thing left from the original was an overdubbed tambourine.

The stress of recording led Fritz into the murky world of drug taking
as Motörhead continued to experiment with various illegal substances.

Other than cigarettes and coffee, I had an absolute ban on
myself taking other stimulants [recalls Fritz]. I strongly believed

MOTÖRHEAD

Ian Gillan told his official website, Caramba!:
*Motörhead were doing an open-air show in Dublin.
I watched the show from start to finish ... it felt as if
I'd strapped a Boeing 747 to each ear. Later in the
dressing room the guitar player said to Lemmy, 'Here,
we never done our new single'. Lemmy turns and says,
'I done it second.' The drummer says, 'I done it fifth!'*

it was a producer's job to maintain a clear and objective mind in order to properly fulfil the function that I'd been employed for. It was OK for musicians to indulge and Motörhead were certainly indulgent. But 32 hours of nonstop concentration had taken its toll. I had been turning up the volume more and more in an attempt to rivet my attention, the amplifier volume control was now at 11 and I was seriously tired. One of the band – who shall remain nameless – breezed into the control room, having just slept off a marathon re-dubbing session earlier in the day, with me as ever still at the controls. Looking at my slumped form at the mixing desk, he said, 'You need a line Fritz, or we ain't going to make it.' He could be very persuasive, taking out the mirror glass, razor and white powder. The band seemed to prescribe one every 20 minutes. Whilst resisting the frequency, I did succumb to his medication, which saw me through the next sleepless 40 hours.

But no amount of drugs could help with plans to get drummer Phil Taylor to sing on the album later on in the sessions. 'Phil was a big asset to Motörhead,' insists Lemmy, 'but one thing he couldn't do was sing. On this album, Larry had sung a few songs, so we thought we'd give Phil a go as well. We tried him out on 'City Kids'. It didn't work. His singing sounded like two cats being stapled together! It was so funny I had to leave the studio. It was pissing down with rain outside, but there I was on my knees in the mud laughing so hard. We had to put an end to that idea.'

The band enjoyed their time at Rockfield. Life away from the distractions of London helped them as they set about moulding their new sound. Life in the wilds of Wales was good. 'It was a great studio. It was full of interesting characters,' remembers Lemmy:

> The two brothers, Kingsley and Charles, were both in charge back then. They were both farmers, but also running the studio. They'd come into the studio during the middle of recording absolutely covered in shit. And they'd simply ask 'How's it going?' They were great.

When recording was over, the band was proud of the material they laid down in Wales. The album was a mishmash of songs culled from the members' various ex-bands, cover versions and a few originals. The overall sound was more hard rock, garage-blues than the band's later faster, heavy metal sound. The title track – and album opener – had originally been written by Lemmy for the 'B' side of the Hawkwind single 'Kings of Speed'. But for his new band, the song was a makeover. It now had a darker, more ominous overtone, in stark contrast to its Hawkwind incarnation. Fritz Fryer recalls the band going to great lengths to get a distinctive opening for the track.

> It was decided that the album should open with the roar of a revving motorbike, which would segue into the opening bars of the band's eponymous track, 'Motorhead'. We had young hopefuls from miles around queuing up the drive of Rockfield on their assorted Hondas, Suzukis and Yamahas. But none of them came anywhere near creating the noise that we were looking for.
>
> Well, Lemmy's contacts cover the entire social spectrum and with one phone call he had summoned the entire West Coast Chapter of the Hell's Angels. When they arrived the next day, Monmouth was boarded up like a Western set out of *High Noon*,

as these bikers descended on the studios. There were about thirty of them, each one insisting that his Harley Davison should have the studio microphone rammed up its exhaust pipe. Each audition had to be played back to the odorous throng that had gathered in the tiny control room, chanting 'Lemmy is righteous'. To say the least, I was nervous about making the decision about which take to keep, so as Lemmy was 'righteous', I let him decide.

Larry Wallis also remembers the day when the band's Hell's Angels friends converged on Rockfield:

The album started with a Harley Davidson kicking up, and then riding away into the distance. And we actually did that. Our Angel friends came down – Tramp, Blue, Charger and Goat among others. We set microphones up outside the studio and the guys kicked up their hogs and rode into the distance and you could still hear them three miles away. We picked one and that's how the album starts.

Before the Rockfield sessions were over, the Welsh studio was to be visited by some VIP guests. Fritz Fryer remembers Motörhead's lead singer was particularly nervous.

One evening, Lemmy told me that his mother and stepfather were coming to visit him the following day so would I mind desisting from swearing in their presence! Sure enough, the next day they arrived, Mum in a royal blue twin-set and pearls, and his stepfather in cavalry twills and navy blue blazer, with the vest pocket emblazoned with the emblem of the yacht club that he was a member of. Having been introduced and exchanged pleasantries, Lemmy and I set off in the direction of the studio. Emphasising some point about his bass playing, I let the F-word slip. His embarrassment was a picture. But I can honestly say that of all the people I met and worked with in the music business, Lemmy was one of the most genuine and decent.

The band and producer left Rockfield feeling that the sessions had been a job well done. They were looking forward to watching the impact of Motörhead's debut album on the music world. But there were troubles ahead. The band returned to London with the master tapes from Rockfield and handed them to the record company. Weeks passed as United Artists stalled on a release date, blaming a range of problems from delays with printing to trouble with the record's sleeve.

More weeks went by, and what should have been the band's debut album remained gathering dust on the shelves at the offices of UA. It soon became apparent that the record company had no intention of issuing the record. Motörhead's frontman finds it difficult even now to restrain his anger at that decision. He takes another big gulp of JD before venting his fury.

> Those bastards at UA began backtracking about its release. For months they strung us along with various lies about when they planned to put it out. But they never did. And in the meantime we couldn't record with another label.

The rest of the band were also deeply upset by that decision. For Larry Wallis, it was hugely disappointing.

> Martin Davies, from United Artists, called us into his office and said, 'No hard feelings. You can keep the tapes and go your own way.' And he wished us the best of luck. We really begged him to release the single 'Motorhead'. We thought it would really sell and change our fortunes. And it would have done. We were on the covers of every magazine and newspaper. And 'Motorhead' was a fantastic song. We used to play it twice at gigs, it was so good. But the record company didn't have the nerve to release it. At time, UA were more involved with Dr Feelgood than us.

With his producing duties over, Fritz Fryer thought the group had a hit album on their hands and was baffled by the record company's decision. 'Ironically, United Artists saw the band as an unmanageable, threatening bunch,' he remembers.

And after a long period of indecision, they passed the tapes on to EMI for release, who had fired the Sex Pistols for similar reasons. But it was only a question of time before Motörhead's powerful sound and image registered with record buyers.

More changes were to follow in the wake of the Rockfield sessions. Larry Wallis decided to call it a day when Lemmy drafted in ex-Curtis Knight guitarist 'Fast' Eddie Clarke to try to give the outfit a heavier, chunkier sound. Larry objected strongly to the idea of having two guitarists and quit the band during the auditions.

It deteriorated pretty badly for me. Suddenly we didn't have a record deal and we weren't really doing that many gigs. I'll be candid with you. I felt Lemmy's royalties from Hawkwind were keeping him quite a happy chappy. There wasn't much happening for the rest of us. I thought about it for a long time, and just got fed up with so little going on. We were Motörhead: the band that wasn't recording or working. I had my other band the Pink Fairies and they were kind of miffed with me going off with Motörhead anyway. So I just went back to them full-time.

Hit hard by their record company's refusal to release their album – the takeover by EMI hadn't led to a change of mind – the band considered calling it a day. A gig planned for the Marquee club in London was their last for that year, and could very well have been the final ever appearance of Motörhead. But Chiswick Records boss Ted Carroll had become a fan of the band and wanted to record that show live. As it turned out, he didn't tape the gig, but offered the band studio time instead. Finally free from UA, the band were only given a day or two to lay down a single. But with all the groundwork they'd done on the songs at Rockfield, they laid down thirteen tracks in that time. So the bulk of the Rockfield sessions were released in 1977 on the band's self-titled debut album on Chiswick Records. The tracks 'Motorhead', 'Vibrator', 'Lost Johnny', 'Iron Horse', 'The Watcher' and 'Born To Lose' would all see the light of day, reworked on this album. The release also featured Joe Petagno's artwork, which would give the band its distinct identity.

More importantly, the album also charted. The band was saved.

The new-look Motörhead eventually transferred to Bronze Records and enjoyed increasing success with the albums *Overkill* and *Bomber*. Then Motörhead returned to Rockfield in 1979, after touring non-stop. They were back enjoying the tranquillity of the Welsh studio for three weeks to rehearse new material for their next project: the *Ace of Spades* album.

That record would propel the band into the limelight and bring them global success. And as a result of this new-found glory, United Artists dug deep into their vaults and pulled out Motörhead's original recordings from their time at Rockfield. They decided now was the time for the world to hear the music that the record company officials had hated so much when Lemmy and Co had recorded it four years earlier. In 1979, the record was finally put out as *On Parole*. Lemmy almost spits with disgust as he recalls the treatment of their first recording.

> We were eventually released from our contract, thankfully. But after *Ace of Spades* was a massive hit, they finally released our first recordings years later as *On Parole*. Fuckers! They were just cashing in.

Lemmy reflects on the band's first record – the one that almost never was.

> We really enjoyed being at Rockfield. The place just had a real rock 'n' roll feel to it and, despite all the problems within that line-up, it gave me a real taste of what Motörhead could achieve. It set the tone.

On that night in 2005, Motörhead played to a packed hall and thousands of fans – thirty years on from their tentative beginnings in Monmouth.

'I'm not ashamed of anything I've done,' reflects Lemmy, 'On my deathbed I'll look back proudly at my achievements.'

Lemmy was a genuine rock icon. Just hours before his band were due on stage at Cardiff University, his face would once again grace the TV screens of the nation. He had been asked to address the Welsh Assembly using an anti-drugs platform to call for the legalisation of heroin.

That afternoon, Lemmy took time off from Motörhead's 30th anniversary tour to warn of the fatal dangers of the drug, and TV viewers across Europe and the US watched the singer explain how making heroin legal would allow it to be taxed and regulated, and would keep users away from drug dealers in order to cut down crime.

Back in the dressing room, I finish my drink, Lemmy shakes my hand and says goodbye, telling me to enjoy tonight's concert.

I leave with my friend Andrew, with both of us looking forward to watching this legendary band in action in just a few hours' time. As we exit the university's main hall and head to a nearby pub to await the start of the concert, I ponder the mark that Lemmy has left on rock music. To me, he came across as a larger than life figure. Lemmy was more than just his music. Part of his appeal was also his full-on lifestyle. The guy oozed rock 'n' roll. He's a musician, a songwriter and a hellraiser. As if to confirm the point, Andrew turns to me with a massive smile on his face and says: 'Wow! You drank from Lemmy's bottle of Jack Daniel's!!'

RECOMMENDED LISTENING

On Parole, Motörhead 1979

Damage Case: The anthology, Lemmy 2006

CHAPTER SIX:
QUEEN AND ACE
RULE THE AIRWAVES

At the time, *A Night at the Opera* was one of the most expensive albums ever made. The cost in terms of studio time was phenomenal! If it hadn't sold as many millions as it eventually did ... EMI might have had second thoughts after spending all that money and might have dropped Queen.

Peter Hince, Queen roadie

It's late at night at Rockfield Studios and Steve Lomax, lead singer of the rock band Tokyo Dragons, is in his room, after a long session putting together the band's debut album *Give Me the Fear*. Steve is tired, and his attention is barely on the music videos which are playing on the TV. Suddenly, though, the singer sits bolt upright as he hears a familiar tune coming from the TV speakers. Freddie Mercury's voice starts to drift across the room and Steve's attention is now firmly fixed on the video in front of him. He's watching Queen's most famous song playing before his eyes: 'Bohemian Rhapsody'. From the window of his room, Steve can see the very studio here where Freddie, Brian May, Roger Taylor and John Deacon put together part of rock music legend:

I thought to myself, 'Bloody hell, that song was recorded here!!' And I was staring at the very place in which Queen had come up with a moment of magic and I said to myself, 'Yeah, I recognise that sound!'

Legend has it that 30 years earlier in the summer of 1975, Freddie Mercury was sitting at the piano at Rockfield Studios. Close to a window, the singer was gazing at a weathervane slowly turning in the blustery wind outside in the courtyard. In that moment of inspiration, the words 'Any way the wind blows' came into his mind. It was the last piece in the jigsaw. He'd found the final line to a song that would catapult Queen on their way to greatness.

And it's also said that on one of the days when Freddie was putting the finishing touches to Queen's masterpiece, the rest of the band were outside in a field playing frisbee. According to the record's producer, Roy Thomas Baker, these stories may, or may not, be true.

Most of the record was, from my perspective, very difficult. If we were doing guitar overdubs, I'd be in the studio with Brian. If there were any piano overdubs, I'd be there with Freddie, and if it was drums, I'd be in the studio with Roger. So from my viewpoint, it felt like I was chained to the control room. So those stories could be true, but I was too busy tinkering away at Rockfield to notice the band's every move.

QUEEN

An English rock band formed by Freddie Mercury, Brian May and Roger Taylor in 1970 with bassist John Deacon joining the following year. The 1986 single 'A Kind Of Magic' topped the charts in thirty-five different countries.

BBC Radio DJ Kenny Everett played a test copy of 'Bohemian Rhapsody' 14 times in two days, despite the single being nearly six minutes long.

Queen first arrived at Rockfield in July 1974 to start work on their third album, *Sheer Heart Attack*. That record would be a turning point for the band. It would bring them their first commercial success, after the relatively slow sales for their first two albums *Queen* and *Queen II*.

Both those records had been made with legendary producer Roy Thomas Baker. He'd started out as a trainee engineer at Decca Records in the mid 1960s, before joining the newly opened Trident Studios as a staff engineer in 1969. There he'd made his name working with the likes of Frank Zappa, Santana, Free and T-Rex. Most importantly, it was at Trident that he first met Queen. The band's first two albums were mostly recorded at Trident before the producer decided to move things out to the country.

> Queen's third album was the first time I'd worked at Rockfield. I think it was a case of getting out of town, getting out of London and all the things that go along with life in the big city. With a lot of bands – though not so much with Queen – if you're within a square mile of a strip club, then you're going to lose them. They will just vanish! Musicians and strippers! You sometimes just can't keep them apart. There are so many distractions in a big city that it's great to get out into the countryside to record.

The band had made great strides on *Queen II*, including the hit single 'Seven Seas of Rhye'. But for *Sheer Heart Attack* they were determined to go one better. 'It was a really good album,' says Roy.

> It was a conscious effort on behalf of everyone to make a great record – to really make a mark. On the first *Queen* album, we recorded it in downtime, whenever there was a gap in studio time at Trident Studios. *Queen II*, on the other hand, was kitchen sink time! We tried every conceivable idea. Freddie would say to me things like, 'Any ideas you've got, just throw them in, so we can have every idea in the mix.' So that was like the pinnacle of overproduction. We tried every trick in the book and quite a few not in it! But for the third record, *Sheer Heart Attack*, we thought,

'Well, we've proved that point. That we are great in the studio and can throw all manner of ideas onto a record.' So for this one, we thought, 'Why don't we move ahead and see what the deal is with making a record, which is more immediate and which the public can really catch on to.' So we were all living in this one area of Wales, and were working together as a unit. It was business. We had few distractions and could focus on the album.

As band and producer grew together, they felt that this third record would be something very special. And Roy Thomas Baker found the members of Queen a joy to work with.

Everyone had written their own songs and so the driving force for each track would be the person who had written it. Then everyone else would join in and add to that. There was no one singular driving force behind the band. My role was everything from producer to throwing in my ideas. There was also the other point of view of acting as interpreter: when someone else came up with an idea, I'd have to help interpret that into a way we could record on tape. Basically, when it came down to the Rockfield side of things, we were more concerned with getting down the backing tracks. We were experimenting with getting different guitar sounds down in different rooms at the studios and recording the drums and overdubs all in different places. Rockfield has loads of great little live rooms to record in. The main vocals, though, were done elsewhere.

Queen considered themselves an album band, but knew that they needed a big hit single to ensure their future. That hit would come in the form of 'Killer Queen'. The first time Brian May heard that song was when he was ill in bed at Rockfield. He'd suffered hepatitis during Queen's first US tour after being vaccinated with an unclean needle and had stomach problems, which needed an operation. A relapse at Rockfield meant Brian had to lie in bed and listen to his bandmates crafting what he could hear was going to be a great song. The guitarist was immensely frustrated at not being able to take part in those recording sessions. But he had the operation, and once out of hospital, he was able to add his input, as the band had left space for his guitar part and solo. They also re-recorded the harmony for the chorus and so eventually 'Killer Queen' was finished. It was the band's first international hit. Upon its release, the album went to number 2 in the UK charts and number 12 across the Atlantic. *Sheer Heart Attack* also contained a number of other classic Queen rock tracks: 'Now I'm Here', 'Brighton Rock', 'In the Lap of the Gods' and 'Flick Of The Wrist'.

Queen were on the brink of international stardom. Everything now rested on the next album and the initial signs were good. The sound of *Sheer Heart Attack*, and in particular the single 'Killer Queen', hinted strongly at the direction the next record would take. For that crucial follow-up album, Queen returned to Rockfield in August 1975. *A Night at the Opera* would be 'make or break' for the band as their record company were getting cold feet. The cost of making each successive Queen album was getting bigger and bigger and EMI were considering the worth of keeping Queen on their books. To make matters worse *A Night at the Opera* was going to be one of the most expensive albums ever. In a bizarre move, the band decided to record it at seven different studios. As well as Rockfield, they used the Roundhouse, Sarm East, Wessex, Olympic, Lansdowne and Scorpion studios. The band were also changing management, and joining them at this time of flux was roadie Peter Hince.

I worked for Mott the Hoople, when Queen were the support act, which is when I first got to know them. I was a drum roadie and had earlier been asked to work for Brian May, but I didn't take it. Then later, with the other guys from Mott the Hoople, we all went to work for Queen. They wanted a whole new crew, you see. That was during the making of *A Night at the Opera*. I came in while it was being done and that whole period was chaotic and disparate. Things were changing. Queen had changed management to John Reid – getting out of the whole Trident thing. They had a new crew and all kinds of stuff was going on with people coming and going all over the place. Before Rockfield, we were at Ridge Farm studios in Surrey. At the time, it was not dissimilar to Rockfield, but it was just a rehearsal place. Back then they didn't have the recording facilities that they have now. But that's where some of the early songs were worked out. We also went back there for the next album *A Day at the Races*.

Given the chaotic recording arrangements, Peter spent a good deal of time travelling between studios and would probably have been better off being paid by the mile than the hour! As such his time at Rockfield was limited.

I only spent a brief time in Wales. I remember driving a van up to Rockfield to pick stuff up and drop equipment off. It was a nightmare because of all the different things going on. I remember there was a pub down the road that everyone used to go to after recording and I recall that the food at Rockfield wasn't very good. I spent more time in London in Sarm, Scorpio and the Roundhouse. It was a hugely chaotic period. Some of the band would be in one studio, while the rest would be in another. All the while us guys on the crew would be moving equipment back and forward. If that wasn't bad enough, at the same time, we were building this complex new stage show up at Elstree Studios. Overall it was a pretty hectic time. The band made it quite difficult for themselves. I don't know why they did it. There was a lot of pressure, so you got a feeling it was a real 'make or break' time for the band. They had just left their old management company and signed up with John Reid. He used his clout as Elton John's manager to persuade EMI to stick a lot of money behind Queen. At the time, *A Night at the Opera* was one of the most expensive albums ever made. The cost in terms of studio time was phenomenal. I think that if it hadn't sold as many millions as it eventually did, there was this feeling that EMI might have had second thoughts after spending all that money and might have dropped Queen. Of course that didn't happen.

A Night at the Opera would be a huge hit, reaching number 1 in Britain and number 4 in the States. Its crowning achievement would be 'Bohemian Rhapsody'. The smash hit single was released on 31

October 1975 to huge acclaim and massive worldwide sales. The six-minute epic swept through gentle ballad into operatic drama and a fiery riff-filled rock-out before another transition into its beautiful conclusion. With one broad sweep, the song sealed Queen's future in the Premier Division of rock performers.

Recording had begun on it at Rockfield Studios on 24 August 1975, after a three-week rehearsal period in Herefordshire. At the time, guitarist Brian May referred to the track's parent album, *A Night at the Opera*, as 'our *Sgt Pepper*'.

The band put all their efforts into getting it right. During recording, Freddie Mercury was quoted in the music press as saying:

> To finish the album, we will work until we are legless. I'll sing until my throat is like a vulture's crotch. We haven't even reached the halfway stage yet, but from the things I can hear, we have surpassed everything we've done before musically.

At Rockfield, the first draft of 'Bohemian Rhapsody' was just Freddie on a piano. Over the next few weeks, the singer's skeleton framework for the song would change many times. Roy Thomas Baker recalls:

> The rough vocals were done at Rockfield, but they were re-recorded in London. There was a room at Rockfield full of saddle bags. It was one of the many rooms we used to hide ourselves away in individually to get away from the studio – to clear our heads and re-energise our batteries. So if people wanted to hide away, there were loads of these little rooms full of saddle bags and farm type things. I remember Freddie playing me 'Bohemian Rhapsody' for the first time on his piano at his place in London. Then later at Rockfield, with the basics mapped out, he focused on pinning down what was right. He played me the beginning part and said, 'Right, now this is where the opera section comes in,' and he'd leave a gap and I'd have to imagine this dramatic opera style segment. And it just kept changing all the time in Rockfield. It took three weeks to record on a 16-track tape machine and we used 180 overdubs, which was very, very unusual for back then.

It was not just unusual. Putting that many overdubs on to one song was unheard of, and trying to squeeze nearly 200 recordings on to just 16 tracks could have led to disaster! 'At the time, we came up with a game plan of what was necessary and we just did it,' recalls the producer.

> It was not until we sat back, listened to it and saw that the tape had started wearing out that we thought, 'Wow, there's thousands of vocals on here.' As 'Bohemian Rhapsody' was entirely done on 16-track, the huge amount of overdubs had made the tape worryingly thin. So much so, that it became see-through as the black oxide had been worn away. When we held the master tape up to the light one day, we discovered it was virtually transparent and decided it was time to hurriedly make a copy!

If the band and production staff were working round the clock to finish the album, life was no easier for the road crew.

> It was very difficult [says Peter Hince] because on other Queen albums you'd be there all the time – like in the later years when we'd just record in Munich or Switzerland – so you saw things progressing. But on *A Night at the Opera*, I'd be in London at the Roundhouse, where Freddie would be doing a vocal, and then I'd have to drive off in the van to pick up a harp, so Brian could play it on 'Love Of My Life'. You got all these little bits, but the 'Bohemian Rhapsody' thing was quite strange. We didn't know what was going on! When I first heard some of the stuff from that song, it was so off the wall that I thought it was an intro that they were going to use to start the live show. But the band – and in particular Freddie – knew what they were doing, what they wanted and how to get it.

And get it right they did. The album launched Queen as a major force in rock music. 'Bohemian Rhapsody' made number 1 in eight different countries, including the UK, Australia, New Zealand and Canada and reached number 9 in the US. The album sold more than half a million copies in the UK in its first eight weeks alone before breaking the million barrier and going platinum, while selling three times that amount in America. 'We were aware of how special the record was,' insists Roy Thomas Baker. 'But I didn't realise just how successful it would become commercially at that time. That all came afterwards when the record simply took off.'

The legacy of Queen's time at Rockfield is immense. Many bands have been inspired to record there to follow in the footsteps of Queen and try to capture some of the sound and magic of 'Bohemian Rhapsody'. Welsh glam rock band Tigertailz – best known for their 1980s hit single 'Love Bomb Baby' – arrived at Rockfield in the early 1990s to record their album *Wazbones*. Singer Kim Hooker says:

> We were there for three months. I went into the studios really late one day and our producer said, 'Here's the tape machine that Queen used to make *A Night at the Opera*', and I thought, 'We've got to use that same machine, because then we can sound like Queen.' But, of course, we didn't! I was talking to some of the studio staff and they remembered Queen. They were telling me how the band got richer with each album they did there. Roger Taylor for the first album drove a Mini Cooper. Then for the next one, it was an MG, but by the end of *A Night at the Opera* it was a Ferrari. The money was now rolling in.

At this point Tigertailz bassist Pepsi Tate chips in proudly with his Queen story:

> They were living in caravans at the studio as the accommodation was being developed, and one day Freddie Mercury was in his leotard playing football with the studio staff and some of their children. One of the kids there cut his knee and Freddie took him to his caravan and patched up his cut. How cool is that to have the lead singer of Queen take care of your football injury?

When in January 2005 The Darkness arrived at Rockfield to record with Queen producer Roy Thomas Baker, one of the group, bassist Richie Edwards, was in seventh heaven!

I'm probably the biggest Queen fan that I know. When I found out that Roy was going to be working on this album *One Way Ticket To Hell And Back*, and it was going to be at Rockfield – probably the most famous residential studio in the world – I was like a kid in a sweet shop. Just walking in there, I really did feel something. It sounds silly, but I could feel that history. And, as you know, Rockfield is not the most palatial studio in the world. It's tatty and you get the impression that it's not been decorated since Queen did *Sheer Heart Attack* in 74. But I loved the fact it's like that, and it really has a vibe about it. You don't get that at any of these other multimillion pound studios, but Rockfield has that vibe in sackfuls. I honestly stood in there, closed my eyes and could imagine all these legendary figures, who changed popular music, working there. You can almost see them in there working on masterpieces that I still listen to today.

But Queen's *Bohemian Rhapsody* was not the only multimillion-selling single of 1975 to have been recorded at Rockfield. The rock band Ace – led by Paul Carrack – would record the massive hit single 'How Long' at the Welsh studio.

The band consisted of Bam King and Phil Harris on guitars and vocals, Tex Comer on bass, Fran Byrne on drums and Paul Carrack on vocals and keyboards. 'It was the summer of 1974 and we went down there for two weeks to record our album *Five-a-side*,' says Carrack.

From that album came the song 'How Long', which became a big, big hit for us on both sides of the Atlantic. The decision to go to Rockfield was taken by the guy producing us, John Antony. He'd been down there with bands before. Now, we were there before the new bit – the Quadrangle – had been built. We were in the original 16-track studio, which was a converted cowshed, I think. But we loved it there and had the time of our lives. The studio, though, looked like it was held together with bits of string. If you leant on the meter bridge of the console, then the back of the mixer fell off! But we simply had a great time. We played football all day and went into the studio to record in the evening. Well, that was the plan.

Paul pauses for a moment as he recalls how easily distracted he and his fellow bandmates were while recording. Ace were at the studio at the same time as Queen. But both approached recording in very different ways. While making *Sheer Heart Attack*, Queen had found Rockfield to be a relatively dull place, with little to do, and surrounded by acres of fields and dozens and dozens of sheep, stretching for as far as the eye could see. Happily for them, it meant they could focus eighteen hours a day on writing and recording with no distraction, as they strove to record their masterpiece. In stark contrast, as a young band new to life in a recording studio, Ace looked a little harder and found that Rockfield did, indeed, have plenty of scope for fun:

> It was my first time in a studio [laughs Paul Carrack]. We were what was known as a pub rock band. We were a gigging band playing the pubs and clubs of London mostly. Basically we booked two weeks at Rockfield to make our album. We just set up our instruments and played live in the studio. To be honest, we were having too good a time in the first week to ten days. I don't think we had anything recorded that was any good.

Paul laughs once more as he thinks back to how little work the band did upon their first arrival at Rockfield.

> We played football during the day, got wrecked drinking in the evening and then maybe played a bit of music later on. Eventually John Antony – our producer – decided to lay down the law. He was in charge of the whole thing – he was the vibe master – and we were having too much of a good old time. But for the second week, he told us to get our heads down and get something proper on record. So we knuckled down and actually recorded some good stuff. When we'd finished recording, we were pleased with every note on the *Five-a-side* album. Plus we had the time of our lives down there for those two weeks. We did a few overdubs on the record back in London, but it was as good as finished at Rockfield.

Listeners agreed and the single from the album, 'How Long', became a huge hit worldwide. The song's lyrics struck a chord.

> Well, your friends with their fancy persuasion
> Don't admit that it's part of a scheme
> But I can't help but have my suspicions
> 'Cause I ain't quite as dumb as I seem
> And you said you was never intendin'
> To break up our scene in this way
> But there ain't any use in pretendin'
> It could happen to us any day
> How long has this been goin' on
> How long has this been goin' on.

'It turned out very different to how I'd originally imagined it when I wrote it,' explains Paul.

> When I wrote the song, I had in mind a sort of stomping northern soul feel and we were playing it live in that style. We actually had earmarked the song as a potential single, because we felt it was very strong. We had tried to record it earlier, during some sessions we'd had in London, so that we could use it as a single. But that didn't come off, so it was down to Wales, and Rockfield, and that's where the feel for the song really came together and it turned out different to the way I had originally envisaged. I think the version we finally came out with had a bit more of a 'late night mellow' kind of feel to it. I felt it was very strong still, but it was a little different from the first plan. It was a big radio hit though, especially in America. Everywhere you went, you just couldn't get away from it.

A few years later Ace went back to Rockfield to try to recapture the magic of the *Five-a-side* album. But the band weren't as happy with *Time For Another*.

'We went back to Rockfield to record that album, but it wasn't such a pleasant experience,' recalls Paul Carrack.

That was nothing to do with the studio itself, but more to do with us as a band. We'd had this phenomenal hit in 'How Long' and we were on the road promoting it all over the place. We were in America for around three months, touring there with prog rock superstars Yes. And then we came under a lot of pressure to record a new album. Obviously, the record company were keen to get another LP out quickly to capitalise on the success of both 'How Long' and the album *Five-a-side*. So we had the stupid notion of going into the studio with no songs written! All we had were a few riffs and bits and pieces. That was a big mistake to make. It was the opposite of what we'd done on the first album and it really isn't the way to put a record together. Even though for the second album we recorded in the posh new Quadrangle studio at Rockfield, it wasn't the same. We just didn't have fun together as a band any more. The band dynamic was way off beam.

Ace released just one more album called *No Strings* before they fell apart and Paul Carrack joined Roxy Music in 1978 for two albums: *Manifesto* and *Flesh + Blood*. In 1981, Glenn Tilbrook recruited Carrack to join Squeeze as a replacement for keyboardist Jools Holland. This new Squeeze line-up achieved international success with their *East Side Story* album on which Carrack sang the band's biggest US hit to that time, 'Tempted'. The singer/songwriter would return to Rockfield again, a year later, to record his solo album *Suburban Voodoo*. It was engineered by Rockfield's in-house specialist Paul Cobbold. Confusion reigned in the control room as both men were known by the same nickname. So whenever someone called out for PC both Paul Carrack and Paul Cobbold would stop and answer. The situation was eventually resolved, says the engineer.

He was very gracious. He simply looked at me and said, 'To make matters easier I'll relinquish the name. From now on you're PC. I'll just be Carrack!' It's stuck ever since. He was a great guy to work with and so talented.

Later in the 1980s Paul Carrack would again find international success as a member of Mike and the Mechanics, with Genesis guitarist Mike Rutherford. Paul sang lead vocals on their global hit 'The Living Years'.

As with most of the musicians who have worked at Rockfield, the studio retains a very special place in Paul Carrack's heart. But it'll always be his first visit with Ace that he remembers with most fondness.

> We just had a ball down there that first time. We were a very tight band back then. We played good music and had great times. What more could you ask for?

Queen and Ace cemented Rockfield's growing reputation, particularly in America. With 'Bohemian Rhapsody' and 'How Long' dominating both the charts and the airwaves, the Welsh studio was soon to find itself inundated with bookings. The giants of rock were about to descend.

RECOMMENDED LISTENING

Sheer Heart Attack, Queen 1974

A Night at the Opera, Queen 1975

Five-a-side, Ace 1974

Suburban Voodoo, Paul Carrack 1982

CHAPTER SEVEN:

JUDAS PRIEST, RUSH AND GILLAN

LEGENDARY NAMES DESCEND ON ROCKFIELD

Pat Moran, the engineer, was a great storyteller and quite a character. He claimed to have this device in his rack of gear, which he called 'The Duff-O-Scope'. He said he used it to 'zone in' to find all the bad notes on any song and it would remove them.

Geddy Lee, lead singer/bassist, Rush

It's December 1975 and it's a cold, grey and slightly damp day at Rockfield Studios. After a temporary lull in activity in the main courtyard for lunch, a group of figures emerge from the dining area in the main Quadrangle studio. Buoyed by a good roast dinner, and no little amount of alcohol, the gang of eight spot another four figures lurking on the other side of the courtyard, who have also just finished eating. No words are exchanged, just a few mischievous glances and smiles. Soon a hail of bread rolls are flying back and forth. The fight escalates as members from both bands dash indoors to grab handfuls of leftover food to be used as weapons of mass destruction: albeit very soggy, gravy-covered ones!

At the end of the messy encounter both sides withdraw, their pride intact, with only the courtyard bearing the scars of battle. This food fight was a clash between two of the future giants of rock, who both honed their sound at Rockfield. Judas Priest returned to work on their second album claiming victory, while a few yards around the corner the producer and members of Motörhead were likewise celebrating a food war triumph.

Judas Priest had arrived at the Welsh studio a month earlier to start work on the follow-up to their debut album *Rocka Rolla*. That album had failed to chart – though it had introduced the band to a wider audience. 1975 was to be the year when Judas Priest would finally capture the sound that would make them famous throughout the world. After years of touring the UK, the band were finally signed to Gull Records by former MCA man David Howells, who'd signed Budgie four years earlier. Howells explains how he came across the Midlands group:

> I was introduced to Priest when their manager at the time, David Cork, came to see me at the record company. He said he had this band playing live at the Greyhound pub in Fulham – an important venue in those days for blossoming rock bands. I went down to see them and I was simply knocked out by what I heard. They were terrific, so I signed them to Gull, but I made a couple of suggestions. Firstly, that they should add a second guitar player and go for that twin lead guitar sound. It was following the format of another band I'd signed called Wishbone Ash, but no one had yet done it in metal. And guitarist K. K. Downing did a great job and found Glenn Tipton and it took shape from there. I also suggested that Budgie and Black Sabbath producer Rodger Bain work with them.

Howells also found the cover for *Rocka Rolla* in a real stroke of good fortune. That slice of luck occurred when he bumped into a friend of his, art designer John Pasche, who is best known for creating one of the most famous and iconic images in rock music: the Rolling Stones'

JUDAS PRIEST

Dubbed 'Metal Gods', with the twin guitar sound of
K. K. Downing and Glenn Tipton and singer Rob
Halford's screaming lead vocals, the band created a
unique rock sound, selling millions of records.

In 1990, Judas Priest were involved in a court case
in the US, which claimed they were responsible for the
suicide of two teenage boys via subliminal messages
on their records. Priest denied the accusations, saying
if they wanted to insert subliminal commands in their
music they would put 'Buy more of our records'. The
case was dismissed.

---

big red mouth with its protruding tongue back in 1971. For that work,
which first appeared on the inner sleeve of the band's album of that
year Sticky Fingers, Pasche was paid £50. The success of the design
saw the band reward him with an extra £200 a few years later and he
sold them the copyright in 1984 for £26,000.

David ran into the designer in London one day and, after ending
up in a pub for a quick drink, the Gull Records boss recalls asking him
about a package he was carrying.

It turns out he'd just come back from Mick Jagger's house. He'd
gone to show him his latest design for the Stone's next album.
The artwork depicted a metal coke-style bottle top covered in
melted ice drops. But Jagger rejected it. So I asked if we could use
it for the first Judas Priest album. I thought the whole idea of the
metal cap with 'Rocka Rolla' scrawled across in 50s-style writing
was such a strong image. John agreed and I later asked the band
if they would write a song called 'Rocka Rolla'. So it is one of the
rare cases of an image influencing the choice of song as opposed
to the other way around.

Rocka Rolla was recorded in Olympic Studios in London in July 1974 and released two months later. The band, though, were disappointed with the final product. They felt technical problems in the studio had resulted in poor sound quality and a hiss through the album. The band were also unhappy with the role of producer Rodger Bain, feeling he'd taken too much control and had ignored much of their input.

For their second album, the band went to Rockfield, and David Howells believes that decision helped Judas Priest establish the sound they were looking for.

> At Rockfield they found an identity. They developed and grew as a band and their songwriting was getting stronger. Priest were out of step with the musical world around them at that time and I found it fascinating.

David Howells' next decision would leave the band in full 'jaw dropped' mode. He decided against hiring a well-known rock producer and made a choice which many – including Judas Priest – might have assumed had been made after a night of heavy drinking! He selected a duo who had scored a number 1 hit just three months before Priest went to Rockfield. The song famously started with an announcement by an airline pilot before ploughing straight into the chorus, in which the singer excitedly sings about his imminent return to Barbados with its palm trees, sunny Caribbean sea and, most importantly, awaiting girlfriend.

The song was *Barbados* by Typically Tropical and having made number 1 in the UK in August 1975 went on to sell more than a million copies worldwide. David Howells' vision was bold, with maybe a touch of craziness thrown in for good measure. He'd chosen producers Geraint Hughes (then going under the pen name of Max West) and Jeffery Calvert. They'd written, performed and produced *Barbados* and made it a huge summer hit. They would replicate that success three years later with *I Lost My Heart to a Starship Trooper*, which they wrote for Sarah Brightman and Hot Gossip. The move was a huge gamble. But it was a call that the experienced record industry executive was confident would bring dividends. There was, it seems, method in his madness:

I didn't want to use a traditional metal/rock producer with any preconceived notions. I'd had this hit on Gull Records by Typically Tropical, which was actually Jeff and Geraint. But they weren't just these two young guys who had made a novelty record. They had a fantastic background in music. Jeff was an engineer at Morgan Studios and had worked with just about everybody from Yes to Rod Stewart and Cat Stevens. Geraint – another Welshman like myself – was a very talented arranger and musician. I chose them for their sonic abilities as they both had a clear approach to what sound should be. So I thought if I put Jeff, Geraint and Judas Priest in a room together, it would bring out the best in the act. I think that was the turning point for the band. The first album was good, but it didn't fulfil the band's potential. But on the second album they arrived. They didn't need a metal producer – just someone who could interpret their ideas.

David makes a good point, but I would still love to have been a fly on the wall for that first meeting between Judas Priest and Typically Tropical at Rockfield. Fair play to the group, they kept an open mind and heard what the duo had to say. Jeff Calvert says it went very well, with the band keen to do anything to improve upon their disappointing debut.

Myself and Geraint had been around studios for quite a few years trying to be as inventive as possible. With Judas Priest, their first record was a typical rock band's album. There was nothing interesting about it. It was boring and a bit weedy sounding. But we helped them introduce things like acoustic guitars and pianos. I think, at first, they were a bit rebellious about certain sounds, but eventually they got to trust us and it all came together. Between us we moulded the sound which they still have to this day.

And, looking back, he claims he and Geraint were the perfect guys for the job.

If I was just a musician, or just a record producer, then maybe I wouldn't have understood what Judas Priest were about. But I was brought up, from the age of 12, in a studio. When I was engineering in a professional commercial studio, I could expect to work with all different kinds of music. One day I would be doing Hot Chocolate with Mickey Most. The next it would be a church choir. So as an engineer I got a good foundation of working with different types of people and music. As a result, it wasn't that difficult moving from a one-off novelty record to a rock band.

Also in Judas Priest's favour was the tremendous working relationship between Jeff and Geraint. As they settled into the day-to-day routine of recording at Rockfield, the pair had clearly defined roles made to bring out the best in the band. 'We always got on very well and still do,' says Jeff.

Most of the time Geraint took care of the musical side of things, while I would lean toward the technical and sound side. You know, making sure we got the best out of the drum and guitar sounds for example. Between us, we were both responsible for different areas, but they all kind of overlapped. He'd predominantly work on the arrangements, while I took care of the sound. The hardest part, initially, was convincing Judas Priest that what we wanted was right. By this stage, the band wanted a bit more 'hands-on' involvement. I gather they were not really happy with the first album as they'd had no input on it and what came out was something they weren't happy with. But we changed all that and took on board what they wanted.

Six weeks at Rockfield also proved an enjoyable experience. Jeff recalls:

There was a lot laid on. It was a lovely setting, even though it was very tempting to wander off on a walk. There was a games room, table tennis and it was a lifestyle there. It was tempting to think, 'Oh, let's go and have a game of snooker or table tennis, or let's wander off and see the cows.' It was my first time at Rockfield. In fact, it was my first time away from Morgan Studios in London, which Geraint and I used as our base. It was also my first time in a residential studio and it was quite interesting to see how things worked out there. You'd begin work on the album in a very disciplined way. You'd start the day early, at a sensible time, but as the week went on, we started staying up later and so getting up later. It got to the point where we were starting at lunchtime. It's funny, because it's not the kind of thing you'd do if you were working in London. There you simply go in, do your time and that's it. But when it's residential you can take your time and have breaks. The whole day ends up moving on. But it was fun. It was a joy to work at Rockfield. The sound was great and the gear was good. Obviously the equipment has to be excellent, but with places like that, it's all about the environment. And they have a great working environment there and that's what makes it.

David Howells commissioned a watercolour from Patrick Woodroffe to grace the cover, which depicted a fallen angel in the flames of hell. The album, *Sad Wings of Destiny*, when released, made number 48 in the UK charts and eventually went gold. It marked the defining sound of Priest with several songs that still feature in the band's live set more than forty-seven years on. 'Victim of Changes' is regarded as a classic Judas Priest song. It starts with a strong, relentless guitar riff followed by Halford's amazing piercing vocals. This song encapsulates what Priest are all about. Another song Priest still play live is 'The Ripper'. It's another soaring, fiery chunk of metal, whereas the track 'Epitaph' is a wonderfully hypnotic song featuring operatic style vocals, which wouldn't be out of place on an early Queen album. The band called it the first 'proper' Judas Priest record and launched a campaign to persuade fans to burn copies of the debut LP *Rocka Rolla*. And producer Jeff Calvert is another who reflects on the album with pride.

When I look back on it, I think – listening to Judas Priest over the years – that I'm proud of it. If you listen to their first album, and then the one we did, I really do believe we helped them create *the* Judas Priest sound. Rockfield and that album was the birth of the Priest sound as it still is. So we created something new. And it's an album people still like, and the band play some of the tracks live. So it was a satisfying job all round.

Priest's arrival at Rockfield was only a little over a year after metal favourites UFO had spent some time there in June 1973 recording demos at the studio. The band had just recruited guitarist Michael Schenker from his German band Scorpions. Without speaking a word of English he managed to find a way of working with the band. Many of the tracks laid down at Rockfield would eventually find their way on to the band's *Phenomenon* album, which would secure UFO a major recording deal with Chrysalis Records. One of those songs was the album's opener 'Oh My', and the record also included the UFO classic 'Doctor Doctor'. The demos were produced at Rockfield by Dave Edmunds.

Following in the footsteps of Priest and UFO, 1976 saw one of the biggest names in rock music arrive at the studio to mix his second solo album. Ian Gillan had left Deep Purple three years earlier, after four manic years as the band's lead singer. During that time the group had challenged the likes of Led Zeppelin for the mantle of the world's biggest band. With critically acclaimed albums such as *In Rock*, *Machine Head* and *Made In Japan*, Deep Purple simply couldn't put a foot wrong. Touched by the hands of the music gods, they quickly carved themselves a permanent place in music's Hall of Fame. But in 1973, Gillan decided to quit, not just Deep Purple, but the music industry as a whole. He spent the next few years pursuing and investing in a wide range of businesses as far removed from the world of rock stars and multiplatinum albums as he could find. For a while he dabbled in a motorcycle manufacturing company in Salisbury and a country club hotel in Thames Valley. The only concession to his former life was a recording studio he set up in London called Kingsway. By 1975, Gillan was bored and had a yearning to return to music. He joined his former Purple bandmate Roger Glover for a live performance of *The Butterfly Ball* at the Royal Albert Hall along with fellow guest vocalist David Coverdale. It was there Gillan met up with guitarist Ray Fenwick, bassist John Gustafson and keyboard player Mike Moran. They would form his first solo group: the Ian Gillan Band.

After their debut album in 1975 called *Child In Time*, the band arrived in Wales a year later to remix the follow-up *Clear Air Turbulence*. Ray Fenwick remembers that meeting the post-Deep Purple Ian Gillan was not quite what he had expected.

> When I first saw him, he'd cut his long hair quite short, which was a bit of a shock. He looked a lot straighter – a lot less rock 'n' roll – than he did with Deep Purple. But by then he'd got into a lot of businesses. He had a studio, a hotel and I think he was also running a travel agency – all kinds of things. If he'd stayed away from music for any longer, I think he'd have become a very successful entrepreneur. I think he'd have been a Richard Branson type.

So why did the band decide on Rockfield, when Ian had his own studio? Ray Fenwick says,

> The reason is that Rockfield was one of the state-of-the-art studios at the time. It had this superb Neve mixing desk, which was just the best thing around. I mean Kingsway had been a great place to record the album, but Ian wanted a better studio to finish it in. Plus Rockfield was residential, so we could all go down there and stay together. That's why we chose it really. And, as a bonus, it came with a reputation.

The Ian Gillan Band settled into the Coach House studio and started remixing *Clear Air Turbulence*. The album was to be a real departure for the former Deep Purple singer. Moving away from the heavy rock signatures of his former band, the music was a fusion of rock, funk and jazz with wonderfully complex and absorbing time changes and melodies. The band members threw themselves wholeheartedly into this new musical direction. And Rockfield proved to be the perfect place to craft the final sound. Guitarist Ray thoroughly enjoyed his time at the mixing desk during his temporary stay in Wales.

For me, there's nothing better than being at a residential studio, because you're captured. You can't go anywhere, apart from the local town. It was a lot more focused at Rockfield. It also helped that we were at the mixing stage, so we were all involved and we didn't have members of the band going off bored when the drum tracks were being laid down, for example. There were some wild things happening to the Ian Gillan Band. But for us Rockfield was a very mellowing place. It's incredibly tranquil and it was a calming experience for us. It's not a place where you want to shout and holler. So we were there with the finished masters, overdubbing and remixing the tracks. The studio was outstanding – that's why Ian wanted to go there, because it had one of the early computer mixdowns.

Ian Gillan has a reputation for being a very determined, forceful individual. But Ray Fenwick says that during those sessions in 1976, the former Deep Purple frontman seemed a lot more open to other people's ideas.

Ian really did want input from everyone. He was so open. Ian had always been with Deep Purple so I think he found it refreshing to be with new musicians, who had different and new ideas. He'd got used to the same guys, and the same problems within the Purple set-up, but we were new and he listened to our input. We were all respected session players and knew our stuff, so if we thought we had a better way of doing something he'd listen. Obviously in the final analysis Ian is the boss and made his own decisions, which is quite apparent [as] he later went back and remixed the whole album.

As with Motörhead's debut album at Rockfield, the original mix of this Ian Gillan Band album would take time to find the light of day.

I thought the mixes from the Rockfield sessions were fabulous. But, at the end of the day, Ian disagreed. He went away and mixed it again at his own studio in London. No one seems to know the reason for that, as the rest of the band were very happy with the finished results at Rockfield.

The album – redone at Kingsway – was released in 1977. The Rockfield masters lay gathering dust in Ray Fenwick's attic for the best part of two decades. The guitarist eventually retrieved them, dusted them down and released them on CD in 1997 as *Ian Gillan Band: The Rockfield Mixes*. He looks back on that period in the late 1970s with the Ian Gillan Band, and that particular record, with pride.

I love *Clear Air Turbulence*. I think the title track is fantastic. One of the unusual things we did on that album was to have a horn section on it. That was due to a friend of Ian's. He [Ian] admired his work and wanted him and his friends on the record. At the time, he took a fair bit of criticism for doing that, but as the years have passed, and that work is reviewed anew, a lot of that criticism has gone. But that's what he wanted to do. He wanted to change the music he was playing. Why should he go from Deep Purple to playing in another Deep Purple-type band? The group he formed later in the 80s – called simply Gillan – was a lot heavier, and much more rock orientated, than we were. But I know Ian loves that jazz, rock, funk period he spent working with us. It was fantastic. We went to Japan, where we had an unbelievable reception. Ian had been there before with Purple, so all the places were sold out. The legendary Budokan Theatre [in Tokyo] was sold out for the two shows we did there, which were recorded and released as a live album. Hiroshima was also a sell-out, while Osaka was another very good gig. Ian felt that concert was a pinnacle gig for the band. We also toured America and Europe. Around that time, we did a lot of work in France, because Ian was a tax exile living in Paris. We did another live album from the Rainbow in London and I think those albums all stand the test of time. We were an unusual kind of band. Ian came from a rock background, but our band was a little bit more fusion. The guys were into jazz and funk, which was apparent in the music and the writing.

RUSH

Strongly influenced by British blues rock, this
Canadian power trio have enjoyed worldwide success
with such hit albums as *2112, Moving Pictures*
and *Power Windows*. In 2006, Rush were placed
fifth behind The Beatles, The Rolling Stones,
Kiss and Aerosmith for the most consecutive gold
and platinum albums by a rock band.

But it was not all work and no play for Gillan and his jazz/funk play-
mates. 'The band was quite a wild one,' says Ray.

> We liked to have fun. It was a time when Ian felt he could let his
> hair down. I always got the feeling with Ian that this was just the
> kind of vehicle he'd been looking for. Of course, he had more
> success later with Gillan, but I always felt he thought he could
> express himself more with us. The chains had been let go. His
> lyric writing in the Ian Gillan Band was great. He always came
> up with fantastic lyrics, which reflected the time. It was also a
> very co-operative band. I always felt I could say what I wanted,
> as did the rest of the band. I never felt Ian wouldn't take my ideas
> seriously, or put them down. He was a great guy to work for.

Ian Gillan would not be the last giant name in rock to descend on
Rockfield in the late 1970s. One big-selling trio would travel more
than three thousand miles to record outside their homeland for the
first time ever.

One day in 2006 my phone rang and I answered to hear:

'Hello. This is Geddy Lee from Rush calling. Is that Jeff Collins?'

It's not often a rock legend calls me at home, but I'd been trying to
get hold of the lead singer of the Canadian hard rockers for a number
of weeks. During that time, Rush had been locked away in their stu-

dio, writing and rehearsing songs for their album *Snakes & Arrows*. Now Geddy Lee has taken a break from the studio to reminisce with me about their time in Wales.

In 1977 Rush were starting to break big. Very big! The previous year they had released two hugely successful albums, the classic *2112* and the live album *All The World's A Stage*. By June of that year, the band had decided to leave Canada and go to the UK to make their next record. Now I get the chance to ask the band's frontman what made them head for Wales. Geddy explains that it was basically all down to the group's love of British rock bands.

> We were looking to record away from home and we were always enamoured with those great progressive rock albums coming out of Britain. We were just big fans of the whole period, so it was natural for us to want to go there and record. Our producer at the time, Terry Brown, did some research and came up with this residential studio, not too far from London, in Monmouth in Wales. He went over and checked it out. It proved to be OK, so we decided to try it out. When we first saw Rockfield, the studios were very funky looking, and very rustic. It was certainly not anything fancy, but that was fine. The people were friendly, though the sun wasn't shining, but we were led to believe that that was quite normal for Wales. We were quite excited to be there. Everything was foreign and just that little bit different, so it took us a while to settle in. The second day we were there, the guys went for a long walk across a field behind Rockfield and ended up getting chased across the pasture by a herd of cows. We realised then it was the rural life for us for the coming weeks.

Once at Rockfield, Rush set up their instruments and started work on what was to become *A Farewell To Kings*. Most of the material had already been written, and some of it had already been played live on the band's world tour earlier that year.

Musically, the Rockfield vibe helped the band put together what was to become their biggest selling album up to that point. Geddy recalls,

It definitely seeped into the record, because we realised we could experiment quite a bit and record some of the acoustic guitars and percussive instruments outside. But the longer we stayed there, the later the recording sessions got, until our time clock went completely upside down. Eventually we were getting up in the late afternoon, having breakfast at suppertime and going on to record until the wee hours of the morning. But some of the outdoor recording we were doing was great. We were out in the courtyard in the Quadrangle part of the farm and we recorded the opening segments of the tracks 'A Farewell to Kings' and 'Xanadu' as well as a few other bits and pieces out there.

If you listen to 'Xanadu', the second track on *A Farewell To Kings*, you can clearly hear birds tweeting. I enquire if they are Welsh birds. 'Indeed they are!' replies Geddy brightly.

In the early morning, the birds would gather round in the court-yard and start tweeting away. And it all got captured on to that disc. Those birds on 'Xanadu', those are genuine Rockfield birds!

The band now felt firmly at home. Well, almost. You can take the boys out of Canada. But it seems you can't take Canada out of the boys!
'We moved in and it was good', says Geddy.

It was our first experience of a residential studio and it was very funny to gather at dinnertime around a big long table and have these ladies come in and cook us these hearty English meals. We loved it at the time because it was something very different for us. But I remember being frustrated as a North American staying up late and trying to find something decent on the TV. When you have just an hour off from studio work to flake out in front of the television and chill, it could be very frustrating trying to find any television programming on past midnight. We were used to cable TV back home with hundreds of channels to watch and suddenly here in Rockfield we only had three! It was hard for some of the guys in the crew, who were always waiting

– always on call – to keep themselves entertained. They had to make do with watching Open University or a darts match very late at night. On one hand it was very frustrating, but on the other, it was quite amusing for them. I mean live darts! That was strange. In those days, it was a nice, unusual experience to be so far from home in a rural atmosphere. Everything culturally was different: the TV programmes, the food, the air and the little town nearby. It was quite different from North American life. But I guess all those things keep you quite vibed up – I was excited and stimulated by that.

A Farewell To Kings was released in September 1977 and became the band's first gold and then platinum record. In June 1978, Rush returned to Rockfield. They had hoped to recapture the excitement of recording in rural Wales. This time they also hoped it would inspire them to write material for the new record. Sadly, their second sample of life at Rockfield would not be as good.

Over the phone from Toronto, Geddy Lee recalls the nightmare of recording *Hemispheres*.

We arrived all excited and rented a house near the studios at Rockfield. But we hadn't written a thing by the time we moved in, so we wrote the entire *Hemispheres* album in that house, and then we moved into the studio and started recording it. Unfortunately, that turned out to be our undoing, as *Hemispheres* was an extremely complex record and a difficult one to make. We were there for what seemed like forever. All the omens were bad. It was a dark kind of summer there, at that time. It seemed as though the sun was never shining. That summer nothing seemed to go right for us. For example, during *A Farewell To Kings*, we would put the initial tracks down live and then lay on overdubs to develop the songs. That all went very smoothly for the first record. But on *Hemispheres* that way of thinking started to slow us down, simply because some of the pieces were much longer and much more difficult to play. I remember on the song 'La Villa Strangiato', we had major problems. It's a twelve-minute long instrumental song and we tried recording it live in the studio in one piece, but we couldn't perform it in one take. In the end, we had to spend the next seven days trying to get the track down in three separate live pieces, which we then had to knit together in the mix. The album took longer and longer and longer to do. We completely overshot the time we had allotted to record there. So our fond experience turned into a depressing one by the end of it, because we spent far too long there.

Rockfield producer John David remembers the visit by Rush – or should that be invasion – quite vividly:

Rush pretty much took over the whole place. The bass player, Geddy Lee, had more than twenty-five bass guitars there, while the guitarist, Alex Lifeson, had probably fifty guitars. I was not working with them, but I remember being in and around the studios at the time, working on various projects and I remember when they spent a whole week just looking for the right bass sound. It was ridiculous and a terrible waste of money. And strangely enough when The Darkness were at Rockfield in 2005 they did a similar thing.

As my conversation with Geddy Lee comes to an end, it turns out to have an uplifting finish. Rather than holding bleak memories, the bassist tells me that, overall, Rush and their crew thoroughly enjoyed their time at Rockfield.

I have very strong, happy recollections of being there and the characters who were there. For example, Pat Moran, the engineer, was a great storyteller and quite a character. He had these phrases we'd never heard of before. Like if you played a bad note, he'd say, 'That was really duff' or 'That was really naff'. We'd never heard those phrases in Canada, so we thought they were quite amusing. He also had this device in his rack of gear, which he called 'The Duff-O-Scope'. He said he used it to 'zone in' to find all the bad notes on any song and it would remove them.

Geddy laughs at the memory.

> It was that kind of place. It was just crazy and the most memorable thing for me was the cast of characters, Kingsley, Pat and Otto the electrician. They contributed to the good vibe the studio had.

With Judas Priest, UFO, Ian Gillan and Rush – as well as Queen – all recording their own pieces of musical history at Rockfield, the end of the 1970s was proving to be a golden one for the Welsh studio. As the 1980s dawned, that legacy would attract a new breed of bands. As well as big rock names, a new generation was about to have their day in the sun.

RECOMMENDED LISTENING

Sad Wings of Destiny, Judas Priest 1976

A Farewell To Kings, Rush 1977

Hemispheres, Rush 1978

The Rockfield Mixes, Ian Gillan Band 1997

Above: Ace take time out (again) from recording to play football at Rockfield in 1974. From left to right Ace are: Paul Carrack, Tex Comer (bass), Bam King (guitar) and Fran Byrne (drums). Phil Harris (guitars) is still in bed! *(Photo by Paul Carrack)*

Below: Killer Queen: Brian May sitting in the Quadrangle studio where Queen recorded 'Bohemian Rhapsody'. *(Photo courtesy of www.brianmay.com)*

Above: Rockfield's farming origins are still evident. They keep horses to this day which the bands can ride – sober or not! *(Photo by Andrew Pritchard)*

Below: The top of Rockfield's main drive. (Coach House studio to the left, Quadrangle to the right.) This is the first sight of Rockfield for arriving bands. *(Photo by Andrew Pritchard)*

Above: Black Sabbath roadie Graham Wright in 2006 at work on The Rolling Stones' 'Bigger Bang' tour at Cardiff's Millennium Stadium, where I met him (see Chapter Two). *(Photo by Jeff Collins)*

Below: Exterior of the Coach House studio taken from the main driveway. *(Photo by Andrew Pritchard)*

Above: Goal! Rockfield, 1995. Oasis play table football in the calm before the storm. Hours later the game had been destroyed, the studios trashed and Oasis had fled Rockfield. *(Photo © Michael Spencer Jones)*
Right: Entrance to the courtyard and the reception area from the main drive. *(Photo by Andrew Pritchard)*
Below: The Coach House accommodation. *(Photo by Andrew Pritchard)*

Above: Backstage with Motörhead in November 2005. Lemmy was the first person to be interviewed for this book, setting the ball rolling. I take notes as Lemmy orders the drinks – 'That's two bottles of Jack Daniels, a crate of beers, and two bottles of coke. That's Coca-Cola of course!' *(Photo by Andrew Pritchard)*

Below: Quadrangle studio, Rockfield, May 2006 – producer Steve Osborne takes a break from producing the band Grace to talk about his time working with New Order and Starsailor at Rockfield. He later reveals a few tricks of the trade to me. *(Photo by Andrew Pritchard)*

Left: Robert Plant listens to the CD he brought to the Robert Plant Band reunion at Rockfield on 15 May 2006. The CD featured a number of rare live tracks to be included on his 2006 box set.

Below: Pictures at eleven! Well, midday actually as Robert Plant meets up with his former band mates – Robbie Blunt (sitting on the arm of the chair) and Jezz Woodroffe (next to Robbie and talking) in a reunion in 2016, while I look on (bottom left). *(Photo by Andrew Pritchard)*

Above: Robert Plant and Robert Blunt outside the Coach House accommodation during the 2006 reunion. *(Photo by Andrew Pritchard)*

Below: Who's the new guy? I sneak into the band line-up during the Robert Plant Band Reunion in May 2006. Left to right: Jeff Collins, Robbie Blunt, Jezz Woodroffe, Robert Plant. *(Photo by Andrew Pritchard)*

Above: Rockfield, Quadrangle Studio, February 2005: The Darkness label up the faders as they spend nearly three weeks searching for the right drum sound. *(Photo by Richie Edwards (The Darkness))*

Below: One of Dan Hawkins' collection of 50+ guitars used on the making of The Darkness's second album *One Way Ticket To Hell… And Back!* at Rockfield in February 2005. *(Photo by Richie Edwards (The Darkness))*

Above: The stray ginger cat befriended by The Darkness, which died shortly after they left. Darkness bassist Richie Edwards reflects on her final few weeks in a positive way: 'She got to listen to a great album being made and got to eat like a king.' *(Photo by Richie Edwards (The Darkness))*

Below: Rockfield's Coach House studio – the main control room – in 2006. *(Photo by Jeff Collins)*

Above: Rockfield's Quadrangle Studio: main control room. *(Photo by Jeff Collins)*

Below: The Tokyo Dragons with Rockfield owner Kingsley Ward at Rockfield Studios in 2005. Left to right: Phil Martini (drums), Pedro Ferreira (producer), Kingsley Ward (owner, Rockfield) and Mal Bruk (guitars). Guitarist and singer Steve Lomax is either taking the shot or in the pub. *(Photo courtesy of Pedro Ferreira)*

Above: Tokyo Dragons guitarist Mal Bruk in action at the 100 Club. He was inspired by Budgie and Motörhead's presence at Rockfield. *(Photo by Andrew Pritchard)*

Right: Tokyo Dragons drummer Phil Martini, during a gig of Rockfield-recorded songs at the 100 Club in London, 29 March 2007. 'We were aware of Rockfield's musical heritage… but we didn't ask to stay in Lemmy's room!' *(Photo by Andrew Pritchard)*

Below: Greg from Killing for Company at Monnow Valley in 2008. *(Photo by Andrew Pritchard)*

Top: An aerial view of Rockfield's sister studio, Monnow Valley. *(Photo © Monnow Valley Recording Studio)*

Centre: The stream outside Monnow Valley, home to many a band's adventure. *(Photo © Monnow Valley Recording Studios)*

Below: The Monnow Valley studios' control centre. *(Photo by Adam Handley)*

Above: Killing for Company and Bob Marlette relaxing outside Monnow Valley Studio in 2008. *(Picture courtesy of Andrew Pritchard)*

Right: The memorable and entrancing doors into the Monnow Valley studios. *(Photo by Peter Britton)*

Middle: Producer Bob Marlette at Monnow Valley in 2008. *(Photo by Andrew Pritchard)*

Bottom: Luke Padfield (left) and Matt Bond of The Dirty Youth recording *Gold Dust* at Rockfield in 2013. *(Picture courtesy of Matt Bond)*

Above: The Dirty Youth singer Danni Monroe. *(Picture courtesy of Matt Bond)*

Below: Luke Morley laying down some riffs at Rockfield in 2020. *(Picture courtesy of Thunder)*

Right: Royal Blood and their producer go all wild west in the Courtyard at Rockfield in 2017. Left to right: Mike Kerr, Tom Dalgety, Ben Thatcher. *(Picture by Libby Burke Wild)*

Below: Fredrik Åkesson during the recording of Opeth's album *Sorceress* in the Coach House Studio in 2016. *(Picture courtesy of Tom Dalgety)*

Above: Luke Morley (left) and Danny Bowes (right) at the mixing desk for Thunder at Rockfield in 2020. (*Picture courtesy of Thunder*)

Left: The BV Queens having laid down their vocals at Rockfield in 2020. Left to right: Carly Louise and Julie Maguire. (*Picture courtesy of BV Queens*)

CHAPTER EIGHT:
THE 1980S USHER IN A NEW BREED

For fuck's sake press the record button!!
Do you realise how honoured you are?
They are ALL in the studio, at the same time,
playing the same fucking song!!!

Joe Strummer, producer, The Pogues

The 1970s had cemented Rockfield's place in the history of rock. The legacy left by bands like Black Sabbath, Queen, Rush, Judas Priest and Motörhead had put the Welsh studio firmly on the musical map. But as the 1970s drew to a close, and the dawn of the 1980s approached, Rockfield's appeal would spread to a younger generation of bands. Adam and the Ants, T'Pau, Echo and the Bunnymen and Simple Minds would head to south Wales as part of a new wave of pop music wanting to embrace the Rockfield experience. Not all of these bands were in awe of the famous rock stars who had gone before them. Many were finding their own path and Rockfield simply fulfilled their recording needs. One such band was The Icicle Works. Lead singer Ian McNabb explains why they chose Rockfield to record their first album in 1983.

We were like a second-generation Liverpool band. We came up behind the likes of Echo and the Bunnymen and The Teardrop Explodes. And they'd all worked at Rockfield with the likes of Ian Broudie from the Lightning Seeds. So we thought it was a mythical place. We'd never made an album before and Hugh Jones, who produced our first album, wanted us to go there. And we thought, 'Wow, that's where the Bunnymen, Teardrops and guys like those worked.' We'd never done an album before, and going away to stay in a cottage in the country for a couple of weeks seemed like an incredibly exciting thing to do when you're 20.

And he admits, that at first, he was unaware of Rockfield's wider musical heritage.

I only found out about all those 70s bands who'd recorded there, much later on. I had been into all that kind of stuff, like Queen, in my teens. But when I got to 20, and had my own band, I was more enamoured of the likes of Echo and the Bunnymen. As a band, we were very dismissive. We were very punk and new wave. We walked around with long coats on, and had spiky hair. When it comes to it, my musical life began with the first Joy Division album. We were kind of iconoclastic. Or at least, that's how we saw it.

Rockfield had a profound effect on McNabb and the band.

The first Icicle Works album was a kind of rural type record. It was steeped in pseudomysticism. You couldn't just write love songs. You had to be incredibly profound about something that was unspecified. So a lot of the lyrics fitted in with the magic of Rockfield, even though they'd already been written. Our location, with regards to the recording of the album, certainly had a big effect on the artwork. The front cover of the album is a tree which was right outside the studio. That is actually *the* Rockfield tree. So it definitely had a pretty profound effect on all of us, and we all took lots of photographs down there – many of which were used on the cover of the American version. Yeah, it was definitely a Rockfield album! We stayed in the house right opposite the studio. Now they have apartments in the main Quadrangle, but for the first Icicle Works album we stayed in the house, which is a cottage in a lane. Every night we'd finish in the studio very late. We'd come out and walk down the pathway in the pitch-black, down this long winding path, where there was no light. We had one torch, but someone lost it, so that was the end of that. It was dark eerie walks home from then on! We'd stumble back to the cottage in the dark, watch TV, drink wine and go to bed. But I suppose the overall abiding memory I have from when we were actually working on the album was when we had our first hit single.

I remember getting a phone call at 7 o'clock in the morning to say we'd been asked by the BBC to do *Top of the Pops*. I remember jumping up and down with joy. We jumped in a van, did the show and then drove straight back to Wales. We were very naïve at that time, so there was no partying in London after the TV show. It was just 'back to work'. A lot of stuff happened at Rockfield that didn't happen again. We were never again as close as a band. It was just incredibly exciting making that first record. But by the time we did the follow-up in the south of France, it wasn't the same. We'd changed. It was a shame. Rockfield, though, was a very special place. When I drive up and down the country, and I see signs for Rockfield, I still get a little tingle. Sometimes I stop and drop in for a chat.

Ian returned to Rockfield a decade later to record his solo album *Merseybeast* – the follow-up to the massively successful *Head Like A Rock*. But the searing heat of the summer of 1995 took its toll:

There was a heatwave. And guess what? The studio's bloody air conditioning broke! Now you don't want to be in the studio when it's that hot. But we were in there far too long. I think we spent a week confined in that heat – it was overpowering.

Ian McNabb's heroes, Echo and the Bunnymen, had first been at Rockfield four years before The Icicle Works in 1979, a year which saw numerous other early pop-punk outfits, such as Simple Minds and Adam and the Ants venturing to south Wales to record. The Bunnymen were hailed as the vanguard of a new psychedelic rock movement. Their debut album, *Crocodiles*, was recorded at Rockfield, as were the two follow-up records, *Heaven Up Here* in 1981 and *Porcupine* two years later.

The third album proved particularly difficult as Rockfield's house engineer at the time, Paul Cobbold, remembers:

> *Porcupine* was quite an interesting album. It was the first time I'd met Ian Broudie, who was producing the album. Apparently the group had taken six months off to write music for this album, but had failed miserably. So they went straight into Rockfield in June 1982 with very little finished, and were told by the record company, 'Right you've got two weeks' rehearsal to get this album together or else!' So I was engineering this record not knowing what they were doing or trying to do. The band were writing melodies and lyrics like mad, while frittering away their studio time. The drummer Pete De Freitas and bass player Les Pattinson would just come into the studio and lay down these backing tracks almost on the basis of 'Well, this is what we want to play, so everyone will have to fit on top of this.' One day, the lead guitarist and songwriter Will Sergeant was in the studio trying to figure out what he was going to play on this one particular song. I was so frustrated that in the end I put the tape machine to record on loop and went out to give my car a quick wash, as it was such a sunny day. I popped back into the studio a while later to see if Will was OK and he hadn't thought of anything. So two hours later I popped out again and the whole day went on like this. By the end of the day, he still hadn't thought of a thing to write or record! I think Ian Broudie found that a hard album to do, because there were some pretty hard-nut personalities in that band. Years later I worked with Ian on one of the Lightning Seeds albums and the first thing he said to me was, 'I want to apologise to you for the way I behaved on the Bunnymen album.'

The Rockfield experience also proved a troubling one for political punk group, the Tom Robinson Band. The outfit were on the crest of a wave having seen their debut album, *Power in the Darkness*, reach number 4 in the UK album charts in 1978. The band went to Rockfield a year later to record the follow-up, *TRB 2*. By now there was some tension between them and the in-fighting and disagreements got worse during recording and hampered progress in the studio. Producer Chris Thomas got so sick of the bickering and politics that he would often down tools and simply leave the studio, telling the band he was 'going fishing'. Only one track from that session – a backing track called 'Suits Me, Suits You' with unfinished lyrics – would prove useable.

Their experience was in stark contrast to that of another young band starting to make headway: Simple Minds.

By 1977, long-time school friends singer Jim Kerr and guitarist Charlie Burchill were growing bored of their punk outfit Johnny and the Self-Abusers. The Glaswegian pair were finding new inspiration from the likes of Brian Eno and David Bowie.

So they abandoned punk and put together Simple Minds. After the release of their first album, *Life in a Day*, the band headed to Rockfield to record the follow-up, *Real To Real Cacophony*.

Their manager at the time, Bruce Findlay, remembers it as an exciting period for the band.

> It went really well down there in Wales. It was still quite early on for the boys, but they were blown away by the whole experience. They loved recording there.

The most memorable part of the recording process was meeting David Bowie. He was at Rockfield to produce a new album for Iggy Pop called *Soldier*. And they were recording it in the studio next door to the star-struck Glaswegians.

> David Bowie is a hero of Simple Minds and Jim Kerr in particular [says Bruce Findlay]. One day he just knocked on the studio door, and asked if we could do him a favour and sing on one of the songs he was doing for Iggy. I remember him saying to the

band in that distinctive voice of his, 'Do you fancy coming in and singing on this song called 'Play It Safe'?' The band were over the moon! They had to sing a line which went: 'I want to be a criminal – play it safe!' They tried various ways to do it, including shouting it. But in the end Bowie said to them, 'Look guys, can you try to sing it with an accent, so it sounds like me?' So these lads from Scotland put on their best cockney accents and were standing in the studio impersonating David Bowie as they sung the line 'I want to be a criminal.' It was hilarious.

The band were thrilled to bits. They were enjoying one of those unique Rockfield experiences of bumping into other musicians, often more famous than you are. Bruce remembers,

> Bowie was a very down-to-earth person, very likeable. It was a very humbling experience to meet him. He's a giant among giants. It was also a thrill to meet Iggy Pop. I remember months later, the band flew to New York for their first appearance there. They were terrified. It was an exciting prospect, but also one that was also quite fearful. It really helped the band to have Iggy's support. When they took to the stage, there he was sitting in the front row. That meant a lot to them.

Meeting Bowie was the icing on the cake for Simple Minds who had already taken to life at Rockfield. 'The band loved staying there,' recalls their former manager.

> The accommodation is great and it's not unlike Scotland, with all the birds flying around over some beautiful countryside. It's lovely. The band enjoyed living together at Rockfield, sharing rooms and cooking in the kitchen downstairs. It was a real bonding experience. It's a bit like being on the road. You've very little contact with people outside the band and their entourage. Though to balance that the band would visit Monmouth occasionally to get some contact with people not involved in music. They would socialise and have a few pints with the locals.

SIMPLE MINDS

Best known for their worldwide smash hit single in 1985 'Don't You (Forget About Me)' from the film *The Breakfast Club*. The song was originally intended for Bryan Ferry who turned down the opportunity to record it.

Simple Minds were produced by John Leckie. He was known for his early engineering work at Abbey Road. Leckie had worked with everyone from George Harrison and John Lennon to Mott the Hoople. He also worked as an engineer on Pink Floyd's *Dark Side Of The Moon*.

Having left Abbey Road, he turned to producing and started working with punk/new wave era favourites such as XTC, The Fall and Public Image. Leckie's first taste of working at Rockfield had been a few years earlier in 1977.

My first album there was by Roy Harper called *Bullinamingvase*. It had a hit single called 'One Of Those Days In England' on it. I eventually did two Simple Minds records. One was *Real To Real Cacophony* and the other was *Empires and Dance*, a year later in 1980. Then I also did Bill Nelson, who used to be in Be Bop Deluxe. He was a great guitarist, and I did his solo record in 1981 called *The Love That Whirls*. I knew all about Rockfield.

I had originally worked at Abbey Road. It's where I started in 1970 as a tape operator. And I also used the Manor Studios. But Rockfield is a dream to be at. It's where you can work in the country and be locked away from everything to make music. So Rockfield was always known about, even from when I first started. It was always known as a crazy place. It was on this farm and people used to tell me that the equipment was all falling apart. But it wasn't. It was always well kept. But that's one of the beauties about the place. You are on a farm and there's plenty of space. That's the main thing, because when you get a band, all their equipment and flight cases, and you go into a small studio like the Manor, then you have no room to move! With Rockfield, you could do anything. Literally, you could do anything you wanted to do because of the space. The other good thing about Rockfield was you always felt it was your place, because it was a bit rough. Like the carpets. Because it was a farm there was always mud everywhere, from the fields. Everyone had muddy boots. But in a strange way, it meant that you felt very at home.

And the Scottish band certainly made themselves at home at Rockfield. They worked hard in the day and played hard at night. John Leckie remembers that being with the band was fun.

It was all a bit crazy. There used to be a bit of a tradition of food fights at Rockfield, particularly involving custard pies and trifle. And this kind of reached a peak with Simple Minds. Every night at mealtime, the caterers brought in a more extravagant dessert and fancy cream cakes. Almost like an incentive for us to fling them at each other. I'd always escape before it happened. As soon as I'd finished my main course, I'd run and hide and then I'd come back. And you'd see the dining room dripping in trifle; it would be running down the walls – it was everywhere. I can remember seeing Jim Kerr and Charlie Burchill coming in and actually cleaning up after the band as they were so ashamed that they'd made a mess of this room. They both had the mops out and were wiping the walls down. I think they were worried in case Kingsley found out what they'd been up to.

The producer also remembers that Rockfield was the perfect environment for Simple Minds to get their act together.

It was a good experience for the band to be sleeping together, eating together and working together. You go through all the ups and downs. It's a bonding time, especially as these lads were only 20 or 21 years old. And because they were there for maybe a month to six weeks, it became their home. Everyone came away with a life experience.

Bruce Findlay agrees with John Leckie's assessment of the impact Rockfield had on the fledgling pop superstars.

> The band were very young when they went to Rockfield. They were teenagers, or in their early twenties. They were overawed by the whole experience. But the studio helped them come to grips with being in a band. They gained in confidence and maturity.
>
> I stayed there a lot with them and hung out with them. They tried to get me in the studio to do some handclapping on the song 'Celebrate'. But I was out of time. I was useless. So the band threw me out of the studio! But, looking back, Rockfield was so vital for the growth of the group. They were a baby band, when they were in Wales. Despite some success, the big time had yet to come.

In July 1980, a new craze was sweeping the UK: Ant Music. Adam and the Ants had just signed a major record deal with CBS. They headed off to Rockfield to record *Kings Of The Wild Frontier*. The album would be an enormous success, hitting number 1 in the UK in January 1981 and reaching the top 5 in America. The album included several hit singles such as 'Dog Eat Dog', 'Antmusic' and 'Kings Of The Wild Frontier'. 'Antmusic' also made number 1 in Australia and stayed there for five weeks.

In April 1987, Clannad arrived from Ireland at Rockfield. The Irish pop band had one objective in moving away from their homeland to record in Wales. They were desperate to break America. Their new record, *Sirius*, was aimed squarely at bringing the band success in the States. Armed with a £300,000 budget, Clannad also brought in famous American producer Greg Ladanyi and featured contributions from Journey singer Steve Perry and pianist Bruce Hornsby.

The band had spent several months writing new songs in their house at the foot of the Dublin mountains before arriving at the Welsh studio, where Paul Cobbold was asked to engineer the album.

'Clannad were so keen to make it big in America,' Paul told me.

I think they had been around all the studios in the UK and Europe, but ended up coming to Rockfield and feeling really comfortable there. The studio just had the most fantastic atmosphere. But it is one of those studios that you either fall in love with, or take an instant dislike to. I remember a number of bands from New York, for example, who couldn't stand the fact that Rockfield is miles from anywhere and wasn't a brand new shiny and chrome studio. It was a bit lived-in and some bands didn't like that. But Clannad loved the place – particularly the residential side. The stuff they'd done up to that date was very good and everyone knew the Clannad sound – it was mix of Celtic music with folk and pop. They wrote some gorgeous melodies. But their record company RCA wanted to break them in the States. It was hoped that the combination of an American producer in Greg and the Rockfield brand would be a major help.

Greg Ladanyi had made his name producing the likes of Fleetwood Mac, Don Henley and Toto among others and was asked to give Clannad a harder edge to their music, while still keeping in touch with their Celtic New Age sound. For example, the vocals on the track 'In Search Of A Heart' were done in the courtyard at Rockfield. Singer Máire Ní Bhraonáin was dispatched outside in the cold wearing two jackets and handed a microphone and headphones. The producer's instructions were simple: 'Sing!' he told Máire and the vocals were laid down at midnight on a clear night under the stars of south Wales. Like the band, engineer Paul Cobbold enjoyed working with the American producer.

Greg was quite funny. He arrived at Rockfield with racks and racks of his own equipment, but not a single transformer to be seen. So the first few days were spent wiring up all this equipment for the UK. Greg couldn't understand why I was getting involved in the wiring. He'd say to me, 'Why are you doing this man? You're the engineer. You shouldn't be doing stuff like this!' So I replied, 'Look. This is the way Rockfield works. At Rockfield everyone lumps in together and if you're not going to bring any leads with you then what do you expect.' That shut him up!

Paul remembers the band also drafted in a familiar Rockfield face in guitarist Robbie Blunt, who'd worked at the studios with Fairground Attraction, Julian Lennon and Robert Plant among others.

They wanted Robbie to give them an electric lead style, which none of Clannad could do. And there was some seriously good guitar playing by Robbie on that album. Overall, it had some great tracks on it – many ending up on *The Best of Clannad*, but I still don't think they broke America though.

Robbie himself recalls,

I enjoyed working with Clannad and became good friends with them, particularly Máire. I did an album with Donovan, where Máire came over with her harp. It was fantastic. She'd sit there, play her harp and sing like an angel.

Other punk and pop bands such as The Stranglers, The Wonder Stuff, The Undertones and The Damned would record at Rockfield during the end of the 1970s and into the 1980s.

But Rockfield remained a perennial favourite of the rock band. In 1983 former Iron Maiden singer Paul Di'Anno arrived at Rockfield with a new band named after himself. Di'Anno was originally called Lonewolf, but there was some wrangling over that name with a band already in existence called Lone Wolf. So they simply changed their name to Di'Anno. The ex-Maiden vocalist initially had doubts about recording in the Welsh countryside, but soon fell in love with the place.

'I'd left Iron Maiden and I wanted to do an album that sounded nothing like them!' Paul pauses and laughs when he recalls those early days after leaving Maiden.

I did one album – my very first – at Rockfield. It was quite a weird experience, because you're miles out in the countryside aren't you? It was the idea of my management company and it was a whole new thing for us. The producer we used was one of the guitar players out of the band Sad Café and he put Rockfield forward to our record company. Our management agreed to go for it. So we went down there. But obviously all being London boys we were like, 'Ooh, where the hell are we?' It certainly was in the middle of nowhere. But we got a lot of work done there and it was a very nice place, apart from the vegetarian chefs we had there doing all the cooking for us. I wasn't too happy about that.

He laughs again before adding,

I remember we were that impressed at the time that we were all actually thinking about buying properties down there in Monmouthshire.

The band recorded some demos at Rockfield before returning a few months later in the autumn to lay down the album. In the mockumentary movie *This is Spinal Tap*, the position of drummer seemed to be a cursed one. The band had a reputation in the film for frequently changing drummers, usually after a mysterious sudden death. Di'Anno also had trouble with their drummers during their stays at Rockfield. Guitarist Lee Slater recalls one unsavoury incident:

We did the usual rock star stuff on both visits, but the worst one was when our drummer Jock Stuart got totally pissed on a mix of beer, wine and scotch. You know, the usual thing! Well, he fell off the toilet whilst having a dump. It was a problem getting the downstairs toilet door open as he was firmly wedged behind it. Anyway, we eventually got the door open and discovered the mess. It was horrific. So we gathered together two spoons and eight forks to draw lots and see who was to clean this up. Whoever got the spoons had to wipe his arse and put him to bed. The two spoons were pulled by band members, but in the end two roadies bit the bullet and sorted him out (on team orders really). It was a case of light the blue touchpaper and stand well back!

Paul Di'Anno's luck with drummers also ran out on another session at Rockfield. They had to fire a drummer brought in temporarily to help with rehearsals. Paul explains,

> We had to fire him during a session. He was OK, but he had this thing about getting himself into horrible situations. He'd laid his drum tracks down and so we were cracking on with some other stuff. Then later he came back with these girls he'd met in Monmouth. They were very drunk and he was very drunk. It was a recipe for disaster but, hey, that's rock 'n' roll! So they'd all gone up to his room at the studios and started acting stupid. The girls were saying things like 'Do this to me' and 'Please hurt me!' So he did. He actually hit one of them over the head with an electric fire, you know, one of those electric fan heaters. So he had to go after that!

After Di'Anno's first album, the band went on tour. But to the dismay of the audiences, the singer refused to play any Iron Maiden songs. After a small amount of success the six-piece group disbanded, once the tour was over.

The rock and roll lifestyle continued at Rockfield as the 1980s started to drift into the 1990s with the arrival of Irish hellraisers, The Pogues. Paul Cobbold was asked to engineer their fifth album, *Hell's Ditch*, working with former Clash star Joe Strummer, who was to produce the record.

'I was never really into The Pogues. I'd just never enjoyed their music,' Paul told me in a very 'matter-of-fact' voice.

> I mean, Shane MacGowan – what sort of a character is he? But inevitably I ended up working with them. Joe Strummer was producing them and I'd never been a big punk fan. I remember Andrew Lauder, who worked for United Artist Records, coming

up to me when The Stranglers were at Rockfield a few years earlier, and saying to me, 'This is what's coming, Paul!' But I was wrong about The Pogues. These guys were great and it turned out to be the most enjoyable album I've ever worked on, for a number of reasons. I remember one day Joe Strummer poking me and shouting, 'For fuck's sake press the record button!! Do you realise how honoured you are? They are ALL in the studio, at the same time, playing the same fucking song!!!' He later told me that the last couple of albums had been 'overdub city', because there had never been more than two members of the band in the studio at the same time. So the albums had been made up by recording the band separately and then dubbing all the parts together. At Rockfield, we kept them together, but we built these little rooms in the studio to separate them acoustically. We had these screens separating them, each with their own bedside lamp and ashtray. But they could all see each other through these Perspex screens. The atmosphere was wonderful.

Wonderful atmosphere or not, the strains and stresses in the band were starting to tell. *Hell's Ditch* was to be the last Pogues record to feature Shane MacGowan. His bandmates were growing sick and tired of his drunken antics.

Paul Cobbold remembers one song which Shane slurred the whole way through, making the lyrics incomprehensible. The engineer had

---

THE POGUES

The Pogues were founded in London in 1982 as Pogue Mahone. The name was an anglicised version of the Irish *póg mo thóin*, meaning 'kiss my arse'. The band specialised in Irish folk music played in an energetic, punk style. The band's popularity was hit by singer Shane MacGowan's relentless drug and alcohol abuse.

to check his copy of the lyrics to make sure Shane was singing the right song. By the end of recording he still wasn't sure! Shane's time with the band was rapidly coming to an end.

> Shane was not well [recalls Paul]. He was taken to hospital during recording and the doctors told him he only had about two weeks to live, because of his drinking. They told him, 'Finish what you're doing and that's it.' But he booked himself into rehab for a fortnight and then returned to Rockfield as right as rain. During recording he could sleep like the dead. No matter how loud the sound in the studio was, he'd sleep through it. Me and Joe would turn the volume on the desk right up until the control room walls were shaking! But Shane still wouldn't stir. You'd have to physically shake him awake.

Paul did strike up a good relationship with Joe Strummer.

> Joe had been there and done it. He knew that to get the best recording you should treat the engineer right and when his ears have gone you may as well pack up. So at midnight – or as near as we could get after a recording – he'd say to the band 'Right! It's 5 past 12, PC needs to get to bed. Let's clear out the studio, so PC can lock up and get some sleep.'

After the album was released, Joe Strummer would replace Shane MacGowan on tour.

In 2002, the former Clash lead singer returned to Rockfield for what would, tragically, be his last record. The music world was stunned by news reports that Joe Strummer had died, aged 50, on 22 December. Initially thought to be a heart attack, later medical tests showed Strummer had fallen victim to an undiagnosed congenital heart defect, one that had likely been with him since birth. The album he was record- ing with his group the Mescaleros, *Streetcore*, was unfinished, having been made in several bursts. After some live dates in the autumn, the band had spent two weeks at Rockfield in December with band mem- bers Martin Slattery and Scott Shields producing. By the end of the session, with some of the vocal parts still to be completed, they had made plans to return in the New Year. Joe died before that could happen but Slattery and Shields finished *Streetcore* in London and released it in Joe's memory. It was a fitting tribute to a man Rockfield engineer Paul Cobbold held in the highest esteem:

> He had so much care. He was the most considerate person I've ever met in this industry. He was totally aware of what was need-ed and how to work as a team. When we finished The Pogues album at 7 o'clock on the final day, he just looked at me, came over and gave me this huge hug and I thought, 'Well there's an icon I've been hugged by.'

The 1980s had seen a more disparate bunch of musicians walk through Rockfield's doors: pop, new wave and punk were having their day in the sun. But the defining point of the 1980s for Rockfield was when they played host to rock's Golden God: Robert Plant.

RECOMMENDED LISTENING

Black and White, **The Stranglers 1978**

Real To Real Cacophony, **Simple Minds 1979**

Crocodiles, **Echo and the Bunnymen 1980**

Heaven Up Here, **Echo and the Bunnymen 1981**

Porcupine, **Echo and the Bunnymen 1983**

Kings Of The Wild Frontier, **Adam and the Ants 1981**

The Icicle Works, **The Icicle Works 1984**

Sirius, **Clannad 1987**

Hell's Ditch, **The Pogues 1990**

CHAPTER NINE:
A LED ZEPPELIN LEGEND REDISCOVERS HIMSELF

You'd go down to the Nag's Head pub and have a few pints of triple Wood's beer and come wobbling back up here. The culture was just great. So I moved here and became one of these dismal, happy, sad, failed musicians that other people cross the street to avoid.

Robert Plant

It's 11 o'clock on a beautiful sunny morning at Rockfield Studios. I'm waiting in the main office along with my friend, and photographer, Andrew Pritchard for the arrival of Robert Plant, the former singer of rock giants Led Zeppelin. I've arranged for the famous singer to be reunited with his first solo band on the 25th anniversary of the recording of his first solo album *Pictures at Eleven* in 1981 here at this very studio. The band also recorded *The Principle of Moments* and most of Plant's third solo album *Shaken 'N' Stirred* at Rockfield as well. Over the past few days, I have phoned the musicians who played with Robert on those first solo albums, and all readily agreed to meet up again at Rockfield to reminisce about their experiences. But, despite their enthusiasm and excitement, one by one they all told me the same thing: 'You'll never get Robert. He's far too busy!' But as it turns out a quick call to the singer's management company eases any worries I have and I'm beaten to the punch as Robert suggests Rockfield, before I can raise it, as a potential venue. He's then delighted to be informed that I've already arranged for his old friends and colleagues to be there to meet him.

So as the day of the meeting arrives, first to roll up at Rockfield is former Black Sabbath keyboard player Jezz Woodroffe, followed closely by guitarist Robbie Blunt. They've been taken to the living room in the accommodation block for the Coach House studio. When we get there, Andrew and I introduce ourselves to Jezz and Robbie, and are told that bassist Paul Martinez has been unable to make the reunion due to a family bereavement. A few minutes later Robert Plant makes his entrance, wearing a blue T-shirt bearing the red square and green star of the Moroccan flag with the word 'Maroc' scrawled below in capital letters. He's also wearing jeans and trainers. With his trademark long blond curly hair, the singer is still easily recognisable. He smiles broadly at his former colleagues and the three exchange greetings, before Robert looks at me and Andrew and says, 'Something's wrong here. I think you two should leave!' I shoot a nervous glance at Andrew and catch my friend's equally puzzled look in my direction. Have we upset the rock legend? Why are we being ordered out of the interview before it's even begun? The singer's face, though, cracks into a big, friendly smile as he explains.

> Me, Robbie and Jezz have not seen each other for a while. I don't think you guys want to listen to us talk about what our kids are up to and what holidays we've been on, do you? Why don't you give us half an hour to catch up and we'll talk then.

Relieved, Andrew and I bid them a temporary farewell and retreat for lunch in Monmouth to allow the former bandmates to catch up on what's been happening to them and their families.

An hour later we're back at Rockfield and Robert greets us and thanks us for giving them some time together. Eventually he sits down on one of three large green sofas in the living room, which are laid out in a 'U' shape around a coffee table. Sitting to the singer's right is Jezz Woodroffe, while Robbie Blunt hovers nearby, lost amid his own memories, on the other side of the room. Andrew starts taking photographs of the three band members, while I sit opposite Robert Plant and read out an email, which I have been sent by another member of this band who can't be here today.

> Dear Lads. Oh the memories. I remember it like it was 25 years ago! If you ever want to do it again, call me. I can still play drums, but I'm better on the slower songs!!! Wish I was there! Phil Collins xxxx

'Well,' laughs Robert Plant, 'having played in Genesis all those years, being with us had to be good fun, didn't it?' Jezz and Robbie both chuckle loudly at their former singer's affectionate barb towards their one-time drummer. Phil Collins was one of two drummers used on those albums: the other being the late Cozy Powell. Phil, though, is 3,000 miles away in New York promoting the Disney Broadway musical *Tarzan*, for which he has written the music, hence the email he's sent me to read out to his former bandmates. At the end of the message, they nod and smile in unison at the memories of the long-time Genesis drummer's contributions to the albums and the subsequent tour of America. They all agree that Phil Collins enjoyed his time at Rockfield, even if he sometimes couldn't take the pace. Robbie Blunt says,

> One of my favourite memories was hearing Phil throw up in the bedroom next to mine, after he'd been on a night out with us. That was amusing!

My mind conjures up a mental image of the Phil Collins *Spitting Image* puppet on its knees, bent over a toilet bowl. I shake my head to clear the bizarre picture from my mind and refocus on the conversation in hand.

'I thought it was great when he played on the road with us,' chips in Jezz.

> It just got better and better, and I loved that old plane we toured on. The five of us rumbling across America in this 60s prop plane.

'That was a 1948 Viscount!' corrects Plant, who's either an aviation expert or simply a stickler for the facts. Mind you, he probably should know as he paid for the plane!

The singer then adds,

> Phil Collins arrived with a different attitude. He was so professional, whereas we were ambling slowly around, saying things like, 'Oh yeah. This is nice'. Phil had just four days with us as his first solo album, *In The Air Tonight*, was just breaking so he had to leave to promote that. It meant we had to be really effective in that short time.

I cast my mind back to four days earlier, when I'd made contact with Phil Collins in New York. He told me how he came to be involved in this project.

> Robert and I had never met, but he asked if I would be interested in playing on his first solo album. I had seen Zeppelin's first UK gig at the Marquee club – they were still the New Yardbirds then – and had been a big fan of John Bonham particularly. I'd followed him since seeing him with Tim Rose. So, all in all it was a great call to play with someone who'd been part of my musical history. Robert said he'd send me some demos that he'd done with Jason Bonham, John's son. Robert sounded great on these tapes. The songs sounded good, and it looked like it was something I could handle. I always had my 'Bonham' hat that I could put on when needed with Genesis or whoever.

By the time Phil Collins arrived at Rockfield, the songs had already been mapped out. 'The material was all written by the guys and Robert,' he explains.

> I had nothing to do with that. I used my marimba on 'Big Log', for example, which may have steered that song a bit. I played what I thought the song needed on each track, but the compositions were already there.

Phil's drums were set up, and recorded, in the Quadrangle studio's table tennis room, which the band thought gave them a better sound. He played on six tracks on *Pictures at Eleven* with former Black Sabbath, Rainbow and Whitesnake drummer Cozy Powell adding his powerful style to the remaining two songs.

There was also a third drummer in the mix. As the band wrote and rehearsed at Rockfield, 15-year-old schoolboy Jason Bonham helped out. Despite his age, the teenage son of Zeppelin's legendary stickman was already a better drummer than most on the scene. But the group decided he didn't have the experience to record the album and so drafted in the differing talents of both Collins and Powell.

When putting the band together, Plant's first port of call was his long-time friend Robbie Blunt, who'd played in Stan Webb's Chicken Shack and the glam rock band Silverhead. 'I first met Robert in 1967 when we were both Mods,' says Robbie.

> He was in a band in Kidderminster, where we both lived. I also remember seeing John Bonham in a band called The Way of Life. You had to see them, because he drummed the same way as he later did with Zep. It was incredible. I've known Robert that long.

The two friends hooked up briefly for Robert's 1950s-style band, The Honeydrippers, in 1980, before deciding to write new material together. Next up, the duo recruited Jezz Woodroffe. Having left Black Sabbath in 1976, Jezz recorded a solo album, which was heard by a friend of Plant's, who recommended the singer snap him up. 'I was based then at my dad's music shop in Birmingham,' explains the keyboard player.

> Robert came in one day and invited me to his house. Robbie Blunt was there playing some guitar riffs in Robert's home studio and we forged a special understanding straight away.

After initial rehearsal sessions at the former Zep singer's home, the three musicians decamped to Rockfield, staying at the Old Mill House – the studio's rehearsal space. 'It was brilliant,' enthuses Jezz.

It was a massive old place. Once there, we tried to get a drummer and a bass player to complete the band. We had quite a few interesting things happen. Simon Kirke, from Free and Bad Company, came down, but that didn't work out too well. We had some young bass players, who played a kind of 'Level 42 style', which also didn't work. Then Cozy Powell arrived and what a smashing bloke he was. We became great friends.

Cozy Powell's enthusiasm and sense of humour endeared him straight away to the band, even if his love of cars and women led to the odd scrape or two.

'I remember Cozy driving this powerful Mercedes with this girl called Emma, from the local college, in the back,' recalls Plant.

Me and Cozy covered the fifteen miles to Abergavenny in about one and a half minutes! He really had his foot down. Her boyfriend, who worked for the music magazine *NME*, was not best pleased and was right behind us. He was in a battered, old diesel Peugeot. But despite the fact that we had this super-quick expensive Merc and he was in an old wreck of a car, we just couldn't shake the geezer. And this girl in the back was saying, 'Well, this is a bit funny isn't it? Shall I get out now?' And Cozy was really baffled. He still had his foot down and was shouting, 'What's going on here? He's right up my arse!' We had a good laugh at that.

And it seems the drummer's stint at Rockfield fulfilled a personal dream. 'One of the funniest things was when Cozy was listening back to the drums on the song 'Slow Dancer' off *Pictures at Eleven*,' says Jezz Woodroffe.

It was the first time he'd heard it back. So he pushed up every single fader, of every single drum, as high as they would go. I think that was one of Cozy's happiest moments ever, because he'd always wanted to work with Robert. Always! And now here he was doing his spectacular, powerful drumming, and smiling from ear to ear.

'I was stood on a chair at the back of the control room pinned against the wall by the noise,' chips in Robbie. 'It sounded ridiculously loud, but great. We had so many good times here.'

Sadly, in 1998 the drummer died in a car crash on the M4 near Bristol. There's a lull in the conversation as Robert, Jezz and Robbie reflect on the loss of their friend and how much they enjoyed the time they spent with him.

The band were in the studio throughout August and September 1981. It was less than a year after the death of John Bonham, and Robert Plant was making the most of his new start: a complete break from the behemoth that was Zeppelin. He'd turned down a chance to record at Zep's old haunt, Headley Grange in Hampshire, choosing instead the rural surroundings of Rockfield.

'Rockfield was a turning point for me both personally and professionally,' states Plant as he looks back at what he considers to be a major landmark in his life.

> At the age of 32, when your career is finished, anything that came after that was a bonus. After all that wild stuff in Zeppelin, this place was an absolute dream. It was pastoral, funny and had a history. I'd lived in this goldfish bowl in Led Zeppelin. All we knew about were security blokes and shadowy figures that came in the night with bags of gear. So when it all finished, it was fantastic to come here and find this whole culture around Monmouth of aspiring, failed, dismal and elated musicians – depending on what day it was. And you could be any one of those at any given time. You'd go down to the Nag's Head pub in Monmouth and have three pints of Wood's and come wobbling back up here to the studios.

Plant's eyes glaze over as the memories of many a booze-filled night in rural Wales come flooding back. Robbie Blunt takes advantage of the pause in conversation.

> The first place we went to was the Old Punch House. The owner endeared himself to us on our first visit by asking, 'What do you

ROBERT PLANT

Plant carved out a place in rock history with Led Zeppelin.
By 2000, the band had sold 84 million albums (second only
to The Beatles). *Led Zeppelin IV* alone sold 22 million copies
making it the fourth bestselling album of all time. When the
band split in 1980, Plant embarked on a successful solo
career with numerous hit albums, including *Pictures at
Eleven, The Principle of Moments* and *Manic Nirvana.*

scruffy buggers want?' There was also a place called The Beaufort.
It was open all the time. They just used to close the curtains at the
end of the night, we'd tap on the windows and they'd let us in.

'It had a strange mix of people,' adds Plant.

You know there's that thing in some parts of Wales: there are the
town folk and then there are the hill folk. And there's always a bit
of friction between the two. Having that, plus musicians and a
weird assortment of people passing through, made it something
like the bar out of *Star Wars*. Still, I moved here and became one
of those dismal, happy, sad, failed musicians that other people
cross the street to avoid.

Robert Plant leans back in his chair as he pauses to remember the
lighter moments of the band's time together, and the three musicians
look at each other and exchange smiles as they reminisce. 'We can all
relate some songs to one funny incident, or another, during recording,'
continues Plant.

The song 'Horizontal Departure' is a great example. We all went
to Ibiza to get in the groove of writing the second album *The
Principle of Moments*. Our bassist Paul Martinez is a lovely guy,

but could come across as a stroppy fucker. He could be so off-hand that people would take it as an insult. One night he was in a club and someone he'd offended decked him. He flew through the door and hit the floor as he came out. We all rushed out into the street after him and there he was lying on the kerb, which was covered in his blood. We'd watched him be punched straight through the door – so that inspired the song 'Horizontal Departure'. So there were all these little innuendos, which were comical to us at the time. It's just the same for any band I guess.

Jezz Woodroffe puts his cup of coffee on the table in front of him as he recalls another inspiring moment.

The song 'Fat Lip' was called that because Robert's son Logan, who was about six at the time, used to walk round telling people he was going to give them a fat lip!

Robert Plant laughs at that recollection before adding, "'Burning Down One Side" was about a spliff. "Big Log" was about a spliff as well. In fact, it's all just one big spliff attack,' he announces with a flourish, clearly warming to his theme. The lyrics of the hit single 'Big Log' have been the subject of much discussion down the years. Are they about the death of John Bonham? Is it a discussion between Plant and God? Jezz Woodroffe shuffles excitedly in his seat and motions with his arm to get everyone's attention.

'I remember "Big Log" was also inspired by that time we were at Roy Harper's house and we'd run out of fuel for the fire. Do you remember that?' he asks Robert and Robbie to make sure his recollection isn't faltering. 'One of the crew came back with this big log that was about eight foot long and hollow. He put one end in the fire and all the smoke was billowing through it and out the other end, straight on to us in the room. Do you remember that?' he says, once again asking for his bandmates' confirmation.

'I remember Paul Martinez rolling a big spliff!' says Robbie Blunt unhelpfully, offering no credence to the keyboard player's curious giant hollow log story.

After the first two albums were finished, the band went on tour in America in 1983, before hitting the UK, Australia and then Japan by February the following year. The Robert Plant tour kicked off on 26 August at the Civic Center in Peoria, Illinois. Despite the singer's insistence on moving as far away from the Zeppelin sound as he could, the legendary status of his former band still cast a big shadow over the start of the tour. Phil Collins told me that sitting behind the drums for Robert was like 'sitting in the master's chair' in reference to John Bonham. Robbie Blunt also had to cope with the thought of taking on the mantle of another Zep legend.

> I felt a lot of pressure going live, because I knew damn well the fans were going to compare me to Jimmy Page. As it turned out, they stopped doing that pretty early on. They said I sounded more like a southern guitar player, which is fine. I love stuff like The Allman Brothers. It was a totally different thing I was looking for – and Robert as well.

Keyboard player Jezz Woodroffe found himself on stage with one of his heroes for the second time:

> The very first gig we did in America was really scary, because we didn't know if we could pull it off. We'd never done a big gig before but it worked. Playing Madison Square Gardens, a few weeks later, on September 12, I think, has got to be a highlight. But then, as a kid, that's what I always wanted to do. I wanted to play at MSG, which I did first with Black Sabbath. As a kid the two bands I used to listen to were Black Sabbath and Led Zeppelin. So it was quite strange that this teenager ended up playing with his musical heroes.

The band had waited for the release of both albums before going live. Jezz remembers,

> The delay was because Robert didn't want anybody asking him to do Led Zeppelin songs, and we hadn't got enough material to do a two-hour show. It was obvious that we needed a fairly

substantial amount of new material before we could put a show together, so we waited until the two albums were done.

Pictures at Eleven had been released the previous year in June 1982, with *The Principle of Moments* issued thirteen months later, as the US tour finally got underway. Both albums made the top 5 on both sides of the Atlantic.

In 1984, the band returned to Rockfield, with Little Feat drummer Ritchie Hayward, to record parts of Plant's third solo album *Shaken 'N' Stirred*.

'Things were a lot different for that album,' reflects the singer.

Everyone had gone on holiday for a while and I'd gone up and done The Honeydrippers project for a while. Eventually back here at Rockfield, Ritchie Hayward had arrived and he was fantastic. It added another whole space to what we were doing. And the thing is, if you listen to the album now I think it's fantastic.

You can feel the tension in the music. If you listen to things like 'Trouble Your Money' it's stunning. It was hard, though, because we were calling on the technology of that time: the 1980s. I knew what we were driving at even if, at times, it was quite painful to do it. I remember poor Robbie had to play this awful guitar synth.

The guitarist groans at this painful memory and adds,

The problem was recording it, because it had this delay. So in your head you had to play few notes ahead, so it came out right. But then you'd get this horrible screeching noise, because it wouldn't track properly. Well, it was tough, but I have listened to 'Sixes and Sevens' on that album and it is good.

Robert Plant's solo catalogue has been remastered and reissued by Warners. The process started with a comprehensive box set called *Nine Lives* featuring all his solo albums, plus bonus live material and interviews. It was due to be released four months after my interview with Robert at Rockfield.

'I was happy to take Warners up on their offer to remaster these albums,' the singer told me.

> At first, I was quite fearful of what it might sound like, but I think it's turned out wonderful. The first three albums, done here at Rockfield, stand up really well. The way that Robbie plays and the way I sing – in fact the way we all played – is great. We were kind of leaning on 80s technology and attitude, but, at the same time, we were coming from a more blues-based sound. I was a bit hesitant about revisiting the 80s, because I tended to embrace every new move that came along to try to get as far away from Led Zeppelin as I could. I wanted to make my own stamp with new people. I wanted to go off somewhere and say, 'OK I can never touch that amazing time, I need to do something different.' So I thought I'd be quite taken aback by what I listened to but it's nice. It's really good. What we did here at Rockfield was quite a good melange between our own styles. Robbie's blues-based but very eloquent style, Paul Martinez's exceptional and unique bass playing and Jezz's wonderful keyboard colours, because there were new keyboards coming along all the time, weren't there?

'And unfortunately I was buying them all!' says Jezz.

'Yeah, but you were getting them at trade prices though,' shoots back Plant with a smile. The singer returns to the subject of the new box set.

> Some of the live versions of these songs were extended to around eight minutes long. I thought we'd have to edit them down. But the studio staff were so helpful and said as they were live tracks we should just let them run.

As it happens, for this reunion, Plant's brought a CD of some early mixes of a handful of the live tracks to be featured in the box set, to play to his former bandmates. Recorded at the Summit Arena in Houston on 20 September 1983, the songs include 'In The Mood' and 'Thru With The Two Step' from *The Principle of Moments*, 'Like I've Never Been Gone' from *Pictures at Eleven* plus 'Lively Up Yourself' – a rare live version of a Bob Marley song.

The hunt is on now for a working stereo. The CD player in the Coach House living room is not working. Typical! You spend the day at a major recording studio and you can't actually play any music. Jezz and Robbie make several attempts to get some sound out of it. Any sound. But the stereo system is having the day off it seems. Luckily, having been told on the phone a few days ago that Robert would be bringing some of these live tracks to play to the band, I brought a portable CD player with me. It's in the boot of my friend Andrew's car. I dash outside to retrieve it, but as I press the key fob to open the lock, I set off the car alarm, not once but twice. I can hear gales of laughter from inside. Embarrassed, I hurry back inside and set up the CD player as the laughter slowly dies down, but not slowly enough for my liking!

As Robert Plant pops the disc into the CD player, 'Like I've Never Been Gone' suddenly booms out into the room. Robert turns the volume up – though not quite to 11 – as we hear Robbie Blunt launch into the song's second guitar solo. The singer tells everyone to listen to how well this has come out. 'That guitar solo is just storming,' beams Robert with pride at his guitarist friend's performance from more than twenty years ago.

Once the tracks end, Robert announces he has to leave to drive to Brecon to rehearse with his new band, The Strange Sensation. As the three friends walk outside into the courtyard, shake hands, hug and say their farewells, they reflect on what was an enjoyable experience two and a half decades ago.

'I was immune to penicillin by the time I left,' says Plant cheekily to the amusement of everyone. 'And I didn't get done for drinking and driving.' 'I nearly did!' interjects Jezz, while Plant points at Robbie Blunt like a naughty schoolboy and laughs. 'But he did!'

In the 1970s, Rockfield's profile had been raised sky high by the likes of Queen, Rush, Hawkwind and Judas Priest. In the 1980s, the presence of rock icon Robert Plant boosted Rockfield's status even higher. Other musicians basked in his appearance at Rockfield. Budgie remember drinking with him in the Nag's Head pub, Di'Anno guitarist Lee Slater will never forget the day Plant came into the living room, with a crate of twenty-four beers, for a chat.

REM and Pavement producer Mitch Easter was delighted to have met his hero during his stint at Rockfield in 1982 with his band Let's Active – even if it was in strange circumstances. His producer John Leckie recalls:

> It was great as there were two studios at Rockfield, so there was always a bit of interaction between them. When I was there with Mitch Easter's band, an army helicopter had landed on the field at the back of the studios on a training exercise. You get a lot of army action around there. So this helicopter had landed and all the soldiers were getting out. And Mitch grabbed his video camera, which had just come out in the early 80s, to record it. He was standing in this field filming these soldiers when all of a sudden someone taps him on the shoulder. He turns around and there's Robert Plant and he says to Mitch, quite seriously, 'You're not allowed to film soldiers.' Mitch didn't mind. He was just completely blown away to be standing in a field with *the* Robert Plant!

Mitch himself remembers the first meeting slightly differently and recalls that the Zeppelin singer had been in touch with him prior to their arrival in Wales.

> It seems Robert had seen my band Let's Active on *The Old Grey Whistle Test* on BBC television, and had enquired about us with the show's presenter. Eventually, through various intermediaries, I was given a phone number and requested to call. So, I'd had this lengthy, and notable, phone conversation with Robert Plant by the time we went to Rockfield. But the circumstances of this, our first rendezvous, was amusing! I had seen a military helicopter in a field along the road to the studio, and I walked back down there for a closer look. As I was walking back, a big brown Mercedes slowed down and somebody called out my name. The driver was Robert Plant, who had somehow recognised me from behind, which is still a bit mystifying. Anyway, he gave me a ride to the studio and he stopped in for a while. He was really pleasant and quite a storyteller. Also, he could do accurate US accents, which is rare!

But not everyone was in awe of their first meeting with the legendary singer.

Sheila Chandra was the singer of the band Monsoon – who mixed Western and Indian pop styles to score a hit in 1982 with 'Ever So Lonely'. While Monsoon were recording their album at Rockfield, Robert Plant dropped into their studio for a chat. Unfortunately, Sheila mistook him for the piano tuner and ignored him!

Being ignored was far from the problem for Rockfield's house engineer Paul Cobbold. His was a case of mistaken identity.

> Robert Plant needed an engineer and I was there at Rockfield, so we got to know each other fairly well. In fact, I used to get mistaken for him in Monmouth occasionally, which was very embarrassing. I had long curly hair – which looked like Robert's. I remember going for a meal in the Rising Sun pub in the town with some friends. The staff greeted me with 'Hello, Mr Plant.' I kept trying to tell them that I wasn't Robert Plant, but they wouldn't believe me. In the end they wouldn't let me pay for the meal.

Robert Plant's time at Rockfield brought the studio even more kudos. It attracted more new bands and musicians, who wanted to record at the home of rock legends. As the 1990s arrived, two of the biggest selling British albums ever would be recorded at Rockfield.

RECOMMENDED LISTENING

Pictures at Eleven, Robert Plant 1982

The Principle of Moments, Robert Plant 1983

Shaken 'N' Stirred Robert Plant 1985

Nine Lives (Box Set), Robert Plant 2006

CHAPTER TEN:

THE 1990S

OASIS AND THE STONE ROSES RAISE HELL

Liam is playing our singer, Darius, rough mixes from the new Oasis album. After hearing a couple of songs, Darius, jokingly, asked him, 'Why do you always rip off The Beatles?' Now obviously this didn't go down too well ... Liam just lost it, threw Darius out of the front door and then punched him in the face!

Neil Cooper, former drummer with Cable

The scene was one of chaos and destruction. Things had definitely got out of hand! Oasis photographer Michael Spencer Jones was horrified at the mess left in the wake of a bust-up between Oasis and another band, who'd been recording down the road from Rockfield, called Cable. Windows had been smashed, bins overturned, with plants and rubbish strewn everywhere. Also lying, almost unnoticed, in the courtyard were the ruined Subbuteo football figures, which the band had bought the previous day in Monmouth and spent all afternoon playing with. Less than 24 hours after that innocent game of table football, Oasis had disappeared: too embarrassed to face the consequences and repercussions of the previous night's spree of destruction.

As the tidy-up got underway, Otto, Rockfield's studio maintenance engineer, surveyed the scene and coolly remarked, 'This is nothing. You should have been here when Ozzy Osbourne used to raise hell. Now that was a mess!'

Oasis – led by brothers Noel and Liam Gallagher – had travelled to Rockfield in April 1995 to record the follow-up to their big-selling debut album *Definitely Maybe*. Choosing Wales to make *(What's the Story) Morning Glory?* had been the decision of their Welsh manager, Marcus Russell. It was just part of the Welsh connection.

'It was my idea to go to Rockfield,' Marcus told me.

> We'd already recorded just down the road at Monnow Valley, owned by Kingsley's brother Charles. And we'd also used Loco studios in nearby Caerleon, so we were very familiar with the area already and were quite keen to try out Rockfield. Plus our producer at the time, Owen Morris, was Welsh. He'd also done some work down there and also recommended Rockfield.

Michael Spencer Jones was given unlimited access to Oasis, both at work and play. He'd known the band since before they hit the big time.

> I'd been doing covers for The Verve and I think Oasis liked the artwork and wanted me to do their sleeve. So they asked to meet me. The first time I saw them was at the Out Of The Blue studios in Manchester, where they were doing a demo of the song 'Shakermaker'. I just shot these fly-on-the-wall black-and-white shots of them. Then, a few days later, they had a gig in Manchester, so I took a contact sheet of the shots down and the band loved them. That cemented the relationship, and they asked me to work on the cover for the first single 'Supersonic', and I stayed with them until the third album. At Rockfield, for the recording of *Morning Glory*, the brief was basically to get some ideas together for the album cover, and spend some time with the band to get shots of them in the studio, which could be used for the album's artwork. It was very exciting. Just to spend a few days with a band, who are recording a top album, was a marvellous experience. I had unlimited access as I photographed

OASIS

English rock band formed in Manchester in 1991 and
led by lead guitarist and songwriter Noel Gallagher and
his younger brother and vocalist Liam. The band sold
more than 70 million albums – with *(What's the Story)
Morning Glory?* alone selling 20 million and becoming
one of the top three bestselling UK albums of all time.

the band in the studio at work, and also during the downtimes
when they were at play. The time at Rockfield was quite short.
The whole album was done in about two to three weeks, but I
had unprecedented access and it was a very privileged position
to be in.

The Oasis camp was buzzing. The band and management felt this
second album was going to be something very special. 'They had
recorded the first album *Definitely Maybe* a year earlier down the road
at Monnow Valley,' says Michael.

And so I'd been there and shot the cover for the single 'Supersonic'
in the studio. But then the original session there didn't work out
musically, so they ended up re-recording some of the songs at
Sawmills in Cornwall. But then, for *Morning Glory*, Noel already
had a huge amount of songs left over from the first album.
And they were great songs. After listening to a couple of the
early recordings of 'Wonderwall' and 'Champagne Supernova',
it became apparent that this was going to be a blinding album.
Marcus Russell said at the time at Rockfield, that if this record
[only] sold a million copies it would be a disaster!

Michael laughs at the memory. 'They were that confident that it would
sell bucketloads, basically.'

Marcus himself remembers that the band were now full of confidence and had a real swagger about them.

> The band had written and rehearsed all the material beforehand. They knew the songs were fantastic. And the relationship – at least professionally – between the band members was really good. Things were really buzzing musically. They got their sound exactly right, so the songs were spot on. The band were delighted with the way the Rockfield sessions turned out. They were so happy once the tracks were laid down, as everyone knew it was going to be something special. The band couldn't wait to get to London to mix the album.

Marcus Russell was the perfect manager for the volatile band. The former British Steel furnace worker and economics teacher discovered the unknown Manchester musicians in May 1993, and guided Oasis to superstardom in a short space of time.

Michael Spencer Jones believes the Oasis manager deserves a lot of credit for the band's success.

> Marcus Russell is a very amiable chap. I really like him and I thought he was perfect for Oasis. He has great managerial skills and knows how to groom a rock and roll band. He's fantastic in terms of getting them exposure and seen by a UK audience. One of the first things he did with Oasis was to get them on the basic pub circuit – I think they call it 'the toilet circuit'.

It may sound like a bit of a derogatory description, but the 'toilet circuit' is a bedrock of British music. It's a network of small, intimate venues, where the bands literally have to change in the toilets. Michael Spencer Jones continues with his memories of those early dates.

> The Duchess of York in Leeds was one of those venues, the Hop and Grape in Manchester was another. They're all these very low-key gigs that bands have got to do. Marcus got them on that tour and it just snowballed from there. When I saw them in the

Hop and Grape – a week after I'd initially met them – there were about 20 to 30 people in the audience. It was empty. But by the end of the tour, Oasis were packing out these venues. On a week-by-week basis, word was spreading like wildfire about this new band and people were being urged to check them out.

Oasis rapidly gained a major following and the support of the music press. When *Definitely Maybe* was released in 1994, it became one of the fastest selling debut albums in the UK ever. It reached number 1 and sold more than a million copies in America. Oasis were riding the crest of a wave. Now settled at Rockfield, the band were enjoying making the follow-up record, *(What's the Story) Morning Glory?* Michael Spencer Jones recalls the camaraderie and high spirits, both in the studio and socially.

I remember one night, at 11 o'clock, we were at a loose end, when we heard some music coming from one of the cottages at the studios. So we went down there to check it out, and went in, thinking it must be a party. And inside there's a guy playing a fiddle in the corner in the midst of this Country and Western, thigh-slapping kind of atmosphere. I thought to myself, 'Oh yeah! That's pretty good fiddle playing.' It turns out that the guy sitting in the corner playing fiddle was Nigel Kennedy, the popular classical musician. So there was a bit of bonding with Nigel, who is a top geezer. A couple of days later, we arranged a football match. The Nigel Kennedy All-Stars versus Oasis. So we went down to the local football pitch in Monmouth to play against them and our jaws dropped when Nigel Kennedy's team turned up in a pink strip. We were all playing in jeans and T-shirts – just a scruffy rock 'n' roll band and their mates! But Nigel's lot were wearing this specially made pink kit to play in. It didn't do them any good as we won. Bassist Paul 'Guigsy' McGuigan and Liam were very good at football, so we ended up hammering them something like 6–1. There was plenty of bonding going on that day.

And it was fun for us in the studio too. One day, after Paul McGuigan had had a haircut at the studio, I remember Owen

Morris doing impersonations of the Gallagher brothers by gathering up huge amounts of the cut hair and sticking it above his eyes to form these monstrous eyebrows! We were in hysterics at that. On another afternoon, the guitarist Paul 'Bonehead' Arthurs had downed a bottle of wine or two and had fallen asleep in Owen Morris' chair. The producer's chair! So Owen thought it was be a good idea to gaffer tape him into the chair. And he did! He completed taped him up – around his legs, arms, everything. Two hours later and Bonehead starts coming around. As he's waking up, he realises that he can't get out of the chair and he's wondering what the hell is going on. Owen Morris and Noel thought I should capture this on film. So I got my camera out and started taking photos of Bonehead strapped in the chair and struggling vainly to get out. He was screaming, 'Get me out! Get me out!' So Owen got one of the razor blades from the tape editing area and actually used the blade to cut the gaffer tape, because there was so much wrapped around him, he couldn't undo it. He had to hack the stuff off with this razor and was actually cutting through his leather jacket. Bonehead's very expensive jacket was being cut to shreds. This enraged him even more! Finally he manages to break free and, because I was taking pictures, he thinks I've organised the whole thing. So for the next couple of hours the chase was on. It was like the hunter versus the hunted as he pursued me.

Michael laughs as he recalls the surreal nature of the pursuit.

He was chasing me with a loaded air rifle around Rockfield. It was quite funny as it was like something out of a spaghetti western! I'd be hiding behind a shed and suddenly I'd see an air rifle poke out from behind the wall. So I'd run and he'd chase me. Then I'd lose him again and hide behind a tree until he tracked me down again and so it continued. It was quite comical in a way, but, in another way, I was terrified. He had a loaded air rifle and if he'd got me, he would have killed me, basically. I finally escaped him at about 5 o'clock in the morning. But later that morning he broke the door to my room down and came in with a baseball bat. Fortunately he'd sobered up by then, so only pretended to beat me up!

I also remember Bonehead's attempt at singing. On the vinyl version of the album, there's a bonus track called 'Bonehead's Bank Holiday'. He was originally going to sing the vocals on this track. But we all went out into Monmouth to the local pub, had a skinful, and then came back to the studio. Bonehead felt his singing ability would be improved by being in the pub for a few hours. But later it became apparent that he'd drunk a little too much. Noel must have lost his patience and so in the end Bonehead didn't deliver the vocal and Noel ended up singing 'Bonehead's Bank Holiday' instead. That was a shame, because it would have been good to have Bonehead singing on one track. He just couldn't do it though. But I've got some great shots of Bonehead and Liam trying to record it together. Of course, the fact he was never actually on the track in the end rendered them slightly redundant, but they are still interesting archive shots to have. My favourite shot of the band, though, is of them playing table football. They went out into Monmouth and bought this Subbuteo table football set and set it all up. They played that game all afternoon. Later in the evening it was a very different story.

Yes, it was that night when trouble exploded at Rockfield and it very nearly put an end to the recording of the album and even the band itself! Liam Gallagher had been out in Monmouth and bumped into another band called Cable while out on the town. He proudly invited them back to Rockfield to hear some of the tracks from Oasis's new album. Cable were recording just down the road in Monnow Valley Studios. A favourite of John Peel, the band were short-lived, but their single 'Freeze the Atlantic' did make number 44 in the UK charts after being used in a soft drink advert.

Once at Rockfield, and with the drinks flowing, the party started to take off. Liam then played a tape of their new tracks, which had yet to be heard by anyone outside the Oasis entourage. Cable drummer Neil Cooper, now with the Northern Irish rockers Therapy?, gave me the full story.

Liam is playing our singer, Darius, rough mixes from the new album. After hearing a couple of songs, Darius, jokingly, asked him, 'Why do you always rip off The Beatles?' Now obviously this didn't go down too well!

The next thing I know, as I'm leaving the kitchen with some beers, Liam drunkenly enters with Darius following him, 'playfully' grabbing him from behind and trying to mount him like a dog!!!! Liam just lost it, threw Darius out of the front door and then punched him in the face! Then all hell broke loose. There was lots of pushing and shoving. Windows and studio equipment was broken. We made a swift exit.

As the arguments escalated, Liam chased his brother Noel and the band's drummer Alan White in a fit of anger. The band had started squabbling among themselves. The pair hid from Liam in Noel's room and then escaped through the window. They both dived into a car and drove off for London with Liam chasing them down the driveway while throwing rubbish bins at their fleeing vehicle. Michael Spencer Jones witnessed the whole incident. He says there were clearly frustrations mounting within the band and the behaviour of the musicians from Cable proved to be final straw, which saw tempers boil over.

I think Cable thought to themselves, 'This is rock and roll. Let's smash the place up!' They behaved like idiots and were very rude. That night they caused a lot of problems. It was the usual scenario. They let a fire extinguisher off, and then smashed it through a door. That was the spark that lit the fuse and caused a lot of the other problems that evening. It led to a major fight. Members of the band were fighting each other in this huge brawl. It ended up with the whole album being aborted for a number of days. At the time it was quite serious and I remember waking up the following day and the scene of devastation was unbelievable! No one wanted to be around in the morning, because they knew the person that was there when the grown-ups arrived would cop for it. I think the following day someone phoned up the repair man. He came around and said, 'This is nothing.' He was going on about the days of Ozzy Osbourne and Black Sabbath. 'They really knew how to wreck a studio,' he told us.

Michael laughs again as he recalls that the poor maintenance engineer only knew half of the story.

We were thinking to ourselves 'Yeah, but you haven't seen Liam's room yet!' It was so bad. I think it was myself and the art director Brian Cannon who were there, and we wouldn't let him into Liam's room. We kept making these excuses and did everything we could to prevent, or distract him, from checking Liam's room, because we knew if he saw that then … well …

As Michael's voice trails off, I ask him just how bad it was.

It was about as bad as it can get really. The bed was broken in half. The television was on the outside of the room, instead of the inside. It was still plugged in as well. At the time, Oasis were pretty frustrated. The band Cable triggered it all, but the frustration was already deep set. They'd just had a huge-selling debut album and had been touring non-stop. They were coming to terms with the whole fame aspect. So their lives had completely changed within 18 months, yet they were still completely skint. That was the frustrating thing as the royalties weren't coming in at that point. Oasis had had a platinum selling album and were performing sell-out gigs, but weren't getting the cheques from the record company. That was part of it.

Another part of it was going into Monmouth and drinking snakebites – this lethal mixture of cider and lager. That was not good. Some pubs banned the sale of snakebite, which was a popular drink at the time. Put all these ingredients into the soup and you end up with a volatile cocktail. But the thing with Oasis is that they seem[ed] to be able to rise above it. Like any professional outfit, when the chips are down, they could deliver. So all this messy peripheral was going off outside, but when it came to, say, delivering the vocal line on 'Wonderwall' in the studio, Liam delivered one hundred per cent. And when it came to Noel's guitar on 'Champagne Supernova', or Bonehead doing the rhythm on that song, they delivered. Outside troubles never interfered. The music was the outlet. It was the positive outlet.

So the band took a short break from Rockfield to let the wounds of the internal fighting heal. Manager Marcus Russell remained philosophical about the volatile nature of the band.

At the time, they needed a break from each other. That was not unusual for the band in those days.

Once back at Rockfield, Oasis finished the album, which would contain some of their best songs: 'Wonderwall', 'Champagne Supernova', 'Some Might Say' and 'Don't Look Back In Anger'. Michael Spencer Jones says he is proud to have witnessed rock history in the making.

The overall memory is of having a brilliant time. When Oasis were doing 'Champagne Supernova' and playing it back in the control room, the atmosphere was just electric. We all thought, 'Wow. This sounds fantastic!' The energy at Rockfield really comes over on that album. The overall impression is that – apart from the one incident where it all kicked off – it was a top atmosphere and I've got some of the greatest memories ever.

During the 1990s, Rockfield was also to play host to another exciting, successful and yet equally as volatile band: The Stone Roses. Formed in 1984 the band were to pioneer the way for a whole raft of new British groups including Oasis and Blur. The band entered the studio in 1989 to record the remaining half of their debut album. The man the band had chosen to produce the record was John Leckie. They were impressed with his credentials, as he'd learnt his trade at Abbey Road Studios under the guidance of The Beatles' producer George Martin, plus some help from the legendary Phil Spector. The producer himself had little doubt of the potential of The Stone Roses. After five years together, the band had perfected their sound and written great songs, such as 'Waterfall', 'She Bangs The Drums' and 'I Wanna Be Adored'. The band laid down some tracks at two recordings sessions in London: at Konk Studios and their record companies' own Battery Studios. The third was at Rockfield.

'We did finish off The Stone Roses' first album there,' explains Leckie.

> We recorded about half the first album – about four tracks – there. That was by far their best album. The last track, 'I Am The Resurrection', which is about ten minutes long, was all done in the Coach House studio. The band wrote it and then recorded it there. I'd say that 'Resurrection' is the best thing I ever recorded at Rockfield, because it captures the band's spirit so well. And you can tell it's a live recording. It's not processed by machines or anything. The whole instrumentation and arrangement was all worked out in that room. That's the one I'm most proud of. Once the sessions were over I told the band, 'Listen. This is really, really good. You're going to make it!'

1989 saw The Stone Roses release the album to huge critical acclaim and sales. But from there on, it was to be a downward spiral for the band. The producer's next meeting with the band at Rockfield would sum up the problems surrounding them, many of which were of their own making.

John Leckie recalls their attempt to record new material in January 1990:

> It was for the single 'One Love', which was to be the follow-up to the Roses' huge hit single 'Fools Gold'. Somehow we recorded it at Rockfield before the band ended up being arrested and taken to a police station!

The trouble started when, following the band's success with their debut album, their former label, Revolver, re-released an earlier single (from 1987) without the band's permission. The band were incensed by what they saw as the exploitation of their old recordings. So, unknown to their producer, who was waiting for them to turn up to Rockfield to record, the band went instead to Revolver's offices in the Midlands seeking revenge. John Leckie admits he was baffled when the band failed to show up on time at Rockfield.

We were meant to start on Monday. So I got down on Sunday evening – the night before – to get everything ready. I had an engineer, a programmer, all the roadies and the equipment. They all came down with me on Sunday evening. So after work that night, we all had dinner expecting the band to turn up the next morning. But Monday went by and nothing happened. We couldn't get in contact with anyone. There were very few mobile phones back then and we just got answering machines everywhere we called. Then on Tuesday after dinner – 48 hours later – just as we were all agreeing that we might as well go home, the door burst open and The Stone Roses fell in. All four of them were covered from head to toe in blue and white paint. They trod paint footprints all over the carpet and they just sat down on the settee and the floor. Then they told us what they done. They had just plastered their old record company in paint.

It was all over the release of 'Sally Cinnamon', which was recorded by an earlier incarnation of the band long before they had success with the first album. Now the Roses were 'the next big thing' this company re-released 'Sally Cinnamon' and claimed it was the Roses' new record. That angered them! The band took them to court, but they lost. The record company owner had a contract and so it was perfectly legal for him to re-release the song. So the band were full of frustration and took their revenge. They had obviously been plotting this for a long time and did it on their way down to Rockfield. They'd bought tins of paint and basically threw it all over his offices in Wolverhampton, and cars in the car park. They caused thousands of pounds of damage.

I knew the police would be on their way soon, but I wasn't going to let the session be wrecked, as we'd been there for two days and had all the equipment set up. So I said, 'Come on. Let's hear what you've got. Let's hear this new song.' I hadn't actually heard the demo yet or anything. And so they went out to the studios, still with paint on their clothes and in their hair, and played me the two songs they had. I put them down on tape and then, after the session, we stayed up, messed around and went to bed around 3 o'clock in the morning. Then at 8 a.m. the police arrived at Rockfield, arrested the band and took them away back to the Midlands.

The Stone Roses appeared in court and were found guilty of criminal damage. They were fined £3,000 plus costs.

The single 'One Love' and its B-side 'Something's Burning' made number 4 in the UK charts, consolidating the band's new-found success. That was the good news. The bad news was that after the release of 'One Love' things began to fall apart at a more rapid rate. The new single was to be the band's last release for four years due to a long drawn-out legal battle with their current record label Silvertone. The impetus was lost and the public began to forget about The Stone Roses.

Three years later the band started work on their second album, *Second Coming*, in the summer of 1993. But they'd be without producer John Leckie. 'We'd done a lot of work on *Second Coming* in other studios,' he says 'but by the time we got to Rockfield I had decided to leave. On our first day there, we had a meeting and I told them I was off.'

It's thought the veteran producer had had enough of the band's overly relaxed attitude to studio time. It was reported that one session at Rockfield took six weeks, costing £60,000, just to produce one three-minute song. Overall, the pace at Rockfield was slow. Very slow. The album reputedly took more than 300 ten-hour days in the studio to record! And the band themselves admit that as much as a quarter of that time was taken up with getting stoned and listening to their favourite records through Rockfield's studio system. As a result, the band went through producers faster than most other groups go through the pre-gig beer and sandwiches!

Leckie was replaced by Paul Schroeder, who'd produced the 1989 single 'Fools Gold' – which was only put on to the American version of the band's debut album. Schroeder, though, quit in February 1994 and was replaced for the final Rockfield sessions by the album's engineer Simon Dawson.

THE STONE ROSES

Fusing 1960s-styled guitar pop with an eighties dance
beat, The Stone Roses defined the British music scene
of the late 1980s and early 1990s. Their eponymous
1989 debut album was a huge hit but the band failed
to capitalise on that success, waiting five years before
they released their second record and then breaking
up eighteen months after its release.

Eventually the album was finished and then released in November
1994, more than five years after their debut. That gap between records,
coupled with the second album's heavier, darker and more rock-
orientated feel, saw the album fail to replicate the band's original
success. Shortly afterwards The Stone Roses would split up.

The 1990s also saw a succession of increasingly popular Welsh bands
decide to record on home soil. Rockfield engineer Paul Read recalls,

> I worked with Catatonia on their *International Velvet* album,
> when they became quite successful. The Super Furry Animals
> and Gorky's Zygotic Mynci came here as well. The Stereophonics'
> first album was done here and the Manic Street Preachers were
> regulars. It seemed all the Welsh bands had to come here at least
> once. But they usually came back.

The Stereophonics recorded parts of their first two albums at Rockfield
with sections of their third done down the road at Monnow Valley
Studios – Rockfield's old rehearsal space.

I caught up with former Stereophonics drummer Stuart Cable in
May 2007 as he prepared to play his first headline gig with his new
band Killing For Company at The Point in Cardiff Bay. Like myself,
his fascination with Rockfield started as a young rock fan. And he was
delighted to be following in the footsteps of his musical heroes.

Obviously growing up being a big Rush fan and reading the credits of their albums *A Farewell To Kings* and *Hemispheres* and seeing Rockfield in Monmouth printed on there, I used to think, 'There's no way they came to Wales to record that!!!' But they did. Also John Brand, our manager at the time, engineered those records and engineered lots of other albums at Rockfield. He was saying that we should go down there, because there was a really good vibe there. And we had a great time down there, especially with the owner Kingsley Ward who was telling us all the stories about these legendary bands. He told me a great story about Rush actually – cos I'm a big Rush fan – and I asked him 'What were they like? What were they really like???' And he said 'They were great. I came back from the shops in town one day and Alex Lifeson and Geddy Lee are there painting our windows.' I said to him, 'You must be joking!' But no! Kingsley said they had the gloss paint out and were doing up all the frames. So while Neil Peart was doing some drum edits his bandmates were painting Rockfield. You just don't think of them that way do you?!

Stuart is a huge John Bonham fan, which comes across in his style of playing as he hammers the drum skins to within an inch of their lives. He recalls being shown where his hero had rehearsed at Rockfield.

Kingsley Ward showed me the studio where Led Zeppelin rehearsed and where John Bonham set up his drums. The room Bonham was in was kind of like a cellar above ground with an arched brick ceiling and apparently that's where they did a lot of Queen stuff as well. It's amazing with all the history behind it. It's so cool.

For Stuart and the Stereophonics the appeal of Monmouth was easy to see.

Its appeal is that it is so far away from the hustle and bustle. Most of the bands who recorded there came from big cities. You look at all the major bands at Rockfield: Queen, Rush, Oasis, The Stone

Roses, Sabbath. They were all from major cities. And I think living in Wales we don't appreciate what we've got sometimes. I really believe that. The surroundings are wonderful and also the thing with Monmouth is that nobody bothers you, do they? When we recorded there, we had people coming over to say hello, but there was no hassle. It's a very friendly town, yet they give you your space. I've been told stories about the Nag's Head pub where Robert Plant used to drink. Now can you just imagine going in there in the 80s and there's Planty sitting there going 'Hi. How you doing?'

The Manic Street Preachers first arrived at Rockfield for their fifth album, *This Is My Truth Tell Me Yours*, the group's most accessible and commercially successfully album to that point. It included the singles 'If You Tolerate This Your Children Will Be Next', 'Tsunami' and 'You Stole The Sun From My Heart'.

'If You Tolerate This ...' was the first song the band worked on at Rockfield in January 1998. The band had little time to arrange it and it was considered little more than an album track, as the band focused on bigger, more dynamic songs. Then fate intervened. The record company paid a surprise visit to Rockfield to check on the band's progress in the studio. Well, any excuse for a day out of the office I guess! But it meant the band had to conjure up something to keep the record executives happy. Singer James Dean Bradfield told the visitors that they had a great song kicking around. Producer Dave Eringa and the band hastily cobbled together a 'monitor mix' for the record company guys to hear. They loved it, and to the band's amazement, told them that 'If You Tolerate This ...' should be the first single off the album.

On its release that August, the song sold more than 100,000 copies in its first week, sending it straight to the top of the UK singles chart.

But the 1990s weren't just success after success for Rockfield. The early part of the decade saw a troubled time for UK recording studios in general. Engineer Paul Read remembers that even Rockfield went through a sticky patch during 1992.

It all quietened down in the summer of that year. The main reason appears to have been the £650m buyout of Virgin Music by
EMI Records. As a result Virgin dropped about seventy bands at
the same time and the British studio business went into massive
decline. There were studios closing down all over the place. Work
was very slow that summer. It took a good 12 months to two
years to pick up to the levels it was before.

Rockfield was Paul's first job in a recording studio and he'd started
there less than a year before after pestering owner Kingsley Ward for
work.

I kept turning up and asking Kingsley if he had an opening for
an engineer or assistant engineer. He'd always say no. Then one
day he phoned up and asked what I was doing the next day. He
said he had Annie Lennox coming down to rehearse for an MTV
unplugged programme to be taped at the Montreux Jazz Festival
in March [1992]. They were going to record the session and he
needed someone to run around making the tea, put the microphones in, shift equipment and instruments or whatever else was
necessary for a week. But I never left really. I also never really got
offered a job! Kingsley just kept asking what I was doing every
week. But that Annie Lennox rehearsal was such a great first experience. It was hectic, because it was a big band style production.
It was based on her first solo album after the Eurythmics called
Diva, which had the hit singles 'Why' and 'Walking On Broken
Glass'. Producer Steve Lipson had done that album with computer
programs and sequences, but now they needed to do it live using
a real drummer, double bass player, harpsichord string section
and backing singers. All of that had to be made to work in order
to bring to life on stage what had been earlier created in a studio.
    Annie Lennox wasn't there for the early stages, but came at the
end to sing her parts. It was an interesting way to start my career
at Rockfield. And it wasn't a typical Rockfield session, in which
most bands tended to be rock or indie – or they certainly seemed
to be throughout the 90s.

Despite the dip in work in 1992, the mid 1990s saw Rockfield's name once again at the top of the charts. In twelve glorious months between 1996 and 1997, Rockfield saw no fewer than five albums recorded at the studios hit number 1 in the UK album charts: albums from Oasis, Black Grape, The Charlatans, The Boo Radleys and Ash.

Ash took advantage of their stay at Rockfield to enjoy the rock and roll lifestyle to the full. Oasis producer Owen Morris was working on their album *1977* when a drunken bout of night-time racing led to the producer's car being damaged. Drunken non-driver Mark Hamilton crashed Owen's Land Rover when the pair were circling the fields around Rockfield Studios in the dead of the night. Following that, the band's manager took out £300-worth of fence with the front bumper of his jeep as bassist Mark played at being a matador using a sheet.

The Bluetones had their own troubles at Rockfield, but it didn't involve mixing fields, cars, alcohol and drunken matadors! In early 1996 their debut album *Expecting To Fly* went straight to number 1 in the UK.

They spent a few months of 1997 working at Rockfield writing and recording the follow-up. But in December there was panic when the finished master tapes went missing. The tapes had been sent to London by train from Rockfield. Their disappearance put the release of the album in doubt, but fortunately the missing tapes turned up at a warehouse in London a few weeks later. Crisis averted!

As the house engineer, Paul Read, clearly remembers, the mid 1990s were a boom time at Rockfield. And – as they say – success breeds success:

> The British band revival – or Britpop – was happening. I did an album with The Boo Radleys, who were well regarded by the music press. Their album made number 1 and the single 'Wake Up Boo' was top 10. Oasis, Ash, Black Grape and The Charlatans all went to number 1 in succession, so it was a really exciting time and we got really busy from that point on. I was working non-stop because everyone then wanted to get into Rockfield.

The hit albums and singles of the 1990s only further enhanced Rockfield's status. From its beginning 30 years earlier, Rockfield was showing no signs of fading into the background. Even though Oasis trashed the place and The Stone Roses brought the long arm of the law into the heart of the studio, both bands recorded landmark albums of that decade. This success simply meant Rockfield entered the 21st century more in demand than ever before.

RECOMMENDED LISTENING

The Stone Roses, The Stone Roses 1989

Walking On Broken Glass (MTV Live Unplugged),
   Annie Lennox 1992

Second Coming, The Stone Roses 1994

(What's the Story) Morning Glory?, Oasis 1995

It's Great When You're Straight ... Yeah,
   Black Grape 1995

Wake Up!, The Boo Radleys 1995

The Charlatans, The Charlatans 1995

1977, Ash 1996

Nu-Clear Sounds, Ash 1998

This Is My Truth Tell Me Yours, Manic Street
   Preachers 1998

CHAPTER ELEVEN:
TOKYO DRAGONS, KASABIAN AND THE DARKNESS

USHER IN THE 21ST CENTURY

Dressing up as ghosts to go and freak out the young man in the studio next door was very childish, but very amusing. Having a 'who could make the most mess with a fire extinguisher' competition was very funny ... all sorts of silly schoolboy antics ... The kind of things you really had to be there for, I guess.

Jim Abbiss, producer, Kasabian

It's 5.30 p.m. in Cardiff on a bitterly cold January evening. Downstairs in the small cave-like venue called Barfly, the Tokyo Dragons are rehearsing for the latest gig on their UK tour. The stage is set at the back of the hall, which has a cramped, rock 'n' rock feel to it. The small space is lined by dark red walls, while the floor is jet black. There are two dark stone and brick archways, which run through the centre of the room, giving it a gothic, hard rock feel. This is not a venue for the faint-hearted. Boy bands and the winners of TV talent shows, like *The*

X Factor, have nightmares about places like this: real venues for real bands, where the paying public expect to be thrilled by an exhilarating night of pumped-up rock.

For the Tokyo Dragons, it's another chance to perform in front of their growing and intensely loyal following. I first saw the band here back in October 2005, when they were part of a triple bill, dubbed *The School of Rock* tour, along with a young band called Sound Explosion and another group tipped to scale the heights, The Answer. That night the Dragons came on last and by the time the first power chords were echoing around the hall, the chant of 'Dragons! Dragons! Dragons!' was almost drowning out the four musicians. This evening I decide to duck in out of the cold and head into Barfly to watch the band rehearse. I head down through the side entrance of the venue, navigating the narrow slippery steps, into the main hall. In front of me, running down the left-hand side of the room, is the bar area, while to my right is the stage. The Dragons' lead singer and guitarist Steve Lomax and lead guitarist Mal Bruk are both taking their instruments out of their flight cases in the centre of the hall. Both wave a quick hello in my direction. On stage, Phil Martini is already pounding away on his drum kit, hitting the same note over and over again. Finally the sound engineer gives him the thumbs up. The drums are sounding good. Then the lanky figure of Mathias Stady cranks out the opening, booming riff of the single 'Come On Baby' on his bass. Baseball cap tilted forward, and his guitar slung low, he looks the part.

'Any good?' he asks the sound guy. 'Rubbish!' comes back the sarcastic reply, which simply receives a V-sign from the smiling bassist.

A group of roadies, all wearing various black tour T-shirts, ranging from Motley Crue through Guns N' Roses to a very faded 1980s Pantera tour shirt, are either chatting, or watching the band run through a few numbers from their set. All the equipment is already in the venue and these guys are taking a well-earned breather. The Dragons' tour manager, Paul Summers, is relaxing at the back of the venue on a battered sofa, where the band have set up their merchandise stall. He's munching on a banana, and has a cup of tea in his hand. His job is done for the moment as the soundcheck continues.

The band look ready for action and keen to get on with the show. Mal Bruk is still hovering near the stage, as the bass player and drummer continue tuning up.

'We've been on tour solidly since the album *Give Me the Fear* was released four months ago,' he tells me with a big smile on his face.

We love it. We had a week off over Christmas, but we didn't know what to do with ourselves. It felt like forever. Man, I'm glad we're back out playing again!

His views reflect the lyrics of one of the group's new songs, 'Let It Go':

This is how I'm living, baby. My life's a show …!!

Mal pats me on the shoulder as he bounds off to join his bandmates on stage, as does singer Steve Lomax. The foursome run through 'Come On Baby', which is about to be released as a single. They also have a stab at a new song, which they've never played live before, but are seriously considering debuting tonight. It's called 'Jack Of Hearts'.

The rehearsal goes well, and even the roadies applaud the band for successfully navigating their way through this tricky new number. All the road crew are now watching the rehearsal, and as ever Paul Summers saunters up to cast an eye over his charges. This time his choice of fruit is an apple, which he eats distractedly while listening. At the song's end, Mal Bruk asks for a bit more volume for his vocals and his guitar. 'No way! Don't do it,' shouts Steve. And the lead singer puts his head in his hands in mock horror at the prospect.

As showtime approaches, the band head into the 'backstage green area' for some pre-gig beers. The Dragons are a band that love rock music. They came together through their mutual love of groups like Motörhead, Thin Lizzy, AC/DC, The Allman Brothers and Grand Funk Railroad.

'Their double live album is just one of the best,' says Steve as he reaches into the fridge for a beer.

We used to play *Grand Funk Live* over and over again. On songs like 'Are You Ready' and 'Paranoid' these guys really rock with the best of them.

That love of rock 'n' roll history is part of the reason the band chose to record their 2005 debut, *Give Me the Fear*, at Rockfield.
'We wanted a studio with a definite vibe,' insists Steve.

> We wanted to get out of London and get to a residential studio. Too many modern studios are very clinical. They simply have no soul. But Rockfield is simply awash with rock history – plus it's also in a beautiful part of the countryside. So we instantly felt at home at Rockfield as a band. It had that vibe, that magical feeling to it! It's an amazing place, a very creative place. When you enter the studio, you can tell it's not really changed. It has that organic feel to it. We felt comfortable being there.

When he joins us later, drummer Phil Martini agrees with his colleague's assessment.

> We found that being away from London meant we could concentrate more. There were less distractions. That didn't mean you couldn't have fun, because boy we did! But you could focus on the task in hand. As it's a live-in studio, you could just wake up and go and get stuck in. And at whatever time of day you wanted!

TOKYO DRAGONS

Mixing the sounds of Thin Lizzy, Motörhead and AC/DC, the Tokyo Dragons play a thrilling brand of classic rock with a smile on their faces. Their 2005 debut album *Give Me the Fear* was described by UK Rock magazine *Kerrang!* as having 'More hooks than a Norwegian whaling fleet'.

We stayed there for around three weeks. We didn't demand to stay in Lemmy's room, or anything like that, but we were aware of the huge musical heritage of the place.

Rockfield's rich musical legacy was what attracted the Dragons and their producer Pedro Ferreira, ahead of other studios. Guitarist Mal Bruk explains:

A lot of great acts have recorded there, so that's a very inspiring thing. In the control rooms you can really hear the vibe from those bands from down the years. We were in the studio where Budgie did a lot of their albums, and as soon as we were in that control room you could just tell that it was where their great records were made. Radio Birdman were there as well, plus all the early Motörhead stuff. It really does have that sound! We'd also get a lot of the studio's history from its owner Kingsley Ward. He's a cool guy. Some evenings, when we'd be in watching TV in the living room, he'd pop in to chat and tell us stories and stuff.

The backstage door opens and drummer Phil Martini joins us. Mal continues with his story about Kingsley's hospitality as Phil grabs himself a beer from the fridge and slumps into a seat next to us.

It's funny because we had a copy of that song by Ace. You know the mega hit 'How Long'. And Kingsley was telling us that the band spent about two weeks there and simply played football the whole time. They'd come in from the field and go into the studio covered in cow shit.

As Mal takes a sip of his beer, Steve steps in to finish the story.

Kingsley would ask them 'Did you record anything today?' and they'd be like 'Naah! We just played football.' And then it got to the last day and they finally recorded that song. They did it on the final day and it's sold around eight million copies. So I guess that was a very productive Sunday! When we were there, we stayed in the Coach House. As Mal was saying, we'd be there at 3 o'clock in the morning after recording, to unwind, and then Kingsley would knock on the door. He'd come in and, it was really funny, but he wouldn't say anything for a long while. We'd all just look at each other and nod 'Alright?' Then he'd launch into all these stories about Sabbath and bands like that and we'd be listening simply mesmerised. We also heard that Mani, the bassist from The Stone Roses, disappeared when he was at Rockfield. The band had been there for ages trying to finish their album when he vanished and they didn't see him for about a month. Finally one day, one of the group went into town and there he was! He'd got a job working in a burger bar, because he was bored.

'It may not be true,' adds Phil, 'but it's a cool rock and roll story. I hope it is true!' The band exchange smiles and Steve suddenly remembers another tale from Rockfield.

'This was great,' he says beaming with enthusiasm.

One day, while we were out horse riding, Dave Edmunds was rehearsing in the Quadrangle studio. We didn't know this. So when we came back and could hear 'Sabre Dance' being played, I was like 'Oh, someone's blasting out "Sabre Dance"' and Mal said to me, 'It's Dave Edmunds!' I looked at him like he was mad and said, 'Yeah I know that's Edmunds' song.' But Mal insisted, 'No, it really is him. Playing the song live. Now!' I was just blown away. So we listened to it from outside against the wall. Mal said we should go and meet him, but I wouldn't. The guy's a legend!

A week into recording at Rockfield and the band's management company Serenity Now! arrived at the studio to belatedly celebrate the Dragons' album deal and the recording of the debut CD. Earlier I'd spoken to the band's manager at the time, Stuart Wright, and he'd explained why they descended on Rockfield at that particular moment.

A few weeks into the recording, myself, Tones Sansom from Triad Publicity and another guy all drove up to see the band.

Because it had all happened so fast, we hadn't really celebrated the record deal. It's unbelievable, but we'd actually succeeded, yet we hadn't, as a group of people, marked the occasion. The band had gone straight to Wales to record, so we didn't get a chance to say 'well done'. And apparently, as the story goes, the band had been quite well behaved up until that point. Then we arrived with about eight million crates of beer and bottles of champagne. So that Friday night, when we turned up, we all went down into the local village pub and had an absolute blowout. Pedro, the producer, joined us as well for the drinks, and we were in some little Welsh village drinking flaming sambucas until 1 o'clock in the morning at a lock-in. Then we all went back up to the studios. There were plenty of drunken antics from that point. Steve, I think, was singing Neil Diamond's hit 'Cracklin' Rosie' on a table. I also found out that it's impossible to play ping-pong drunk! Simply impossible!

When I mention the management visit to the band backstage in Cardiff, it's greeted by groans and laughs.

'We just let go that night and had a great time,' says Phil Martini.

It had finally all come together and we were in the studio making the record. So that Friday night, two weeks into the recording, was a particularly amazing time. Everyone was in such high spirits. It was brilliant. The Serenity Now! visit was a major highlight. But we had massive hangovers the next day.

Despite the alcohol-induced headaches, it was straight back into the studio the next day for the band. All the main tracks had been recorded. All that was left were the extra tracks to flesh out some of the songs. So the band were working out ideas with Pedro for the song 'Do You Wanna?' And because they had the extra pairs of hands, in the shape of their management, they came up with an idea for the beginning of the song: get the management to do some handclapping and shout the chorus line 'Do you wanna get high?' Stuart had told me earlier that it was a nerve-wracking experience.

We were standing round a microphone with all the band singing, 'Do you wanna get high?' and clapping their hands. But if I
remember rightly one of our team had to be thrown out of the
recording session because his hand claps were out of time. So we
lost a pair of hands part way through recording it. And despite
doing a great job, we are not credited on the album!

But Stuart recalled how the band loved Rockfield's vibe, and how,
along with the work ethos of producer Pedro Ferreira, it really suited
the band's love of playing live.

The Dragons do play a lot live. They'd actually played a gig live at
the Barfly in London right before they drove off to the studio in
Wales. It was like the end of a soap opera.

We'd got the recording deal, and then the band disappear with
their gear to Wales. They'd done a lot of the pre-production
in London, though. So they'd basically been rehearsing the
songs and getting the arrangement right in between gigging
everywhere in the UK. So by the time they got into the studio,
they were so hot and so tight as a unit that when Pedro was
saying, 'Right we'll do the first guitar track for this song', it
went with military precision. There wasn't really any doubt in
their minds what the songs were going to turn out like. They'd
really shaped them before they arrived at Rockfield. But being
there helped inspire the band. Any group that has a fondness
for what makes rock and roll great would start to breathe that
in a little when they arrived at Rockfield. And that's what they
did. There's no denying that they felt they'd arrived, because
here they were playing in a place that's a big cornerstone of rock
and roll history.

It's a point the band's lead singer heartily agrees with.

The high points were the album being released, and that it had
been recorded at Rockfield. Our album was recorded there!
That's enough. Wow! You think this is such an opportunity to

record in a place with such a heritage. You'd think recording an album at such a famous place would involve huge pressure, but it was so relaxed. We were very sad to leave.

Just before the band head on to stage, Steve Lomax again reiterates their classic rock credentials.

At Rockfield, we wanted to make a proper rock record. That's why we chose the place. It's where real fantastic rock records are made. We wanted to make one that had a classic rock feel, but was also a real party record.

He looks back as he opens the door and adds,

But despite our time in the studio, we still feel that the live sound is a massive part of this band.

Phil Martini nods in agreement as he also leaves the green room.

Yeah. It's still the best way to connect with the fans.

With that, as the chanting for the Dragons gets louder and louder, the band take to the stage and give the hundreds of assembled fans the kind of rock and roll party they've been waiting for.

Another new rock band descended upon Rockfield that same year, 2005. The Darkness headed to Wales to record the follow-up to their massive selling debut album *Permission to Land*. The band gained widespread publicity with their retro sound – influenced by bands like Queen, Aerosmith and AC/DC – and lead singer Justin Hawkins' falsetto vocals.

Permission to Land hit number 1 in the UK, selling one and a half million copies. The record would eventually notch up three and a half million sales worldwide. It was hardly overnight success, though, for a band who'd been playing the live circuit for years trying to get their brand of rock out to the masses. At one gig in 2002 in Wolverhampton, The Darkness played to just five people: their soundman, their manager and her brother, a journalist and a photographer. The story goes that as the band starting playing, a mobile phone started ringing on the stage. The lead singer broke off mid-song, turned to bassist Frankie Poullain and asked him to answer his phone. A crest-fallen Poullain took the call and quietly asked his mum if she could call back as he was on stage.

The success of *Permission to Land* catapulted The Darkness into the limelight: hit singles, sell-out audiences and coverage in the UK's national press were now the order of the day. For the band's much anticipated follow-up they recruited legendary producer Roy Thomas Baker.

It was his idea to return to the place where he'd scored such creative success with Queen.

'It was like the good news and the bad news,' said the veteran producer when I interviewed him.

> The bad news is that Rockfield hasn't changed in twenty-odd years. The good news is that it hasn't changed in twenty-odd years. So basically it was very familiar to me even though I hadn't worked there for some time. I remembered where various things would work, and where various things wouldn't work. It was a bit like getting back on a bike for the first time, having not been on one for a few years. It was very easy for me to slide back into the whole Rockfield thing. It was another seven days a week record. We went into the village maybe twice. One time it was Dan Hawkins' birthday. So we went there to celebrate. Then we went back straight back into the studio.

On that occasion, surprised locals were joined by members of The Darkness, eager to let their hair down for guitarist Dan's celebrations. After a day's recording the band ploughed into the alcohol as flamboyant lead singer – and Dan's brother – Justin led a singalong towards the end of the night on the bar's piano. The band also spent time on the quiz machine and played pool with the customers. The Nag's Head grew busier as the night wore on and customers began texting their friends with the news that The Darkness were in party mood. 'That was one of those mad nights' is how Roy Thomas Baker refers to the party celebrations.

THE DARKNESS

Their debut album, *Permission to Land* went straight to number 2 in the UK charts upon its release in July 2003 and made the top 40 in America. The band recorded the follow-up with Queen producer Roy Thomas Baker at Rockfield. The nucleus of the band, brothers Dan and Justin Hawkins and drummer Ed Graham, played in a band together but Justin only became lead singer when the rest of the band were impressed by him singing a karaoke version of 'Bohemian Rhapsody' at a New Year's Eve party in 1999.

Overall our time at Rockfield was a real bonding experience. But unlike touring, you are not in a different location every night. We always went back to the same place. We had this amazing routine at Rockfield. First we booked the whole studio, so we had both the Coach House and the Quadrangle. We did the recording in the Quad and used the Coach House for odd experimentations and overdubs, or if anyone needed to rehearse their parts, then they'd go to the Coach House. We had a good routine. We'd be up in the morning for breakfast – the usual mundane stuff. Then we'd go into the studio. We'd break for lunch for half an hour or so before returning to the Quadrangle for more recording. Then we'd break for dinner, before one last session in the evening. Then it was tools down and we'd go back to the residential part of the house. I think myself, Dan and Justin were in the main house together and we had a fixed thing. We'd say, 'Right we've finished! Let's open the champagne. Let's have our Campari and sodas, watch some movies and go to bed.' So that was different from being on the road.

Working on the second album wasn't easy going. It was dubbed in the press as 'the difficult second album'. Lead singer Justin Hawkins at the time dismissed those claims – with tongue firmly in cheek – by announcing it was 'the painstaking second album'.

Despite the flippant remarks, the band were finding live recording at Rockfield quite tough and, by their own admission, were falling apart. Many of the early sessions saw the foursome recording separately and, at one stage, Justin Hawkins abandoned the sessions altogether and considered leaving the band. But Justin, and his brother Dan, saw a hint of magic in the early backing tracks and decided to press on with turning their follow-up album into a masterpiece. So it was bassist Frankie Poullain who was dismissed and replaced by Dan's former guitar tech Richie Edwards. He'd been at Rockfield the whole time with the band and found it easy to step in to the breach at short notice.

I knew there was something going on between the band and Frankie. There were a lot of conversations in corners and it was quite apparent that everything in the garden wasn't rosy. But it was none of my business at the time. I only became aware of how serious it was when Dan turned around to me one night in the control room and said, 'Frankie's out of the band; we want you to be our bass player.' I thought 'Fuck' but was delighted. The transition from being part of the crew to band member was really quite smooth and easy. But it was weird as I was still seeing the same three guys, but I was now part of the band. A lot of things were the same, yet different! Overall, although I wasn't involved in Frankie's departure, I think the band would have folded had he stayed. To keep the band going he had to go. It's happened now and that's it. But it needed to happen for the band to carry on. From that moment things became a little easier. All of a sudden all the negativity surrounding everything lifted and we could concentrate on being a band and recording the album. It made the rest of the recording a lot of fun.

The band were now determined to take their time. The first album had been rushed, as the band were unsigned at the time of recording and financed a large part of it themselves. With the help of Roy Thomas Baker, this album was to be done the way they wanted. The producer revived his 'throw the kitchen sink at it' mentality, which he had used with Queen three decades earlier. The band had around fifty guitars in the control room, there were more than 100 guitar overdubs on some songs, plus a similar number of vocal overdubs. Then thrown into the mix were an orchestra, sitar, pan pipes and bagpipes. By the end, the band had recorded 400 reels of 24-track tape ready for mixing into the finished article. No problem then!

Fellow Rockfield producer John David had some reservations about the approach.

> They had the Queen producer Roy Thomas Baker, who's as eccentric as they come, working for them. He was acting as if it was still the 70s. The Darkness hired the whole place. Both studios! And they spent the first two weeks or so just looking for a snare drum sound! That was just throwing money away for something that, at the end of the day, isn't going to make much difference. I don't know if they'll ever make back the cost of that album, *One Way Ticket To Hell ... And Back.* They must have spent a fortune.

Richie Edwards also remembers only too well how meticulous Roy Thomas Baker was during those early days in Rockfield, trying to find the very, very specific drum sound that he wanted.

> Roy and I went to Rockfield about two weeks before the rest of the band arrived. We started getting the equipment set up and ended up spending that fortnight just on getting the drum sound right. We were moving microphones a quarter of an inch here and a quarter of an inch there, and it just seemed to take forever. Roy would go into the control room, listen back to the sound and he'd say, 'No. No. Move the mic a couple of millimetres that way!' And we'd go through it all again. And then there was like an epiphany when he said, 'Right. That's it. We can start!' and to his credit I think the drums sounded absolutely amazing.

But when I spoke to Roy Thomas Baker he had no regrets and was happy with the work that went into the making of *One Way Ticket To Hell ... And Back.*

> I'm very proud of that record. We spent a lot of time out in the barn, which is Rockfield's rehearsal studio. Later I went on the road with them during their tour and we also laid down a couple of tracks in America. But the work we did at Rockfield was the most intense. The critics seem to come down very hard on the band. I see The Darkness get voted in various magazines as Best Band and Best Album, and the critics will say, 'We didn't want to vote for them, but we had to because these guys are really good.' And that's the point! When I was in the studio with them at Rockfield, we never cut any corners. It was very professional, and the guys are really, really talented musicians. Dan's a great guitarist, Justin's a really talented singer and is great at working out parts, plus he's an excellent keyboard player. They've got a certain flamboyance about them, particularly Justin and the way he bounces around and he's very tongue in cheek. He's laughing at himself. He laughs all the time as he writes and sings, because there's a major amount of humour to it. I think a lot of people don't take them seriously as a result. But they write really good catchy melodies and good songs. We pulled them all together at pre-production and they got even better when we were recording at Rockfield. It all gelled together after the vocals were put on.

And of the comparisons The Darkness draw with Queen? Who better to judge than the man who put together 'Bohemian Rhapsody'?

> This is the way I see it. If you're like myself and into great red wines then you can taste the difference between one red wine to another and you can even tell what year it was made. But if you're not into red wines, then they all taste the same! So bearing that in mind, compared to anyone who is not as affiliated with music as much as I am – in terms of my knowledge of music – I can hear distinct differences. I only hear a small percentage of

Queen's influence on The Darkness. I also hear influences from a bunch of other bands including AC/DC. People say they are a clone of Queen, but I just don't hear that.

Mind you, for the making of the album, Justin Hawkins did play the piano which Queen used for 'Bohemian Rhapsody' and Roy Thomas Baker could still spot the stains where Freddie Mercury had spilt a glass of red wine onto it thirty years earlier.

The only downside of the Rockfield experience: 'Still the same as thirty years ago,' says Roy Thomas Baker.

The owner Kingsley Ward is a great guy, but he will insist on driving his tractor around at 6 o'clock in the morning, when we were trying to sleep, and mowing the lawn and stuff like that. And I can quite do without the smell of manure, thank you very much.

Eventually *One Way Ticket To Hell ... And Back* suffered from poor sales compared to the band's debut album, despite receiving widespread critical acclaim in the music press. But bassist Richie believes the album is not yet receiving the praise it deserves:

Obviously the first album was hugely successful and I suppose there were a lot of people who wanted their pound of flesh and wanted to see the band fuck up. The Darkness never should have been big in a lot of people's eyes. So there was pressure in that respect and also because the band had pretty much been on tour solidly from 2003 to the start of recording in January 2005, so they'd had no time to write as such. So they went to Rockfield with ideas rather than songs. Saleswise, the album is on just over a million worldwide. Obviously it's a big drop from *Permission to Land*. It's the old cliché to say we don't look at sales, though, yes, it would have been nice if it had sold 30 million copies and made us a truckload of money. But it was far from being the failure that the press claimed it was. I think *One Way Ticket* is a far better album than *Permission to Land*. Sonically it's outstanding and

Roy Thomas Baker has proved once again that he's still got it. If you doubt that just listen to the album! There are some great songs on it and I personally believe in ten or twenty years' time you'll still be able to listen to the album and go 'Wow! Actually, that's a really good album.'

Rockfield holds a special place in Richie's heart as his life changed there when he was offered the job of bass player in the band. But he also has another special memory from his days at the Welsh studio.

There was this stray ginger cat, which started hanging around after we'd been there for a couple of weeks. Now I'm a huge animal lover, so I took her under my wing. Well, the food at Rockfield was great so we were eating spectacularly well. So I used to sneak out some smoked salmon, fresh mackerel fillets, fresh trout and sirloin steak and she just had the time of her life. We left there in May and I had a phone call from Rockfield a few weeks later saying she'd died. That really upset me at the time, but then I thought, 'Hold on. She's a stray cat, who just happened upon Rockfield and decided to arrive there when some sucker like myself would look after her. So the last few weeks of her life were spectacular. She got to listen to a great album being made and got to eat like a king.' So that was a nice memory to think that I made the last few weeks of a cat's life special.

While The Darkness found the early part of their time at Rockfield hard going, they did come out of the other side in one piece and having produced a great sounding album. Most of that pressure and tension stemmed from the huge success of their debut album. But The Darkness weren't the only band who turned up at Rockfield in this decade feeling the weight of expectation. Huge success was predicted for Coldplay when they entered Rockfield in late 1999 and early 2000. The band had met while studying at University College London four years earlier. Having completed their exams, they signed a major five-album record deal with Parlophone but entered the studio off the back of a huge rift, which saw drummer Will Champion fired and then reinstated. The internal rift resolved, the band pressed on with their sessions in Wales for what would eventually become the multi-million selling album *Parachutes*. Rockfield house engineer Paul Read worked on that first Coldplay album and witnessed the band suffering this major crisis of confidence.

> It's funny because they were new to recording. This was the first album they'd recorded and it really was a bit of a struggle for them. They weren't really sure what they wanted to achieve. About a week in, we didn't have anything on tape that was useable. It just wasn't good enough. And a guy from Parlophone Records came down to see them to check out their progress, because so much money had been invested in them. The band were worried that they were going to be dropped, because they'd been in the studio for a week spending lots and lots of money and hadn't come up with anything.

The visitor from the record company was Dan Keeling, who was looking after the band. He left Coldplay to their own devices at Rockfield, confident they could organise themselves, despite this being their debut album. But Keeling was shocked when he received the band's first demo tape from the sessions on his London desk. The songs lacked passion and energy, so Keeling headed straight to Rockfield for a frank meeting with the band. Coldplay were a close unit and disliked outside interference. But this time they had to sit and listen as they were basically told to 'do it all again'.

Ultimately, his advice proved best for the band as they looked to find their feet in the studio. Paul Read recalls that the meeting with Keeling had the desired effect.

> At the end of the day, Dan Keeling could see that this project was well worth sticking with in the long run. So he wasn't going to drop the band, despite their fears. He basically reassured them that all was well and told them not to worry, to relax and do some recording. But it was a surprise, in some ways, that the record even got finished – let alone that it was such a big success.

Rockfield was to provide much inspiration for *Parachutes*. The anthemic hit single 'Yellow' was inspired by a Welsh sunset. The band were working in the main Quadrangle studio one night, when they went outside during recording into the open courtyard. As opposed to the city, the beautiful darkness of the countryside made the stars glisten, causing bassist Guy Berryman to exclaim 'Wow, look at the stars! See how they shine.' And so the song's now-famous opening line was born.

Parachutes was begun at Rockfield but the band also recorded parts of it at Matrix Wessex in London and Liverpool's Parr Street. Given it was the band's debut, the record company were hoping for a very healthy return of at least 100,000 sales. *Parachutes* eventually went on to sell more than five million worldwide. Despite, or maybe because of, their huge success, at the time the band remained fearful of the world outside their unit. They were paranoid about their material getting out into the public domain when it wasn't ready. So much so, that the band often attached a false name to early CD pressings, so that if they were stolen from cars owned by record company employees, or left on public transport by careless journalists (heaven forbid!), the new owners would not know that they had stumbled upon a lucrative early copy of a new, unreleased Coldplay album. The name they used, more often than not, for this purpose was *The Fir Trees*.

While Coldplay struggled with the weight of expectation surrounding their first album and their massive record deal, other artists can sometimes simply feel the pressure of recording at such a legendary venue as Rockfield.

Scottish singer/songwriter KT Tunstall started work on her second album at the Welsh studio in July 2006. She was working on the successor to her big-selling debut *Eye To The Telescope*, which featured the hit single 'Black Horse and the Cherry Tree'. But the recording sessions hit a snag when Rockfield's own rock 'n' roll history got in the way of making the album.

A few months before arriving in Wales, KT had recorded some demos for her next CD, *Drastic Fantastic*, in a tiny basement studio in London. After moving to Rockfield, she tried to recreate the vibe of that small studio but failed, finding it difficult to create in a place which had already been claimed by rock history. Rockfield's name and prestigious past became a big obstacle to the creative process and KT called it a day halfway through recording the album. This is how she jotted down her feelings in her website's online diary.

> We started recording album 2 at Rockfield out in Wales, but to be honest it just didn't suit me – too many options and too much space. I still need it low-key and wee. We'd done some demos in a great little 70s studio in London and found ourselves trying to emulate the wicked vibe we had going, so we thought arse to the big studio, let's do it in a little smelly studio! So I'm now really excited about making an album in London. That city vibe must make its way under the door.

But despite that, during her time at the studios, the singer enjoyed her fair share of bizarre 'Rockfield moments': the surreal occasions that most bands encounter when recording at the farm-cum-studio. Again KT's diary entry sums up the incident best:

> Recording in old stables; there's more old stables next door, but they still have horses in. They talk to each other. The horses. Not the stables. We've built a campfire, bought crates of booze, employed a chef, absolutely sorted. It was pretty funny. We went to the supermarket on a wine run and the checkout girl asked Arnie if he was on holiday. Arnie says, 'No, I'm recording on the farm.' She says, 'Oooh! We've had all sorts of famous people, Ozzy Osbourne … oooh, you're not from Pink Floyd, I'd die if I met Pink Floyd. But I've never met anyone famous. Who do you play with?' Arnie says he plays with me, and the woman says how she thinks I'm grand and she's got my album. I'm standing right next to him and wave in her face going 'hiyaaaaa!' and she goes bright red and screams. Brilliant!

KT had been working at Rockfield with legendary producer Steve Osborne, whose CV lists U2, Peter Gabriel, The Happy Mondays and Placebo among others. A Rockfield veteran, Steve had started the decade at the famous studios in December 2000 with New Order for their CD Get Ready – the band's first album in seven years following on from 1993's Republic. At the same time, Steve started working with Starsailor. The band spent January working on the single 'Good Souls'. Steve remembers the excitement surrounding the project.

'Starsailor had a lot of expectation placed on them. But it was a great experience,' insists the producer.

> For the first single 'Good Souls', I was also doing the New Order album at the same time. We broke up for Christmas with New Order and I came back over here for three days to do 'Good Souls', because the record label wanted that out before we started the album. So when we came back to do the whole album *Love Is Here*, we'd already had that dry run. It meant when we got back here, we could focus on making an album – as opposed to getting the first single ready.

The band returned to Rockfield in May 2001 for five weeks to make *Love Is Here*. Five years on from that, Steve is once again back at the Welsh studio – this time with the band Grace, who are hotly tipped by their record label EMI to be the next big thing. It's a sunny day in May, and once again my friend, and photographer, Andrew Pritchard is with me at Rockfield as we wait for Steve to take a break from his session with Grace to speak to us. We're waiting in the lounge next door to the Quadrangle studio. As we walk into the room there's a dartboard hanging on the wall, which looks like it's seen some major 'battle of the bands' action. We take a seat on two sofas with an oak coffee table in front of them. On the table, there's a poker set, complete with chips and instructions, plus a half-empty bottle of Teacher's whisky (the lightweights!). Next to the bottle there are – bizarrely enough – a packet of water bombs, complete with an easy-to-fill funnel. I guess musicians have enough to worry about already without having to struggle to refill their water bombs! An acoustic guitar is propped up against the wall, while in front of the TV is a stack of DVDs, including the movie *The Incredibles*, two seasons of *The Sopranos* and *Kylie Live in Sydney*. As Andrew and I resist the temptation to watch Kylie strutting her stuff on stage (to appreciate her unique musical style obviously and nothing else!), Steve saunters into the room and introduces himself. We move into the studio to chat about his work at Rockfield. Just inside the studio door is a small sign printed on white paper. It should read 'Illegal Substances are NOT to be brought onto the studio premises.' But someone has crossed out the word 'Not' so it now states: 'Illegal substances ARE to be brought onto the studio premises!' Damn. Andrew and I have forgotten to bring ours, but we're allowed into the control room anyway, where Steve sits at the mixing desk, lavishing praise on the studio.

> Rockfield is my favourite. It appeals to me, because it's away from everywhere. It's not like a studio, really. It's like going to someone's house. It's a big farmhouse in the country, where it just so happens that you can record. It doesn't have that soulless generic studio feel to it. If you go to a studio in London, you feel like you are going to work. You definitely have that vibe where you are going into a work environment. Here it's like you are on holiday, but you're doing music at the same time. In a sense, the equipment is almost irrelevant. What Rockfield has is space. There are not many studios left with a lot of different acoustic spaces. What you've got here is a number of different areas with different sounds – live sounds, flat sounds, ambient sounds – and then lots of little booths to put in amps and stuff. There's also a fantastic sounding piano. So the mixing desk and the technology is almost kind of irrelevant. For me, the great thing is that you can put someone in a room with a guitar and start recording. Then, if that's not the right ambience, you can put them in another room and check out the sound there. You can find the right space for whatever sound you want. That's the important thing.

Back in May 2001, Starsailor were awestruck as they settled in to put together their debut album. 'They loved it,' says Steve.

> Kingsley Ward would always end up popping into the studio. He loves to tell bands the history and they love hearing it. Starsailor revelled in that history. There's an inherent vibe in the place, because of that history. That is part of the whole reason why it's

a great studio in the same way that The Beatles' history is in the walls at Abbey Road Studios. That also helped Starsailor. They are all really good players, they have great vocals and very organic sound. With that record it was all about getting them to perform and the reason Rockfield was perfect was that we had them set up together in a room playing as a band. We were recording an old-school performance record, which was great for them as that's the kind of band they are. I particularly loved working on 'Good Souls' – the first single. Quite often the first thing you do with a band is the thing you love best. I think that overall what was nice for me, with that record, was getting rid of the whole Pro Tools digital editing stuff and all the gadgets of modern recording. I went back to old-style working and recording something very real and tangible. We didn't use a modern way of doing it.

Love Is Here was released in October 2001 and made number 2 in the UK album charts, putting Starsailor on the road to fame and fortune.

Unlike Coldplay and KT Tunstall, Starsailor positively thrived at Rockfield. As did another eager young rock band. Kasabian had a ball recording their 2006 number 1 hit album *Empire*.

It was the Leicestershire band's second album and they found being at Rockfield a home from home as producer Jim Abbiss explained to me.

I got involved on their first album, but I took over at quite a late stage. It started out as 'Let's see what they have and see if I can mix it' and then I discovered that it was a bit more complicated than that, and I needed to do quite a bit more recording. It was much different for the second album. We had long discussions about how we should approach it. I was involved from the start, from hearing the very rough demos, right through to the end. For the first album, the guys used to live on a farm in Leicestershire, and they used to do all their recording in a disused dairy shed. They basically spent a couple of years making their first album with a huge amount of freedom. They were able to work in their own time and were completely free to be able to jam stuff and record whenever without disturbing anyone.

KASABIAN

Leicester band often compared to Primal Scream and Oasis. The group were named after Linda Kasabian – a get-away driver for the Charles Manson cult, who later turned state's witness against them.

During the recording of their number 1 hit album *Empire*, one of the band's chief songwriters, Christopher Karloff, left due to musical differences.

On tour in the US, they once left their drummer behind in Baltimore, when the tour bus went without him. None of the band noticed he was missing until Philadelphia!

After the first album – which was released in 2004 and made number 4 in the UK and the top 100 in the US – the band toured almost solidly for two years. It meant they'd had little time to write and rehearse new material. Jim Abbiss thought working at Rockfield would be the perfect solution.

I thought it was pretty important to take them somewhere with a lot of different recording spaces and try to recreate some of the elements they'd had on the farm, which they used to rent out and record at. So Rockfield was a home from home. And the beauty was that we took out the Coach House, which is the smaller studio, but it gave us the bigger accommodation house. So we used one of the spare bedrooms as a demo studio. That allowed us to work on something in the main studio, while also doing stuff in the demo studio. It meant the writing process could be ongoing, and within two days of being down there the band said they felt completely comfortable and it reminded them of how they'd made their first record. Having been away from home on tour for two years, it was kind of important to have that.

Whilst at Rockfield, Kasabian liked nothing better than a good lock-in at the legendary Nag's Head pub. They also launched the odd raid into Monmouth to stock up on fish and chips and alcohol. As the producer said:

> I had a great time … The thing about the band – which adds to the experience of being at Rockfield, because they are good friends of mine now – is that they know, and admit, they are very lucky people doing the best job in the world they can do. None of them would rather do any other job. Many musicians you work with are very po-faced and serious about it. Kasabian are serious about their music, but they are not serious about life. They want to have a good time and don't see any point in doing what they love and being miserable about it. So any evening could become a party and many did. It meant we had a giggle together and started a bit later the next day. But that's just part of it, as far as I'm concerned. It's not often people get the work done, and then think how they can enjoy themselves. But we had so many great times. Dressing up as ghosts to go and freak out the young man in the studio next door was very childish, but very amusing. Having a 'who could make the most mess with a fire extinguisher' competition was very funny. We did a lot of dressing up. The band used to buy loads of clothes from second-hand shops and we'd assume roles – all sorts of silly schoolboy antics that made it very funny. The kind of things you really had to be there for, I guess.

But, as well as their schoolboy antics and generally enjoying themselves, Kasabian also spent time absorbing the studio's forty-year history: messing around with the numerous old instruments left lying around the place and listening to many original recordings, including the master tapes of 'Bohemian Rhapsody'. Jim Abbiss was likewise enthralled.

> I love it. It has an amazing heritage and equipment that is still relevant today and still sounds fantastic. The studios sound outstanding and the echo chambers – which you don't get in any other studios these days – sound great. It's all part of the charm

of the place. The band knew the heritage. They are friends with, and fans of, Oasis, who'd talked about their experience there. So they were keen to experience that kind of history. I'd rather be somewhere with character, and with equipment of character, than some soulless space where you just have the ability to record. Rockfield's just inspiring.

And Kasabian needed to be inspired. As the band had spent so long on the road, they entered Rockfield with more than a few gaps in their list of songs to record. Jim Abbiss explains:

The guitarist Sergio Pizzorno is the main writer and he had enough ideas to do an album, but they weren't all completed. What we did was to start recording the five tunes that were finished. And while that was going on, the band were in the demo studio trying to take the other stuff to the next stage. Over the course of our time at Rockfield, there were a couple of songs that were just little ideas, which we didn't even know would make it. But they came off amazingly well eventually. It was a very fluid process as the guys jammed them and they became complete ideas that we could work with. There are two big examples. 'The Doberman', the last song on the album, is one of my favourites. Yet it started out as a very simple idea of Serge's on acoustic guitar. But the guys jammed it and made it into a full-blown, long, complex arrangement. Then there's a track called 'Seek and Destroy', which again was just a little two-bar synth loop. Hidden in there was an idea for a melody, which we didn't know would work or not. But that came together in the space of a day. We recorded it very quickly and all just instantly fell in love with it.

At the start of the record, we didn't think we'd have those two songs yet they're almost two of my favourite tunes. Though possibly my overall favourite is called 'Me Plus One'. It started life as a little simple, sweet song. Serge, though, had this idea to do this glorious end to it – a summery Motown kind of feel. We'd talked for a long time about doing something different, maybe using string players. So we contacted some Algerian musicians in Paris and – on a bit of a wing and a prayer – we went to Paris for the day and just booked a studio there and then. Next we rounded up a bunch of guys into the studio and said to them 'OK can you play us some riffs?' And they just jammed these amazing hooks and tunes, and from that moment we knew the song was going to be amazing. It was a real 'Thank god we've followed the idea through' type of moment. We had no idea what we were going to get. It was a case of 'Let's see what happens.' But when the strings come through at the end, it lifts the whole thing up. Nobody expects that Arabic folk tune to come through. It's become one of our favourites.

Hit albums for Kasabian, The Darkness, Supergrass, Starsailor and New Order, among many others, saw Rockfield's profile as high midway through the first decade of the 21st century as it was three decades earlier when the likes of Queen, Rush and Black Sabbath were bringing the studio's name to the music world's attention. And a decade or so later, the studio would be brought to a whole new audience by the medium of film.

RECOMMENDED LISTENING

Love Is Here, Starsailor 2001

Get Ready, New Order 2001

Give Me the Fear, Tokyo Dragons 2005

One Way Ticket To Hell ... And Back,
  The Darkness 2005

Empire, Kasabian 2006

CHAPTER TWELVE:
ROCKFIELD ON THE SILVER SCREEN

On behalf of the Ward family, I would just like to say a huge 'Thank You' ... The film is a triumph! ... You perfectly captured our Rockfield life with all of its quirkiness.

Lisa Ward, Kingley's daughter

Footsteps trudging through thick, slick wet mud. Each footstep squelches, sinking deeper into the treacherous dirt. The wet, sludge-like mud now covers a pair of fashionable black boots and has splashed up the hems of a pair of flared jeans. The camera pans up over a yellow T-shirt covered by a very big, furry sheepskin coat. There, surveying the scene, with long blond hair and wearing sunglasses despite the overcast sky, is Queen drummer Roger Taylor (played by actor Ben Hardy).

'Recording studio?' He gazes at a big brown barn in front of him, incredulity barely disguised in his voice. But he has indeed arrived at Rockfield Studios.

'Well, the idea was to get away from all distractions,' announces one of the entourage for the band.

Shortly afterwards there is a scene of Freddie Mercury, played by Rami Malek, in which the band's frontman is scribbling ideas for a new song on to various jumbled pieces of paper. In the background you can clearly hear the noise of birds, chickens and horses in the fields outside his bedroom window. As he leans back in a rocking chair, he smiles and simply says, 'That's really good,' as he reflects on how well his new track, 'Bohemian Rhapsody', is coming together.

These are scenes based around the time Queen spent at Rockfield Studios in 1975 to record the multimillion selling, iconic song that would also become the name of this big Hollywood movie. The band has decamped to Rockfield to record their album *A Night at the Opera*.

The 2018 film *Bohemian Rhapsody* tells the story of Queen from the formation of the band up to their 1985 performance at Live Aid. It emulated the legendary, titular song in terms of commercial success, making more than £650 million at the box office, having been made on a relatively small budget of £35 million. That makes it the highest grossing biopic in movie history.

On top of that, it won four Oscars: for Rami Malek as Best Actor, Best Film Editing, Best Sound Editing and Best Sound Mixing. (The film was also nominated for Best Picture, but it was beaten to the Oscar by *Green Book*.)

Clearly, Queen still have that Midas touch more than four decades after 'Bohemian Rhapsody' was recorded in south Wales. The actual scenes of the band recording at Rockfield, though, weren't filmed there. The movie's producers visited the Monmouth studios two years before shooting started. When they announced they were making a movie about Queen, the studio's owners assumed that scenes of the band at Rockfield would actually be done at the studio.

But the film's producers, having taken extensive pictures of where Queen had recorded back in the 70s, decided to mock up a version of Rockfield elsewhere. The movie uses Stockers Farm, in Rickmansworth, in Hertfordshire. So in the movie, it's tagged as Rockfield Farm and not Rockfield Studios.

Characterisation was key to the film's success. New Zealand screenwriter Anthony McCarten worked on the script, insisting he start by interviewing the band. He wanted their telling of the Queen story and not the word of published biographies or news articles, and spent many hours with Brian May and Roger Taylor so he could hear the Queen story as they had lived it.

Freddie Mercury really enjoyed his time at Rockfield Studio as its being a little left-field fitted his vibe. It was the perfect environment for making music. You get a sense of this later in the film when Freddie is seen walking out into the studio's courtyard. He is smoking as he strolls outside, very deliberately and slowly taking in the rural scene in front of him. He looks content. He throws his cigarette to the ground, marches purposefully into the main house at the studios and then the scene cuts to him playing the opening of 'Bohemian Rhapsody' on a grand piano. Then, he suddenly stops singing, smiles a very big smile and looks satisfied at the progress of his fledgling masterpiece.

As recording carries on for days and then weeks, the movie shows the band express concern about the spiralling costs of the sessions and, crucially in the expensive analogue recording days of the 70s, the very real possibility of running out of tape. The band are already three weeks over schedule.

'Dub 26 of Fred's Thing,' sighs the actor playing slightly frustrated producer Roy Thomas Baker. Mercury's vision is pushing analogue tape technology to its limits. The real Roy Thomas Baker recalled to me that was how the song was known during recording, due to its constantly evolving nature.

> I walked in to the studio one day and, of course, he was doing the finishing touches to 'Bohemian Rhapsody'. It was called 'Freddie's Thing'. It wasn't called 'Bohemian Rhapsody' yet. It had no name at that point.

The movie's Oscar-winning rapid editing shows Freddie Mercury, Roy Thomas Baker and the band recording vocals, editing overdubs and, all the while, having fun. '"Bohemian Rhapsody" was wild. We enjoyed every single minute of it,' recalled Roy Thomas Baker when I interviewed him. 'We had to record it in three parts. We did the whole beginning bit, then the whole middle bit and then the whole end. It was complete madness. The middle part started off being just a couple of seconds, but Freddie kept coming in with more 'Galileos' and kept on adding to the opera section so it just got bigger and bigger. We never stopped laughing.' As is shown in the final vocal session in the film when the band all collapse in a fit of giggles, demolishing the Rockfield vocal sound booth as they fall over. Pride and relief at the same time.

As the film also shows, the record label were less impressed.

'Well, I'm not entirely sure that's the album you promised us,' is the withering verdict of Ray Foster, played by Mike Myers, going on to say, '"Bohemian Rhapsody": it goes on forever. Six bloody minutes!'

Here comes a great example of the witty dialogue the screenwriter gleaned from his time talking with May and Taylor to get the historical detail: Freddie replies, lightning-quick, 'I pity your wife if you think six minutes is forever and do you know what? We are going to release it as our single.'

Moments later, the movie contains a nod to a famous scene in Myers' worldwide hit film *Wayne's World* (1992). That saw Mike's character Wayne, and his best friend Garth, in a car with some friends. When a cassette of 'Bohemian Rhapsody' is popped into the car's tape deck, the rock fans all start singing along, finally headbanging to the hard riffing latter part of the track. (Much like me in Chapter One of this book, just with bigger hair.)

In the film, back in the record company offices after his visit to Rockfield, Mike Myers' character suggests releasing 'I'm in Love with My Car' instead.

'Well, that's the kind of song teenagers can crank up the volume in their car and bang their heads to. "Bohemian Rhapsody" will never be that song,' the dialogue continues with knowing self-parody.

In fact Mike Myers had a hard time getting to use the Queen classic as they'd been slightly forgotten in America by the 90s. The producers wanted a Guns N' Roses track instead as they were all the rage at the time. Myers, though, fought tooth and nail for 'Bohemian Rhapsody'. And he won. Freddie Mercury was said to have been a big fan of that scene. *Wayne's World* was released shortly after the singer's death but the film studio had sent the band an advanced video tape of that scene, so they could give their views on what they thought of the homage. Queen guitarist Brian May took the tape to a very ill Freddie Mercury, who watched it, loved it and declared it to be very funny. It seems Queen always thought their iconic track was a little tongue in cheek. They even claimed to headbang along to the song whenever they heard it played on the radio. May sent Myers a letter thanking him and a signed guitar as a show of appreciation. Search for the scene on YouTube and you'll see the top 10 clips have racked up millions of views. It's as popular, and as funny now, as it was 30 years ago.

The *Wayne's World* scene also brought the band to the attention of their current singer Adam Lambert. To his generation in America – Lambert was born in 1982 – the band weren't as well known as they were in the UK but he watched *Wayne's World* with his brother and father and found the 'Bohemian Rhapsody' homage resonating with him most of all. Later at home, his father pulled out some old Queen albums. Adam was now a fan.

There are some critics and moviegoers who point to historical inaccuracies in the movie. They say that, among other things, it simplifies the band's formation and misses out the fact that John Deacon wasn't the original bass player. Similarly Freddie didn't meet Mary Austin on the night he joined the band. Many also point to the fact that Queen did not split up ahead of Live Aid.

But Brian May and Roger Taylor view the film as a resounding success. They have both said that people need to remember that *Bohemian Rhapsody* is a movie and not a documentary. May saw it as an emotional story about a band coming together as family. It's about everything that happens in a family: some good, some bad. But ultimately there is always that bond. That togetherness. As Freddie Mercury himself would often point out, being the lead singer of Queen didn't make him the leader of the band.

Even though they weren't actually filmed there, the film's extensive scenes of the band at Rockfield once again saw the studio's name prominently back in the popular culture mindset; its role in music history secured on celluloid forever. The film also highlighted the camaraderie of the band, as they enjoyed living and recording at the residential studio, an asset of Rockfield many other bands would later discover for themselves.

Two years after *Bohemian Rhapsody*, Rockfield would once again feature on the silver screen. This time it *was* a documentary focusing purely on Rockfield's illustrious history and telling the story of how brothers Kingsley and Charles Ward turned their family dairy farm into the first-ever independent residential studio. The documentary also featured interviews with some of the legendary musicians who'd spent time at Rockfield and helped it become one of the most famous studios in the world.

Hannah Berryman was inspired to make her film after watching a programme about the famous Alabama studio, Muscle Shoals, where the likes of The Rolling Stones, Aretha Franklin, Willie Nelson, Lynyrd Skynyrd, Joe Cocker and Cat Stevens have recorded. Hannah told *Rolling Stone* magazine that she wondered what a really unusual British equivalent studio story might be and came across Rockfield. The documentary team were struck by Rockfield's impressive studios combined with the homely charm of a rural country retreat. They recognised there was a great film to be made about how a farming family had created a recording studio with love and over five decades attracted a startlingly impressive roster of bands and musicians. How had a small Welsh farm become a major competitor in the music business, holding its own against any of the larger and more well-known studios?

The documentary premiered on BBC Four in July 2020. Straight after its screening, Lisa Ward posted the family's praise for the film on the Rockfield Facebook page.

> On behalf of the Ward family, I would just like to say a huge 'Thank You' and 'Congratulations' to Hannah Berryman and Catryn Ramasut [the producer]. The film is a triumph! We absolutely loved it. Seeing the footage of band's times here, their videos and photographs, as well as hearing their own memories was just lovely. The response we've had has been incredible. So much so our website has crashed, due to the sheer volume of people checking them out as soon as the film finished, and this morning I'm overwhelmed with the number of emails coming through. You perfectly captured our Rockfield life with all of its

quirkiness. Rockfield is so much more than work for us. This is our home and we absolutely love what we do, so this was a very personal story for you tell, however you did so brilliantly.

The documentary reflected the attachment many musicians have to the studios. Ozzy Osbourne stated,

> Rockfield will always be a part of me, because we started Black Sabbath there. I started my solo career there. I can go and live in Beverly Hills, but for some reason, I end up back in Rockfield. It's magic!

RECOMMENDED VIEWING

Bohemian Rhapsody 2018

Rockfield: The Studio on The Farm 2020

CHAPTER THIRTEEN:
MONNOW VALLEY

THE SISTER STUDIO

**I was struck by just how remote
the location was. We drove right
through the wilds of Wales and
beyond, down country lane after
country lane and then through
a couple of orchards ...
So we left the rest of the world behind.**

Cormac Neeson, lead singer, The Answer

It's a gloriously sunny day in June 2008 and I'm turning into the
driveway at Monnow Valley Studios, which winds gently into a courtyard outside of the main building, set in beautiful countryside along
the river Monnow. The studio is surrounded on three sides by tall
trees and on the fourth side by a large field. The river snakes around
the old manor house, which gleams shinning white in the midst of all
this greenery.

Alongside me is my friend, Andrew Pritchard, who will be photo-
graphing today's recording session. The band, Killing For Company,
are here to record with LA-based producer Bob Marlette, who's best
known for his work with Black Sabbath, Alice Cooper, Rob Halford

of Judas Priest and Lynyrd Skynyrd. He's flown in from the States
to produce a demo for the band formed by the former drummer of
Stereophonics, Stuart Cable.

Andrew and I stroll up to the entrance, where we are greeted by the
owner Jo Riou. Not only does she own Monnow Valley Studio, but she
is also the manager of Stuart's band. It's almost a quarter past eleven in
the morning and Jo explains the rather empty studio.

> I'm afraid the band are still not up. They had a bit of late night
> drinking and celebrating the end of a long, tricky recording
> session.

Monnow Valley is Rockfield's 'sister' studio, having started out as a
writing and rehearsal facility for Rockfield. When Charles Ward
branched out on his own in the early 1980s, he turned it into an independent studio. Ozzy Osbourne may have loved Rockfield, but he and
Black Sabbath also spent time at Monnow Valley, as have the likes of
Motörhead, Simple Minds and Oasis.

You couldn't imagine a more delightful setting to record in. The
original Old Mill House is around 600 years old. It's a huge building
with eleven bedrooms, a big kitchen, two lounges and the studios.
It also has three acres of gardens and a mile of fishing rights along
the river Monnow. The lead singer of the Northern Irish band The
Answer, who recorded some of their debut album *Rise* here, sums it
up perfectly.

> I was struck by just how remote the location was. We drove right
> through the wilds of Wales and beyond, down country lane after
> country lane and then through a couple of orchards. As we walked
> through the door of this beautiful mansion, we realised this was
> gonna be our habitat for the next month. So we left the rest of
> the world behind. I think that's part of the joy of the place. You
> don't have too many distractions at all, apart from what you're
> going to drink that night whenever the studio tracking finishes.
> Everything about the place lends itself to an extended period of
> very focused creativity. Musically, I have very clear memories of

sitting in the tracking room with this great ambience and a kind of wooden, organic feeling with lovely, earthy smells around the place. And I remember sitting down at the back of the studio as Andy Bradfield, one of our producers, was working on the song 'Always' with our guitarist Paul Mahon. The song finishes the album *Rise*. I remember the delight at watching this track come together. That was a very special moment.

As the clock ticks past midday, Killing For Company slowly emerge one by one. Guitarist Andy Williams is first up and heads straight into the kitchen, closely followed by producer Bob Marlette. Rhythm guitarist Richie King stumbles past eating a bowl of Cheerios and is happily chatting away with Stuart Cable. Singer Greg Jones is by far the perkiest of the bunch. He breezes into the kitchen with an uneasy smile on his face. This is because today it's his turn in the studio. They will be laying down vocals for a song called 'Surrender'. As Greg steels himself for the session, Bob Marlette sets up the studio and chats to Andrew and me about what it was like working with Black Sabbath and the different merits of Yes drummers Alan White and Bill Bruford. Then Andrew mentions that, on the drive to the studio, we were listening to the debut album by the Kentucky band Black Stone Cherry, telling him we thought it was 'really, really good'.

'Ahh then I've a treat for you,' says Bob very enthusiastically. He pulls a home-made CD case out of his bag. 'I've just recorded their second album. It's even better than their debut. How would you like to hear the first two tracks?'

Andrew and I are gobsmacked. We're being offered the chance to sample some new music that hardly anyone else has yet heard, and from such a good band.

'Yes please,' we both reply without hesitation.

We all sit in appreciative silence as the tracks 'Blind Man' and 'Please Come In' blast out of the studio's speakers. It's bliss just sitting here taking in the perfect sound quality and thoroughly enjoying new tracks from a band both Andrew and I really admire.

Minutes after the tracks finish, and we have congratulated Bob on an amazing job on what would become the album *Folklore and*

Superstition, Greg wanders in. The studio is ready, as is Greg – albeit a little nervous. This is Bob Marlette who is producing, after all.

Before they get underway, Bob coaches Greg on how he thinks the vocal should go.

'How good's your range? How high can you go?' he asks. 'Let's do this in the chord G. Let me see what you can do,' he challenges Greg.

The Killing For Company frontman sings the chorus of 'Surrender'. Bob shakes his head. He's sitting, leaning back in his chair, his expression impossible to read with his eyes hidden behind dark shades. He tells Greg he needs more emotion and more yearning. After another three attempts both Bob and Greg are happy. Bob slaps Greg on the shoulder: 'Job done'.

Later everyone is sitting outside in the courtyard, around a large, long table, shielded from the summer sun by a big patio umbrella. It's a sort of impromptu musical picnic, but with beer instead of sandwiches. Bassist Steve Williams (now known as Wendell Kingpin with his current band Pearler) is totally chilled, sitting at the end of the oblong table in a green, long-sleeved T-shirt and wearing a thin blue beanie hat. He's content to listen as guitarists Andy and Richie both gently strum classic rock tunes on their acoustic guitars. Stuart Cable is floating around, his loud voice booming out as he cracks joke after joke and tells tale after tale about life in music and with the Stereophonics. Sitting next to the two guitarists is Greg, who is also happy to sit back and take in the relaxed vibe. Next to him is Bob Marlette in black jeans, black polo neck and dark shades, holding a fat cigar.

Bob is regaling the band with tales of his days playing in a group in LA in the early 70s. He's explaining how they were always broke and always looking for a place to crash. Either with fans, fellow musicians or whoever. Needs must.

One night, this woman I was talking to after a gig in LA said I could stay at her place,' he explains. 'Well, she said it wasn't her place really, but was owned by her boss. He was away for a month in Switzerland and she was house-sitting for him. So I turn up with my stuff and the first thing I notice on a shelf on a wall is a row of Ringo Starr bobbleheads. Wow. I thought, her boss must be a real big Beatles fan. As we walked into the main room, there was this amazing replica Beatles drum kit. It was the centrepiece of the room. I also noticed there was a lot Beatles memorabilia. Seeing my interest in these items, she revealed that her boss was none other than Ringo Starr. So I spent a few days crashing at the house of one of The Beatles. Later in the week, the doorbell rang. I opened it and there was George Harrison standing in front of me. I was stunned. He asked if Ringo was in. I simply said 'No' and closed the door.

More recently the producer told me how he first came across Monnow Valley Studio. It was all down to some metal legends.

It's funny because I first got introduced to both Rockfield and Monnow Valley through Black Sabbath and Ozzy Osbourne, while working with those guys. Instinctively, just because of the history of Rockfield, I was going to choose there over Monnow Valley. But the deal breaker was that Monnow Valley had a better console and live room. So I ended up going to what could be considered the lesser known studio, but I actually preferred a lot of the characteristics of Monnow Valley over Rockfield.

His first impression of Monnow Valley?

I loved it straight away. I've worked for years in a lot of big studios in America and London. But there's just something so endearing and engaging about Monnow Valley, which I saw from the first moment I walked in there. I loved the vibe. I wanted to hang out there and make records. And they let me smoke my cigars in the control room. That had become a real 'no-no' in the US, but Jo was very benevolent and would allow me to smoke my cigars. But I feel that at Monnow Valley, the dynamic is right. Right for me. What I like about it most is the fact that I'm not a 'clock in and clock out' kind of guy when it comes to making music. If it's two o'clock in the morning, and an idea hits me in the head, then I'll want to record it there and then. You can do that there.

Bob's favourite memories of Monnow Valley?

> Obviously, Black Sabbath first comes to mind. It's [also] where I was first introduced to a band called Heaven's Basement. I enjoyed working with those guys a lot. Another [favourite] was a band called Slaves To Gravity. That was really one of those records where I really loved the music. I loved the band and it's a shame that the record just never had its day in court. Then obviously there was Stuart Cable in Killing For Company. Those guys were wonderful. Stuart was such a great character. Such a cool dude and I really enjoyed working with them.

So Bob Marlette liked Killing For Company and Killing For Company liked him. The band's Singer Greg Jones looks back on that time at Monnow Valley, and working with Bob, with great fondness.

> I'd never been to a residential recording studio before, so I didn't really know what to expect. I remember it all really clearly. So there's lots of pivotal points for me. Obviously me singing in the booth, but also watching the guys playing, rehearsing and writing new material while we were there. And working with Bob Marlette was just an incredible experience. I'd never worked with anybody like him before. He's got that incredible prestige that comes from working with the calibre of artists he's worked with. And he knows his stuff inside outside. He was always striving to get the best out of you, whether you were the singer, the drummer, guitarist, bass player or whatever. He used to make me laugh. He always had this big grin on his face behind his dark glasses and his big cigar. He'd tell us to take our performance up a level. When I was doing my vocals, he would push me and push me and push me. He was always telling me that I could do it. So working with Bob Marlette was a game changer.
>
> As a band, we enjoyed the whole residential experience. I'd get up early to go for a run through the lanes. I'd sunbathe, go for a swim and then we'd do some recording. Later friends of ours would pop in and we would go into town for some beers.

STEREOPHONICS

Stuart Cable formed Stereophonics in the south Wales valleys' village of Cwmaman in 1992 with friends Kelly Jones and Richard Jones. He left the group in 2003 after disagreements over the band's musical direction

The drummer formed Killing For Company in 2007, and after extensive touring of the UK, the group recorded six songs at Monnow Valley that were never released. In 2010, Killing For Company officially released a nine-track limited edition taster of what would have been their first album – *The Lost Art Of Deception*. But sadly, that same week, Stuart died at his home in Llwydcoed in south Wales after a heavy drinking session.

The coroner recorded a verdict of accidental death.

I guess the big thing about it being residential is that you're constantly in and around music. Before, when going about your day-to-day life, you might rehearse for a few hours, but then you'd go home and life would carry on as normal. Whereas at Monnow Valley, you were eating, sleeping and breathing music. That's the difference.

Charles Ward ran Monnow Valley for 17 years. It was then bought by John Roberts, which is how Jo Riou ended up owning the studio. Sitting in the kitchen with her husband Phil in February 2022, she chuckles as she explains how it came about.

It might have been a bang to the head I suffered on tour some-where! I was managing People In Planes and, of course, John, who was the dad of the band's guitarist Pete Roberts, owned the studio. He'd bought it from Charles Ward. I was helping him run the place. Then we got the band a massive record deal in America and we all shipped out over there. The studio was just sort of left to tick along, as we were on the road with the band for a year. I was getting to the point where I wanted to put down some roots. I knew the studio had potential and could be run better. It just needed a bit of love. It had been unloved for a long time. I thought I'd it a give it a go and sixteen years later I'm still here.

She pauses and laughs again, remembering the reality of taking over after four years of helping John.

And we have given it a lot of love. One of the things that attracted me to it is the fact that all these people over the years have obviously loved it. There's a reason for that. And if they love it, then you can guarantee other people will love it. Obviously, it has that history with Rockfield, which is hard to decipher. Sometimes it's hard to tell which stories came from what era and from whom. A lot of those people aren't with us anymore, so we've had stories handed down to us. A lot of them have been from neighbours, who remember hanging out with those people.

Phil now chips in, eager to reinforce the point with some rock history.

A farmer up the road told us he'd met Freddie Mercury, who told him that in a room here he'd written the song 'Bicycle Race'. It was a room in which bikes were stored. That's what Freddie told this farmer. Then, again, you often read interviews with Queen where they say that Freddie wrote it after watching the Tour de France. So who knows.

History and memories are notoriously fraught with problems. Memories can be very unreliable, but it's all part of the fun of warm and nostalgic recollections from our past.

Jo adds to her husband's point. It's second-, or third-hand, memories versus those direct from the source.

We have people who will say they remember meeting Phil Collins here years ago and stuff like that. So a lot of the stories are not necessarily from the horse's mouth. But then you'll speak to a band like Simple Minds. They told us amazing stories about how they'd written their first four albums here. And how they'd spent so much time here, they felt like part of the fabric of the building. They said it was amazing to come back years later and actually record an album here. So, when you get it directly from the source, it's really nice. But, as I say, a bit like Rockfield, I imagine it's developed its own sense of history. Maybe things got a little bit embellished, but who cares. It's rock 'n' roll.

Owning Monnow Valley Studio has led to some good memories and also some not so good. As Jo points out, 'When the Scottish band The View were here, it was an horrendous time. Shall we say it was challenging.'

She rolls her eyes, but smiles at the same time. Looking back on their turbulent visit seems less fraught now time has moved on. Well, slightly less fraught!

That was a month of our lives that might as well have been a year. It went so slowly and they were so naughty. I just felt I couldn't keep telling them off. But then, they would do something even naughtier to top their previous misdemeanour.

She emphasises the word 'naughty' in the same way a head teacher would explain a child's bad behaviour having summoned their parents to the school. But there is some affection for the wayward band there, even if it is buried deeply. The View were produced by Owen Morris, who has worked with Oasis, Ash and The Verve among others. Owen and The View were definitely willing partners in crime in Jo's eyes.

Owen has spent a lot of time in Monmouth and knows it really well. I think he really enjoyed leading those young boys astray in ways that they probably wouldn't have figured out themselves otherwise. One day, they built a raft and sailed down the river

Monnow into Monmouth. Well, they got halfway there when it sank with Owen and the singer Kyle Falconer on board. Phil and I were coming back from Monmouth in our pickup truck, when I saw this half-drowned boy walking down the main road. And I thought, 'Oh, God, it's one of ours.' We stopped and asked Kyle what the matter was. He told us they'd sailed down the river, the raft had capsized and that Owen was dead. We got back to the studio and he's telling everybody that Owen's been killed on the river. What we didn't realise was that Owen was actually in the telephone box on the village green ringing the police.

Phil adds, 'He was telling the police that they had to come because of this river disaster and how Kyle is dead.'

Jo continues,

Two hours later, he'd managed to walk the half a mile from the telephone box, back to the studio. Everyone was now in a joyful mood, because both Owen and Kyle had survived drowning on the raft ... They had a mass celebration for about two days, because nobody had died. Days later, they had a superglue fight in the studio. They glued anything that they could find to their heads. I can still recall one of them glued beer cans all over his head. He'd go to the pub every day with this ring of beer cans around his head. Eventually, they had to shave his hair off to get this beer can hat off. Yeah, you could say they were challenging.

But the likes of superglue incidents and near-death rafting experiences are few and far between compared to the good memories. Jo recalls some of the many highlights.

Since I've been here over the last twenty years, Black Sabbath have been here a lot. I love being in the studio and hearing new stuff being created. Especially watching bands like Sabbath. When you watch them rehearse, it's essentially a concert just for you. You're stood there while they're playing all their famous songs. Sometimes in their pyjamas! We've also picked up some new 'older' clients as well, like the band Yes. They've been here a few times to rehearse. They love us now and we love them. They've become like family.

Between 2013 and 2018, Yes rehearsed their live sets at Monnow Valley ahead of tours where they played whole albums from their back catalogue, such as *Going For The One*, *Drama* and *Tales From Topographic Oceans*.

Yes keyboard player Geoff Downes says,

The guys love Monnow Valley, but I don't think the WiFi was that good. So that didn't good down well with some of the band. But kidding aside, we had all the crew with us and guitarist Steve Howe was well catered for with his vegetarian foods. So that went down well. And it's nice to be able to take a break from the studio and take a walk by the river. I think everyone had a good time.

California-based Yes bassist Billy Sherwood has one very special memory of his experience in south Wales,

Lovely people and just a really nice place to work. Of course, you have no choice but to work. I'm used to a little of the city madness, so I was a little stir-crazy at night. But it was fun. I have one vivid memory of being in the rehearsal studio. It's pretty rural and there' s no one around. So as we're playing, I looked through the window and I see this guy walking down the road toward us. It's a very long road and I'm watching this guy getting closer and closer. I'm thinking who is this? He finally makes his way into the building and, lo and behold, it's Robert Plant. I was just floored. He was one of my heroes growing up.

Geoff Downes recollects that day too.

He strode in as cool as you like and simply said, 'Hi guys, how's it going?' It was great, because our road crew were huge Led Zeppelin fans.

Another time [in 2016] we had my former Buggles bandmate Trevor Horn drop by. We were at Monnow Valley rehearsing for a tour where we were to play the whole of our album *Drama*, recorded more than three decades earlier, when we had both first joined Yes.

That was a period of huge change for Yes. In 1980, both singer Jon Anderson and keyboard player Rick Wakeman left the band. At the time, Yes were in The Town House Studios in Shepherd's Bush in London rehearsing a new album. They were now reduced to a trio: bassist Chris Squire, drummer Alan White and guitarist Steve Howe. But help was on hand from a very unexpected quarter. Working in the studio next to them was the band The Buggles, who a year earlier had had a worldwide smash hit with 'Video Killed The Radio Star'. As it turned out, both members of The Buggles, singer and bassist Trevor Horn and keyboard player Geoff Downes, were big fans of Yes. Each group also had the same manager, Brian Lane. So the solution was for Downes and Horn to replace the departing Anderson and Wakeman. And later that year, the new Yes line-up released the album *Drama*. It reached number 2 in the UK album charts and number 18 in the US.

Geoff Downes continues:

Trevor was going to do some songs live on stage with us for our 50th anniversary. Having Trevor there at Monnow Valley meant we had most of the original *Drama* line-up in the studio. Only bassist Chris Squire was missing. We all miss him since he sadly passed away [in 2015]. We played tracks from the album, like 'Tempus Fugit'. I enjoyed it because I was playing Yes material that I had originally been involved on, rather than playing keyboard parts previously recorded by Rick Wakeman or Tony Kaye. That was a good tour and great rehearsals. I suggested Monnow Valley as I know it well, because it's just down the road from my home in Raglan. Its rural location is perfect. There are no time constraints. You are not going to get stuck in traffic. There's a lot more togetherness and you get a lot more time to work on things. And people can't sort of say, 'I'm just off to feed my dogs,' or something like that. It keeps everybody in one place.

Having bands like Black Sabbath and Yes rehearse at their studio are among the high points for Jo and Phil, but there are many others to choose from. Such as Tom Jones' visit to the studio in 2020. Phil recalls,

It was the first time he had ever recorded in Wales. Can you believe that? Eighty years old and [he] hadn't ever recorded in his home country. *Surrounded By Time* went to number 1 here in the UK. It made him the oldest male vocalist ever to do so.

'I'd met him a few times in the past,' says Jo. 'You know, from my days with the Stereophonics and things like that.'

He is absolutely charming to everybody. He had a chat, and did a selfie, with the plumber, who came to fix our boiler. And he would wave and say hello to anyone passing by … He was lovely.

Phil rounds off the memories of Tom Jones' stay:

He'd do a few hours in the studio singing. And then, at about four o'clock, he'd go into the lounge to watch the quiz show *Eggheads* on TV, which is his favourite programme.

Jo and Phil look at each other as they recall other memorable moments. Jo says,

We've had some really funny times. I remember the violinist Nigel Kennedy was sat on our sofa one morning, having a beer. Our cat brought a squirrel into the house. It dropped the squirrel, which then made a run for it – right over the top of Nigel Kennedy … The squirrel ran round and round the room for about ten minutes, while about six of us tried to catch it. Nigel was extremely bemused by the whole thing.

Jo continues,

> Then, obviously as we're in the middle of nowhere, we'd often take bands to the village hall for bingo nights or the quiz night. Things like that. So you can imagine loads of local farmers and, say, a rock band from America mixing in the town hall. I remember taking a New York band called Deadbeat Darling there. They didn't have a clue how to play bingo. Every number that came up, they would all shout 'Yeah' and put their hands up. We'd be telling them, 'That's not how it works.' But [they're] a lovely band and we are still friends to this day.
>
> The Scottish band Frightened Rabbit came here and we took them to a bingo night as well. We didn't win at bingo, but we cleaned up on the raffle. We came back here with loads of bottles of booze, like advocaat. So that night, we mixed a lot of snow-balls. We were so drunk that we nearly bought a miniature horse on the internet. I think we had £500 on the table. We needed another £50 to win it, but nobody was prepared to put any more money in. I dread to think what would have happened a week later, when a miniature horse would have turned up.

Jo and Phil break into laughter at their lucky escape from accidentally starting a small farm and Jo moves on to another happy memory. She smiles as she says:

> I remember the 80s band The Blow Monkeys came in when they were doing a Pledge campaign for the fans. One of the items was a private gig for ten people. So we laid on a full spread and turned the studio into a bistro wine bar with the band in one corner. The Blow Monkeys were so lovely. They asked us if we wanted to invite all our neighbours round. So we did. We all stood at the back while the fans had this intimate gig. We became really good friends with the band's Dr. Robert and his wife Michele.

While musicians appreciate the studio's beautiful scenery, pleasant and fun-loving owners, and the great equipment and space, there is one other topic, which is often mentioned when discussing Monnow Valley. Ghosts.

It's not unusual for recording studios based in old buildings to be haunted. The bassist from Yes, Billy Sherwood, shared the following experience.

> I went to Jimmy Page's old studio at The Mill House in 1993. They told me how haunted it was and were trying to freak me out, but I'm kind of sceptical. So I was working late at night, sitting in the control room with this guitarist called Ian. We were minding our own business and talking about rock and roll. I had my feet up on the console, leaning back. Then suddenly, this huge heavy speaker, that was on the left of the console, just flew across the room. I turned to Ian and asked, 'Did you just see what I just saw?' We were both freaked out. It was the most bizarre thing I've ever experienced. It was just so off the chart. The speaker ended up on the other side of the room as if somebody had just shoved the damn thing seven or eight feet. It's almost like the spirits just wanted to prove themselves to me, which they did.

Billy never encountered any ghosts at Monnow Valley but other musicians certainly did. Two of the band The Answer were so spooked during their time recording there that they refused to sleep upstairs in their bedrooms and crashed downstairs on the sofa instead. Their lead singer, Cormac Neeson, said that

> There was definitely something strange going on there. A weird kind of energy in a few specific rooms. Not in every room, but a couple of the bedrooms. I remember getting up after the first night there and everybody had a story about this weird feeling. Like the temperature dropping or a feeling like you aren't alone in the room. A couple of members of the team did request to switch rooms ... but it only added to the fun and the mystique of the place.

Greg Jones, from Killing For Company, said his band also felt an un-worldly aura about the place.

> You had that sense of wanting to look behind you to check everything was OK. The house was split into two: one part was the old original building and then there was the newer exten-sion. There was a definite change of vibe and feeling when you crossed over from the extension back into the old building. It just adds to the overall feeling. I guess really you just can't put your finger on it.

But as Billy Sherwood proves, the spirits don't appear for everyone. Producer Bob Marlette never encountered any ghostly goings-on at the studio. But rather than feeling relief, Bob was disappointed.

> It's so funny, because I've said my whole life that I've been waiting to see a ghost. You know, to actually witness something super-natural, because to me that sort of says that there is something else. But no, I've never witnessed anything like that at Monnow Valley sadly. I wanted to so much.

I mention the studio's reputation for being haunted to Jo and Phil.

Phil Riou excitedly gives me an update. 'We had a seance, Jeff. A seance!'

Jo takes up the story.

> There was a Brazilian band called Breed 77. One of them would sleep on the sofa in the daytime and then stay up all night because he was too scared to go to bed. The band just wound each other up. Later on, we had this seance. Kind of by accident. This medium came to the house for something totally unrelated and stood in the dining room telling us she could see a lady in there. She said the ghost knew I [Jo] could see her. Anyway, she walked around the house and said, 'Oh my gosh. I've got to come back and do a seance here, because there's so much going on in this house.'

We were a little unsure, but eventually agreed. We set up microphones to record the event. Some in the studio and some in the dining room, because that's where we would all be sitting. There was about ten of us. We had all the lights off and a couple of candles lit. We all had to hold hands. Suddenly the medium was saying, 'Oh, this girl's come through. She's called Beth.' She asked Beth to tap on the table to let us know she was there and to walk around and touch someone. I was thinking, 'Please don't touch me.'

Anyway, she [the medium] carried on and we went into the studio, where she announced that there was a spirit who was not very nice. She calmly informed me that this ghost wanted to get rid of me. She looked and me and warned me, 'You don't want him here. So we're going to get rid of him by opening up a portal and sending him to the light.' So we went upstairs, where she opened up this portal and started chanting. It turns out she does exorcisms for the Catholic Church. Anyway, she got rid of this guy, but then she says there's now other people coming out of the woodwork. Lots of ghosts from all over the house. We had a little girl ghost in one of the upstairs bedrooms. But eventually they all went to the light.

And you know, it was quite bizarre, because afterwards it did feel different. It was like a thunderstorm that happened and the studio room, especially, just felt really different. So anyway, all the ghosts went. Days later, we played back the recording we'd made of the seance. My jaw dropped. As she said 'walk among us', you could hear footsteps on the recording. And when she said 'tap', you could hear something tapping on the table. We were spooked and decided we were never going to listen to that again. But a couple of weeks later we went to listen to it again. Now, bear in mind that in the studio we record to a hard drive and we have two backup drives, so nothing ever gets lost. So we went to play back the recording from the drives in the studio, but everything had gone. All gone. Disappeared from every single drive. Now they were password protected and nobody messes with the backup drives. But it had all disappeared.

Jo laughs. Phil hums the theme tune from *The Twilight Zone*.

Jo concludes, 'I was a cynic beforehand, but now...'

She pauses before continuing,

> The only ghost left is the lady in the dining room. The original one. She wants to stay here. She likes us apparently. So we've let her stay, so we still have one ghost.

RECOMMENDED LISTENING

Cross Purposes, Black Sabbath 1995

Rise, The Answer 2006

Hats Off To The Buskers, The View 2007

Underwaterouterspace, Slaves To Gravity 2011

Surrounded By Time, Tom Jones 2021

CHAPTER FOURTEEN:

THERE'S A HORSE OUTSIDE MY WINDOW!

MORE TALES FROM THE STUDIO-CUM-FARM

**Rockfield keeps on bringing me back.
I've done such a variety of different things
there that all seem to work.**

Tom Dalgety, producer, The Damned

Its early morning in spring 2012. The Scottish rock band Gun are at Rockfield to make their first full-length album in 15 years. Their last record was 1997's *0141 632 6326*, an album title that, at the time, was a live phone number for updates about the band. (It later became the number for a driving school.)

The band's singer, Dante Gizzi, is getting up ready for another day in the studio working on what will become *Break The Silence*. He slowly walks across his room, draws the curtains apart and takes a startled step back. Instead of the rolling countryside of Monmouth, he is confronted by a pair of intensely staring eyes, a long brown face and jet black mane. He tells me when I interview him for this book, 'It's a bizarre thing to wake up and find a horse looking back at you. What a way to start the day.'

But if you record at a studio-cum-farm, you're likely to come across more horses than a steward at the Grand National and Gun's drummer Paul McManus also had an equine experience.

> Sometimes you'd be walking back into the house after a good session so you could have a bit of a kip. It would be pitch-black outside and you'd end up stumbling head first into a horse.

Break The Silence was the band's second visit to Rockfield. The first had been for 1994's album *Swagger*. That record features Gun's most successful single: a cover of the song 'Word Up!', originally by the US group Cameo. Gun have a specific view on how cover versions should be done. They felt it would be too easy for a rock band to cover songs by the Foo Fighters or Nirvana, for example. So they would record songs from different genres instead, meaning they could reimagine the track by stamping the Gun sound on them. So down the years, Gun have covered hit material by Hot Chocolate, The Beastie Boys, Blondie, Stevie Wonder and Rihanna among others.

For 'Word Up!', Gun transformed a rap pop song into a hard rock anthem. Talking about their first foray at Rockfield, Dante Gizzi remembers, 'When we were there for *Swagger*, we were aware of all that was happening around The Stone Roses.' This was the dispute with their record company that got out of hand and ended up with the band being arrested for criminal damage.

> I remember bumping into them and they were down-to-earth guys [recalls the Gun frontman]. It would have been the tail end of 93. Later, for *Break The Silence*, Kasabian were at Rockfield with us. I loved chatting to those guys because I'd toured with them with my other band called El Presidente. But it's incredible the amount of bands who've been there and made music history. You can't help but feel in awe of it. And then you want to create something as iconic as any of the albums recorded there. And we were often invited to have dinner with the Ward family. Kingsley would often ask us to join them.

Paul reinforces the point that the family do look out for their guests.

> One day Kingsley came up to the accommodation when I was there on my own. He asked me what I was up to and I explained I was doing nothing as our producer was doing some editing. So he took me to the main house, where he sat me down in the lounge. We chatted about the musical instruments that were in the room. Each instrument had a fascinating story attached to it … he'd show me a ukulele and tell me it was the one Dave Edmunds always used to play. Once we'd stopped chatting, he turned the TV on for me, as if you were turning the cartoons on for your kid to keep them occupied. The film *Good Will Hunting* was on. I remember watching the whole movie. I think Kingsley was worried about me being at a loose end. So I felt obliged to watch the whole movie. I thought it would be rude not to.

Paul also recalls one very emotional time at Rockfield, where he says the support from the studio was moving.

> One thing that will live with me forever is that as we made the record [*Break the Silence*], my grandmother [who] was ninety-eight took ill. I was brought up with my grandparents. Sadly, she died while we were in the middle of recording. But during this period, I would drive from Rockfield back to my place in Scotland several times a week, because I wanted to be with her as much as I could at the end. So those memories are imprinted in my mind. It was such an emotional time and Rockfield was fantastic for me. If there is anywhere [to find solace when] you need comfort during that kind of suffering, then this was the place. You were part of the Rockfield family and I'll never forget that. Mind you, it was good for the Chancellor as well, because I got caught speeding about four times a week. So I don't know how much money I handed over to the government.

Dante agrees that this remote location was absolutely what the band needed.

That was one of the great things. The freedom of being in a residential studio in the middle of nowhere. I remember recording the song 'Innocent Thieves'. Paul and I put the bass drum out in the courtyard and recorded at midnight. Can you imagine doing that anywhere else? There wasn't a house for miles around, so we disturbed no one. If you had a buzz for something then you could create it there and then.

They say that you're at your most creative through the night. Well, we were staying up to the early hours of the morning because of that residential element. It means you can just come and go as you please. You'd record for a bit, then have a wee bit of a chill, before returning to the studio much later.

Paul believes Rockfield has a special atmosphere too.

We've done a lot of sessions over the last 15 years or so. We've recorded all over Europe. But without being disrespectful at all to those other magnificent studios, with magnificent people, I can, more or less, remember every single part of all the sessions in Rockfield. It was just that memorable being there, because you had that aura. That's one of the things that still lives with me. There was a sense of something I've never experienced in any other walk of life. Forget even making a record. I've been in some iconic buildings. Some genuine historic buildings. But the sense of history seems stronger in Rockfield.

'I agree,' chips in Dante.

There is definitely aura around that studio. And it's great to have the time to just absorb it all. It helped us create a fantastic album there.

Talking of the other studios that Gun have recorded in around Europe, one in Brussels sticks in their minds for a few reasons.

Dante explains first.

This studio, called ICP, has got equipment that they have been collecting since the 1960s. So they have all this great old equipment, like old Moog synthesizers.

But some of the equipment proved to be a little too vintage, shall we say.

One mic stand had a Swastika on it. The studio was absolutely gorgeous, but it felt a bit odd singing into a microphone with a Nazi symbol. The reason was because they had this historical collection of old German microphones, from the Nazi rallies in the 40s. A Neumann Mic. It felt strange when you went to sing into it.

Paul then shares his embarrassing experience before they had even started to record.

I'd been in America, so I was flying back into Gatwick, where I jumped on a plane to Brussels. The rest of the boys were already in Belgium. So I got a taxi from the airport.

'Now I'm still struggling with English,' laughs the Scotsman, 'so I've no chance in French.'

But I gave the taxi driver the address and he took me to a place in a strange semi-rural and semi-commercial area. He points to a door. I can see nothing obvious that's a studio. So anyway, I knock on this door and an old lady opens it. I try to explain who I am and what I'm there for. She lets me in and the first thing she did was get some lunch. She brings me some food and I'm just looking around thinking this is a kind of mad place. What's going on? But I didn't want to be disrespectful, so I ate the food and enjoyed her company. Eventually, I ask her where the rest of the band are. As it's a residential studio, I thought maybe the boys were in their rooms. But she told me it wasn't a studio. So I asked her again where Jools and Dante and the others are. She says that she had never heard of them.

It turned out the studios were next door and the old lady was their neighbour.

Fortunately, given its isolated location, Paul couldn't turn up at the wrong place in Monmouth.

Paul also remembers recording *Break The Silence* as being a huge bonding experience for the band. They had broken up in 1997 and reformed in 2008 with Toby Jepson on lead vocals for some live gigs and an EP, before Dante stepped in to take over vocal duties.

Looking back over the sessions in 2012, 18 years after first recording at Rockfield, the drummer says they brought the band closer together as a unit.

> We recorded *Break The Silence* in both studios: The Quadrangle and The Coach House. That's because Kasabian left Rockfield before we did. So we changed studios. I did drum tracks in both of those wonderful rooms. But we didn't have any crew with us. It meant we had to move our own gear. I remember using an old farm trailer to move my drums and amps up and down all those bumps and cobbles at one in the morning. What a way to make a record! So not only was it wonderful recording at the studio, but it was a remarkable team-building venture as we had to do everything together. We came out of that studio as a really tight bunch.

As Paul pauses, deep in thought and memories, Dante fills in for him.

> I think Rockfield was well ahead of its time back in the 60s and 70s. Being residential would be a fairly new concept. The level of equipment, the set-up of the studios and, above all, the sound. What a sound you get in the rooms! So I can easily imagine how back in the day, it was so attractive to bands and how so many great records were made there.

Paul has now been jolted out of his reminiscences, and with a beaming smile concludes,

I was so grateful to have had the opportunity to go and record there. I'm so grateful for those moments. And to meet Kingsley and all his family and hear all those stories. What a huge honour.

South Wales rock band The Dirty Youth also had a blast recording their first two albums at Rockfield. The band got together in 2009, formed by lead singer Danni Monroe and guitarist, songwriter and producer Matt Bond. They signed to Universal Records a year later. At Rockfield, they crafted two excellent albums: 2011's debut *Red Light Fix* and 2015's *Gold Dust*. Matt says,

The Dirty Youth always went in hard when an album was finished. I remember, we had a two-day listening party for one album at Rockfield. One of the guys from our label, who was frankly a pain in the arse, ending up getting his drink spiked with magic mushrooms by someone. So this guy went on a mystical tour into the night. He was found in the morning lying in a bush by one of the guys from The Proclaimers, who were also recording at Rockfield at the time.

He sings the first line of The Proclaimers 'I'm Gonna Be' as he remembers. Matt's first experience at Rockfield, though, was making an album with the UK metal band Bullet For My Valentine.

I found the place magical when I first went there. Knowing the history of the artists that have been there before sparks an energy and excitement that you can hear in the records made there.

He returned to produce records for other artists as well as recording with his own band.

I think the best record I've worked on there is a track I wrote and mixed with NBLM and Randy Jackson, the youngest of the Jackson brothers. The song featured some unreleased Michael Jackson vocals that Randy had. It's really hard to put into words how special that was on so many levels.

I also really enjoyed listening to all the stories from Kingsley and Lisa Ward, while drinking champagne into the early hours. But making music there is what it's all about. For me, that's when I felt The Dirty Youth had made it as a band. The albums we made there were my favourites. We recorded the next one at Abbey Road, but the vibe was just not there.

In 2012, the Pixies decamped to south Wales from Boston, USA, to make a series of EPs that would eventually result in a new album. Part of the reason they choose Rockfield Studios was because it was their producer Gil Norton's favourite place to work.

The US indie band may not be one of the biggest selling bands to have recorded at the legendary studios, but they are certainly among the most influential. Back in 1994, Kurt Cobain told *Rolling Stone* magazine that when he was writing Nirvana's debut album, *Nevermind*, 'I was basically trying to rip off the Pixies.' David Bowie referred to them as 'The psychotic Beatles'. And the band Radiohead are huge fans – singer Thom Yorke proclaimed that the Pixies changed his life.

The Pixies were due to be at Rockfield for six weeks, but potential disaster struck after just a fortnight. Key member of the band, bassist and vocalist, Kim Deal, quit. She met the band at a local coffee shop and stunned them by saying her goodbyes. The band teetered on the brink of splitting up. But, after much soul-searching, they decided to remain at Rockfield and recruited bassist Simon Archer, who had played with The Fall and PJ Harvey. The three EPs were finished and eventually became the 2014 album *Indie Cindy*. So once again Rockfield became part of music history as the place where the Pixies could have broken up, but instead decided to carry on and make groundbreaking music for years to come.

One of the biggest selling albums recorded at Rockfield in recent years has been the debut album by Royal Blood. Formed in Worthing in 2011, the duo is made up of Mike Kerr, who sings and plays bass, and drummer Ben Thatcher. Mike says he was never interested in any other type of band and they revel in being just a duo. Sometimes live on stage, Mike will ask the audience to 'put your hands together for the rest of the band. And they are Ben Thatcher!'

Royal Blood's stripped-back blues rock sound has drawn comparisons with the likes of The White Stripes and Queens Of The Stone Age. It is rooted in Mike Kerr's unique bass playing, with various effects pedals used to make the instrument sound like an electric guitar and bass guitar at the same time. Their album was produced by Tom Dalgety at Rockfield, who says the genesis of the band also happened at Rockfield, but years earlier.

> I met Royal Blood there around 2010, but, at that time, they were part of a different project. They were basically the session players for a pop singer making a record there. I remember getting there the night before and they'd arrived early as well, whereas the artist hadn't. So we were hanging out and I thought we might as well set up the studio to save a bit of time for the next day. I set them up in the live room, where they started playing some covers of songs by Muse and Queens Of The Stone Age. They played them extraordinarily well. I remember thinking that this was better than I was expecting. At the end of the session, I said to them, that if this project doesn't pan out, maybe we should do something together. And that's what eventually happened.

> Later we did a few demos at the studio in my house and also some studios elsewhere, before eventually going back to Rockfield to make the album. Three of those demo tracks ended up on the first album. By now the band had signed to Warner Records, which gave us a much bigger budget. It was great going back there as that's where we had first met. Overall, we did that first record very quickly. They get the Rockfield vibe. They like the weirdness of it.

I asked Tom whether it was easier, or harder, working with a two-piece rather than a bigger group.

> It's a bit of both. There's something about the musical challenge with that which I relish. If you've only got two musical ingredients, you have to try and make them both as big and bombastic

as possible. So you need a really huge drum sound that occupies a lot of space, and this octave divided bass for a massive wall of sound. I enjoyed the challenge. So on the first record, it really is just the two of them.

The album made number 1 in the UK and was in the Official Top 25 bestselling albums in the UK for 2014.

Tom Dalgety says he was slightly surprised by just how well the album sold.

> I really didn't expect it to be as big as it was. I thought it would be a cool underground rock thing. Initially I thought the band would get signed by a small indie label. So it was very interesting when they were taken on by a big label like Warner. One night on iTunes, Royal Blood were in the top downloaded rock singles. And then, as more singles came out, we got to the point where, before the actual album had come out, there were three or four BBC Radio One playlisted singles. Then I realised the album was going to do something. Of course, it went to number 1 in the charts and stayed top 10 for quite a long time. That really blew my mind.

2019 saw Tom Dalgety return to Rockfield to produce punk legends The Damned.

The band formed in 1976 and the original line-up included lead vocalist Dave Vanian along with guitarist Captain Sensible and drummer Rat Scabies. It's said that they were the first punk band from the UK to release a single, 'New Rose', which came out in the year they formed. Their first album, *Damned Damned Damned*, came a year later. The band did two albums and an EP at Rockfield in the 80s: *The Black Album* from 1980, the *Friday 13th* EP a year later and then the 1982 album, *Strawberries*.

That album's working title was *Strawberries for Pigs*, inspired by the reception the band's newer music was getting from some of their older fans. The band, at the time, had been playing a lot of new material. But it seems the audience at their gigs didn't want to hear the newer material, just the classic early punk tracks. So lead singer Dave Vanian described it as 'like giving strawberries to a pig' and the name stuck for a while.

Working titles rarely make it on to the final cover, as demonstrated by Liverpool band, The Teardrop Explodes. They were at Rockfield in the autumn of 1980 working on their hit debut album. Ultimately called *Kilimanjaro*, its original working title was Everyone Wants to Shag The Teardrop Explodes. Mind you this did resurface in 1990 for their final studio album, which was made up of never-before-released material.

Back to The Damned, who, 43 years after they first formed, were back at Rockfield to record a new EP.

Tom Dalgety loved working with them, but given their colourful history at the studios, he was surprised Rockfield hadn't told the band never to darken their door again.

There's a great story from when they were doing *The Black Album* in the 80s. The singer, Dave, was dressed as Dracula as he was into his vampires. Apparently, for a few mornings, he walked into Monmouth dressed as Count Dracula and loitered around some graveyards. A little later spooky stories started emerging. Tales of 'The Monmouth Vampire'. There were dozens of sightings of this monster. But it was really just Dave out on his morning stroll.

I also remember [in 2019] that one of the group had a wasps' nest just outside the window to their room. Wasps were swarming in. It was funny seeing Kingsley on a stepladder trying to deal with the wasps and hearing the kind of very colourful language he was using. Not your usual day-to-day studio activity.'

The EP, released in 2020, was called *The Rockfield Files*. The front cover showed the band in a field, leaning against a fence, petting a rather large bull. Very apt. At the time, Captain Sensible told the music press how much he'd enjoyed working with Tom.

[He] was brilliant. He is great with guitars and bass. He makes everything sound good and it was fun cranking the amp up again after the last album *Evil Spirits* in 2018, which had been more keyboard led.

Tom also plans to return to Rockfield to record in the future.

> Rockfield keeps on bringing me back. I've done such a variety of different things there that all seem to work. And I like having that extra distance from London. It's less inviting for hangers-on to come and encroach on your creative space. In London, it can be a bit of a drag with management, the label and friends all popping in the whole time. But as soon as people find out that they need to get two trains, a bus and maybe a taxi, suddenly they don't want to be there, which for me is great. Leave me and the artists isolated somewhere and we will just to get on with it. There's something really fantastic about that.

RECOMMENDED LISTENING

Red Light Fix, The Dirty Youth 2011

Break The Silence, Gun 2012

Indie City, The Pixies 2014

The Rockfield Files, The Damned 2020

CHAPTER FIFTEEN:
YOU BROKE FREDDIE MERCURY'S PIANO?

THE ADVENTURES OF THUNDER AND OPETH

Residential studios are so few now, so it's fitting that Rockfield is still going as it's the oldest with the greatest tradition. The greatest history.

Luke Morley, lead guitarist, Thunder

It's a cool summer evening in July 2020. The crew for the band Thunder have almost finished setting up their equipment and lights in the studio. The group are here for a special live performance of their recently recorded album *All The Right Noises*. Guitar pedals are readied for action. The drum set is carefully assembled and keyboards are wheeled into place. A set list can be seen taped to the floor. All this work is being carried out by crew wearing face masks at the height of the COVID-19 pandemic when various kinds of 'lockdown' were in place and certain precautions had to be followed to allow people to meet.

At that moment, the band take to the stage and, once settled, they break into 'You're Gonna Be My Girl' from the new record. To promote it, Thunder are playing some tracks from it right here where they were recorded: Rockfield Studios. These live tracks will eventually be included on the album's deluxe edition.

Roll back the years and Thunder's first experience of Rockfield was in April 1996. Then they were here to record *The Thrill of It All*. Produced by the band's lead guitarist, their fourth studio record was a big success and made number 14 on the UK Album Chart nearly 25 years ago.

Luke's first impression of this unusual set-up?

Obviously, we were very aware of the history of Rockfield before we arrived. Now we'd worked before in various other residential studios, such as Great Linford Manor and Ridge Farm. So it was our preferred way of recording even back then. When we turned up, the most striking thing was the family who run it all. The Ward family. They are simply amazing. All that history of rock unfolding on their doorstep. They've seen it all, done it all and they don't care.

He laughs, and smiles at the memory of meeting them for the first time, before continuing to recall that first impression of this unusual recording studio in rural south Wales.

Unlike a lot of other recording studios, it has a very relaxed vibe and was civilised down to the ground. Kingsley and the whole family are such really interesting people and they welcomed us. One of the lovely things about working there is that, at any time, Kingsley, or any one of the family, could just wander in to the studio control room, sit there and start chatting away to you. Kingsley, in particular, is hilarious. The stories? Well, crikey. I don't know how many of them are printable!

The guitarist lets out a huge, loud belly laugh.

But they're extremely amusing and entertaining. Kingsley is a complete maverick. A one-off. But you just accept that they [the family] are part of the package. If you're one of those precious artists, who has to work in silence, not being disturbed, then this definitely isn't a studio for you. But, in Thunder, I think we're all naturally very laid-back. We welcome a little break every now and again. And that's what happens. Sometimes, you'll be in the middle of a very tricky guitar overdub and in walks Kingsley, completely ad hoc, and he'll start talking about all kinds of things. From his views on the world to what he thinks of Covid, or the government. Anything. But it's always very entertaining. As a result, we've been going [there] for the last 30 years.

Back to the summer of 2020, and the latest album. Why had they decided to return to Rockfield for the live performance? Luke reflects for a while.

It was because it's such a relaxed place for us. A home from home. So, we thought what a great place to do it. We wanted to record this during the lockdown. We wanted to do some live content as we couldn't do any gigs, because of the pandemic. So we thought, we'll all get tested and go to Rockfield and do it there. It was a good thing to do, because we had the space to get that separation. That social distancing. We arranged for screens everywhere to keep everyone apart and we stuck the backing singers in their own booth. But we all still had eye contact so it felt like a performance, even though there was no audience. It was a really cool thing to do as Rockfield is one of the few studios where you can still do a live performance. I mean not many studios have that capability in terms of size and isolation rooms.

Behind the band, as they perform in the studio, is a video backdrop of the cover of the album, which features a very striking sculpture called 'The Singing Ringing Tree'. The band found the album cover using a slightly unorthodox method: a Google search for 'bizarre musical instruments'.

Says Luke Morley,

We had the album title. *All The Right Noises* comes from the lyrics of one of the songs on the album called 'Destruction'. I thought it's such a cool phrase that we need to use it more on the album. Maybe on the album cover. So I started thinking about what makes a noise. Engines maybe? But that seemed sort of predictable. I then thought about musical instruments and the noises they make. So I googled 'bizarre musical instruments' and up came The Singing Ringing Tree.

Sitting on a hill above Burnley, The Singing Ringing Tree is a three-metre high, wind-powered sound sculpture. It's made out of steel tubes, with each one tuned to resonate a different note and resembles the funnel of a violent hurricane. The band thought the image was perfect for an album cover, describing the artwork as 'like an alien that's landed and sits watching over the town – but making music when the wind blows through it.' Luke Morley, along with his friend and photographer, Jason Joyce, drove to Burnley to take photos of it at various times of the day and night over the course of two days. The one finally picked as the main image was taken at 3 a.m.

Danny Bowes recalls the discomfort his friend had to endure to capture the image.

Luke and Jason both said it was absolutely freezing. Luke sent me video footage of the two of them all wrapped up against the elements with little head torches on. I was so glad I wasn't there.

But it was worth it: the image – which is untouched – came third in the Best Art Vinyl Award in 2021. Fifty other album sleeves were nominated, 'So I was chuffed with third place,' says Luke.

Danny recalls the original recording sessions for *All The Right Noises*.

We did it at Rockfield in three sessions in the summer of 2019, November 2019 and then January of 2020. Then we had to wait for the producer, Mike Fraser, to mix it in Vancouver. He was working with AC/DC at the time. Why he couldn't drop them, I don't know? But he got his priorities all wrong.

Bowes giggles quietly at the thought of Fraser dropping AC/DC for Thunder.

> Then everything went haywire as the moment he'd mixed it, lockdown began. It was apparent straight away that we couldn't release the album in September 2020 as planned. So we post-poned both the release of the album and the tour. We were sitting on this record for nearly a year. I've never before been in a posi-tion where we were forced to wait around for more than twelve months before anybody could hear our new material. That was a very strange thing to handle. But in the grand scheme of things, we're all pretty lucky in this band. We've got houses. We've got gardens. We've got places to go. Some people were cooped up in flats with kids, or they'd have to work from home and maybe homeschool their children at the same time. The lockdown was very frustrating for many people. My heart went out to them. So at the end of the day, if our record is delayed 18 months, who gives a damn? It's not really important. Not when you think about what's going on in the world with people suffering and losing their lives. Well, it's only rock 'n' roll, isn't it?

The live performance featured two backing singers: Julie Maguire and Carly Louise, otherwise known as the BV Queens. Due to Covid, they were separated from the musicians on stage, as Luke said, by a booth of their own.

'Yeah, it was a wonderful experience,' recalls Carly when I spoke to them in February 2022, 'but we were in this little, tiny booth. Well, it was actually more like a little cupboard.'

'But,' says Julie, grinning, 'it was great just to be singing again. And with that band. It sounded so good. Didn't it, Carly? It was amazing.'

'So right,' replies Carly. 'We were saying exactly that afterwards as well, weren't we? I mean just to be playing live again after lockdown was something. And live with Thunder too. Just being on a stage with them. The songs, that night, sounded just like the studio tracks. They are just the most incredible musicians. The performance was flawless.' Carly continues, 'It was something of a surreal experience, because we had been listening to Thunder since we were kids. And they are just the loveliest guys and made us instantly feel so comfortable.'

Julie, eyes wide in excitement, agrees. 'I was such a massive fan of the band already. So to be asked to come and sing for them was incredible. I got to know them when Luke and Danny came to see Cats in Space on tour, when my band was supporting them. Carly and I were a bit nervous of meeting them, but they were just so lovely.'

Back at the Rockfield performance, the band are getting into the groove. There may still be a pandemic, but by summertime 2020, many of the restrictions have been lifted. This allowed the band to reconvene and re-record eight of the new songs live. In the absence of any live touring, it's the best Thunder are going to get. Danny Bowes found Rockfield a wonderful place to make a record.

> The people who run it are so fun-loving and entertaining. They're nice people to work with. We've worked in other studios, which are state of the art, but you're frightened to put your feet up. Frightened to mess up their studio. We like things to be a bit grubby. To have a bit of history.

Luke Morley agrees with his friend.

> One of the great things about Rockfield is that you can relax and be yourself. Over the years, I've been in some studios where they're so clean. Overly clean. So much so, that you worry about where you're going to put your coffee cup in case it leaves a stain. So you start looking for coasters to put down. But at Rockfield that's not important. You can simply put your feet up on the desk and, if you spill a cup of coffee, well, you can clean it up later. It's nothing to worry about. I like that aspect of it.

Talking of stains, I ask the Thunder guitarist if he's noticed the grand piano on which Freddie Mercury played 'Bohemian Rhapsody', and spilled red wine on.

Yeah, and there's much more than red wine been spilt on it! When we were recording there recently, we had one song, which was very piano based. And we broke a string on it. We actually broke a string on the 'Bohemian Rhapsody' piano.

He laughs in disbelief at this memory.

Nobody's ever broken a string on the Freddie Mercury piano before. We were mortified. But, actually, it was quite funny. We were sitting there listening while our keyboard player was at the piano. And we could hear these bizarre noises. He stopped playing. When he started again, we could still hear these strange noises. It turns out that the string had snapped and flown off the piano. But, you know what? We recorded it anyway. It was such a bizarre sound that we actually used the noise of the string breaking at the start of the song. The studio is just such a relaxing place. It has such a creative vibe. It's why we keep going back.

And Thunder do, indeed, keep returning to Rockfield. They made their 2015 album *Wonder Days* there. They returned for 2017's *Rip It Up*, once more for 2019's *Please Remain Seated* and, after *All The Right Noises*, they headed back again in 2022 for their next album *Dopamine*.

Pleased Remain Seated was an unusual album for the band. It was one where Thunder deconstructed a collection of their own songs and then re-imagined them in mostly acoustic, slowed-down blues or a jazzy style. It was still a success and made number 8 on the UK Albums Chart. But Bowes recalls that not everyone appreciated the reworked versions of their rock classics.

'A lot of people thought, maybe, we were now ready for our pipe and slippers,' he recalls, a slight touch of hurt in his voice.

It is a great record. But it is also clearly very different to anything Thunder has ever recorded before. As I listened to the album, there was one thing that intrigued me. How hard is it for someone, who has been singing those songs for years in a hard rock style, to then have to sing those tracks in a completely different musical style? How difficult is it to forget the original songs and re-record those vocals in a different way?

'You're the first person I've spoken to … that has asked me that question,' responds the Thunder singer.

> I thought that would be the real obvious question that someone would ask me. But nobody has. And you're right. It's very, very hard indeed. Because you've got a muscle memory happening when it comes to singing songs. Especially songs that we've been singing for nearly 30 years. So to sing them in a different style, a different tempo and a different key, in some cases, is a weird one. I certainly I found it very difficult to do, especially playing live. When we did the tour, there are lots of key moments in certain songs, where I tend to do some physical things. But now I couldn't do that as I was sitting down, because of the more mellow nature of those versions of our songs. I felt like a caged animal. You've got to remember for 30 years, we've been rocking out and telling people to jump up and down. So, on this tour, to ask them to sit down for two hours was a bit of a turnaround. But many of our fans said they loved it, because they got a chance to actually sit and take it all in. You know, the musicality of the thing.

Well, the album was called *Please Remain Seated*, so I guess it did what it said on the tin. But having felt like a 'caged animal' in the context of that record and tour, Bowes says it was great twelve months later to come back with a really good rock record. And once again, that's what *All The Right Noises* and *Dopamine* are: a hard rock tour de force.

Guitarist Luke insists that the band can keep getting better.

> There's no reason why you can't improve as you get older. I've met so many people over the years who've said to me that we will never again make an album as good as our 1990 debut *Backstreet Symphony*. I find that really depressing. Because, although I think *Backstreet Symphony* was fantastic at the time, you can't stand still.

In Rockfield, Thunder have found the perfect environment to record in. They like that the studio, with all its rock history and quirks, is a treasure trove for musicians. Luke Morley describes the studio as 'unlike any other'.

> On 2017's album *Rip It Up*, there's a song where we needed this loud, metallic clang. So we found an old milk churn and Harry, our drummer, just stood in the middle of the courtyard banging it. Absolutely pounding it with a hammer. It was fantastic. So we kept all the natural acoustics from the courtyard. You've just got to embrace it. … What I adore about working there is the fact you're allowed to completely indulge your creativity, without wishing to sound pretentious. You can use anything that is there. The owner, Kingsley, has a cupboard full of old musical instruments. For one session we needed an old Wurlitzer organ. Kingsley told us he thought he had one somewhere. So we went into the barn, kicked a few chickens out of the way, moved a few bales of hay, and, sure enough, there was this old Wurlitzer. It had one key missing. Fortunately, it wasn't a key that we needed for the song. So we cleaned it up and it worked brilliantly. So that makes you realise it's a farm first and a studio second. And you have to embrace that.
>
> Residential studios are so few now, so it's fitting that Rockfield is still going as it's the oldest with the greatest tradition. The greatest history.

And Rockfield simply knows how to use that history, that ambience, that vibe. Luke continues,

> That's the whole point of working there. I did an album at Rockfield back in 2011 with a band I was in called The Union. That would have been the first time I'd been back there since 96 with Thunder. That time we were in the Coach House studio. But it was the same wonderful experience. So no, nothing had changed. Not in 15 years.

Dopamine, Thunder's fourteenth studio album, once again recorded at Rockfield, is the band's first double album.

> We didn't set out to make a double album [says Luke]. But as the writing and recording process went on, we wandered into some interesting areas, which meant I didn't think we could afford to leave anything off it. In the end, we did cut it from twenty tunes to sixteen, but it wasn't easy.

The BV Queens got to return to Rockfield to add their vocals too. Julie Maguire agrees the standard of the new songs meant it was difficult to cull the sessions down to one single record.

> Luke is incredible. He is so prolific. It was so wonderful to be a part of those songs and watch them grow and come together.

As she says this, in her excitement, her arms and hands automatically play air guitar. Her enthusiasm is shared by her singing partner, Carly Louise.

> They had so many amazing songs. It was almost like how could they whittle it down? I actually think lockdown did Luke good, giving him that extra time to do things. I think *All The Right Noises* was up a level for the band and then this one's just even better again.

There are big smiles and excited laughter when the duo recall that this most recent visit saw them stay in Freddie Mercury's room.

'Amazing.' Carly actually sings the word rather than says it.

> You can almost feel the energy of everyone who's been there. I loved hanging out in the control room and listening back to the songs. You're sitting at the recording desk looking above you. And you see all the people who've signed their names in there. It's just magical.

Julie nods, 100 per cent in agreement,

> Yes, hanging out in the control room was such a thrill, especially
> when we did the live tracks for *All The Right Noises*. I found
> myself sitting there every so often looking around and thinking,
> 'This is just crazy.' The amount of people that have just sat in
> this room and probably done exactly what we're doing right now.
> Yeah, just amazing.

Being at Rockfield can feel like being part of the family. That type of
bond is important to both Bowes and Morley, who first met at school
nearly 50 years ago. With the constant laugher and wisecracks between
the two, one reviewer compared them to the legendary duo Morecambe
and Wise, referring to the iconic sketch in which Eric Morecambe
grabs the classical conductor André Previn by his suit jacket lapels and
insists: 'I am playing all the right notes, but not necessarily in the right
order.' Bowes is a huge fan of Morecambe and Wise.

> Their comedy looks so effortless, yet it was so well rehearsed.
> And that's what we have tried to do. We may not have always got
> away with it, but we tried.

It isn't only English bands who have enjoyed multiple visits to
Rockfield throughout the 21st century.

Rewind to 2014 and the leader of progressive rock giants Opeth
Mikael Akerfeldt is standing by the roadside entrance. Behind him are
two stone columns, either side of the long driveway up to the studios.

It's a very cloudy and windy day, despite it being almost summer.
But this is south Wales and hot weather is definitely not guaranteed.
Mikael is dressed all in black: black shades, black jeans and a black
T-shirt with a colourful face made out of a collage of various images
on the front of it. The collage is from the cover of *Zarathustra*: a pro-
gressive rock album from 1973 by the Italian band Museo Rosenbach,
regarded as one of the best Italian progressive rock albums of all time.
Mikael knows his genre.

At this moment, Mikael is being filmed.

'Welcome to Rockfield Studios,' he announces to the camera. The Opeth frontman is embracing social media and today he is making a video for YouTube.

'We are here making our twelfth album.' He pauses and gestures towards the studio with a sweep of his arm. 'Let's take a look.' With that he invites thousands of Opeth's fans to have an access-all-areas look at the place their favourite band will make their next record, *Pale Communion*. That album gave Opeth their highest chart positions ever, reaching number 19 in the US, number 3 in Sweden and number 14 in the UK.

That was the first time Opeth came to south Wales. Two years later they returned for the follow-up album, *Sorceress*. Both albums were produced and mixed by Tom Dalgety, who has been a regular visitor to Rockfield for the past two decades.

> In the nearly 20 years of taking people there, I can't think of anyone that's hated it. But then, if you're used to working in London studios, where you can order a takeout at two in the morning and things like that, then, it's probably going to be a culture shock for you. But that soon eases. I loved it straight away, because I'm a country boy. I grew up in a farm-like environment. So it felt very homely to me.

In five different YouTube videos, featuring all of the band, every one of them mentions just how easy it was to get along with, and work with, Tom and he, in turn, thoroughly enjoys working with them.

> We were very, very comfortable around each other by the time we were working on the second album at Rockfield. And we're very good friends. Whenever I'm working in Stockholm, I'll always go to see Mikael and Fredrik Akesson, the guitarist in the band. We love hanging out together. We had dinner at Mikael's house the last time I was over there.
>
> That was really a lot of fun working with them, because, me, Mikael and the rest of the guys have a similar taste in music.

We just love late 60s and early 70s British rock. Up until then, I'd been at Rockfield a lot with mainly indie bands, like The Maccabees and Delays. They are great bands, but they were more drawn to Rockfield because of the connections with The Stone Roses and Oasis. So when I was first there with Opeth, it was just really great to be there with people that were as excited about proper rock albums made there such as A *Farewell To Kings* by Rush and *A Night at the Opera* by Queen. We just loved those kind of records.

The band spent twelve days recording at the countryside studio enjoying its serene and inspiring surroundings. For Akerfeldt, the historic setting was perfect for this landmark moment in the band's history. He wrote on the band's website,

> *Sorceress* is our twelfth studio album, since our beginnings in 1990. I find it difficult to understand that we've been going for twenty-six years. Let alone that we've made twelve records now, all of which I am very proud of. *Sorceress* is no exception. I love this album, as does the whole band. I wrote the music during five-to-six months and we spent only twelve days recording it at Rockfield Studios in Wales. I find that once again we've taken a step forward. It's different! It's extremely diverse. And, if I may say so myself, extremely good. I feel the right to say that since I like to think I know this band better than anyone on the planet. Also, I always manage to detach myself from the record and listen as a fan. It's a fine little record. My favourite in our discography right now. Of course. That's how it should be, right? It's both fresh and old. Both progressive and rehashed. Heavy and calm. Just the way we like it. Hopefully there'll be others around the globe sharing this opinion. It was a joy to make it. A joy to record it, and a sheer joy listening to it. So there you have it!

But back to 2014 and YouTube and Mikael Akerfeldt is smiling and delighting in showing the band's fans on camera exactly where *Pale Communion* will be born.

Well, we're in the Quadrangle studio, which is the second studio to be built here at Rockfield. I think it was built in 1973. We won't be using this studio. We will be in the other studio: the Coach House. But I wanted to show you this studio. It's famous. The band Queen recorded *Sheer Heart Attack* here in 74 or 75 and *Night at the Opera* and 'Bohemian Rhapsody' was also recorded here. Not only that, the song was recorded on this grand piano here.

He pauses to admire the historic instrument and decides to give everyone a demonstration.

'This is how it sounds.'

He plays a few chords on what is probably the world's most famous piano. Even watching on YouTube, it sends a tingle down your spine as the notes ring out. As you take in what's being played, you can't help but smile at the history contained in those black and white keys decades later, simply due to its link to one of the world's most famous and epic rock songs. By playing the piano, Mikael has direct physical contact with that history. Those watching him on social media get to feel that as well. The Opeth frontman smiles mischievously as he prepares to make an affectionate and gentle joke in homage to the former Queen singer. Playing a few more delicate notes, he jokes, 'Freddie Mercury was a little sloppy. So my touch is a little bit more sensitive.'

The cheek. But we forgive him as we feel his sheer enthusiasm for music.

Tom Dalgety says, 'He's one of those annoying people that's pretty good at every instrument you can name. So that's just the type of joke he's likely to make.'

Tom also remembers another day when Rockfield's history came alive in front of the Opeth singer, absolutely making his day.

When we were there to record *Pale Communion*, Mikael had become obsessed with the group Spring, a progressive rock band from Leicester. Spring were a very unique early 70s prog band, in which three of the members played mellotron. Anyway, one night, when we were finishing up, Kingsley came into the control room and asked if he could use the tape machine to do some transfers after we'd finished. I asked him what he was transferring. It turned out he was doing the masters of the Spring album! The look on Mikael's face was incredible!

As you can read in Chapter One Rockfield played a key part in landing Spring the audition that led to their one and only album being recorded and released. That was in 1971 when they were rescued by Kingsley Ward after their van gave up the ghost nearby. He was fascinated that they owned a mellotron. The early polyphonic sampling keyboard has just thirty-five notes but, when you press a key, a strip of magnetic tape passes over a playback head playing a sound like a tape recorder. The strip only lasts about 8 seconds. But when the key is released, the tape rewinds, ready to be played again. It was a very popular instrument with bands like Genesis, Yes and King Crimson among others.

Spring's singer Pat Moran went on to become a sound engineer at Rockfield Studios, bassist Paul Martinez later recorded at Monmouth with Robert Plant, and, just out of interest, another of the band's members, Pick Withers, later found fame as the drummer of Dire Straits.

Mikael continues with his video tour and his own gentle brand of humour.

So Bohemian Rhapsody was recorded on this grand piano and Roger Taylor's drums were recorded in there. Well, maybe. That's what I'm told. I don't know. I wasn't here. I was barely born at the time.

As a music aficionado, you can tell Mikael is having the time of his life. He steps out of the Quadrangle studio. A chill wind is whipping around the courtyard and catches the musician, who is just wearing a T-shirt, by surprise.

So this is the courtyard. It's basically an old farm. So you can see horses and stuff. This is also a residential studio. So we live here.

He enters the Quadrangle accommodation living room. It's a big room with three very comfortable sofas arranged facing each other in one half. In front of them are big patio doors leading outside. To one side of the room is an old metal wood-burning heater. In the other half of the room, there is a large wooden dining room table. Mikael continues his YouTube tour.

My room is nice and tidy. I won't show you the rooms of the other members of the band as they are not as clean. We also have a laundry room, a TV room and patio out back, so that we can sit and drink beer after a full day's hard work. Inside, we come into the living room. This is where we dine. We get in-house cooked food, so we have two chefs cooking for us. It's great. It sounds really luxurious. And it is, but of course, we're paying for it.

He considers the irony. Yes, famous bands get great treatment. But they are also paying for the privilege.

Cut to January 2022, and Mikael Akerfeldt is among many who respond to the sad news that a musician who made his name at Rockfield has passed away.

Mikael posted on Facebook,

I almost choked on my coffee, this morning, when I read that one of my idols, the great Burke Shelley of Budgie, had passed away. What a terrible loss! Most people know Budgie as the band that Metallica covered ('Breadfan', 'Crash Course in Brain Surgery'). They remained underdogs in the scene, even if they're right at the beginning of the creation of hard rock/heavy metal music. Burke was one of those guys, who was quite uncomfortable with the heavy metal tag, but it's undeniable that they were instrumental in bringing it to the masses. I stumbled upon them in the 80s. A friend of mine … played me 'Bandolier' from 1975. It wasn't the heavy side of their music that sucked me in, but rather the gentle side. Songs like 'Slipaway' are beautiful. And the majestic 'Napoleon Bona-Part 1 & 2' showcased dynamics that a lot of their peers simply didn't have. Since then, I have [a] rather impressive Budgie section. Their softer side remains my favorite part of their music. Burke had a jazzy quality to his voice as well as the ability to scream like the best of them. We recorded 2 albums at Rockfield studio in Monmouth in Wales, which was the go-to studio for Budgie. I remember waiting for them to drop by, but they never did. Why would they? Childish dreams on my behalf. So I've never met them unfortunately. I did however manage to see them live twice, and they were fantastic! Thank you Burke, for all your fantastic music! And our sincere condolences to the Shelley family as well as to the remaining band members, past and present – Mikael.

Burke Shelley and Budgie will be forever linked to Rockfield Studios. The band were often described as a cross between Black Sabbath and Rush. While they may not have enjoyed the greatest success, their influence was far-reaching with members of Metallica, Iron Maiden and Van Halen among their fan base, as well as former Judas Priest guitarist KK Downing. The respect he had for Burke Shelley shone through in his own online post:

I have so many treasured memories when supporting Budgie on those great and extensive tours of the UK. I think we felt a special bond as both bands were perusing [sic] a direction together that was different to everyone else back in the late 60s and early 70s. Before I knew the band, I was a huge fan. I used to look forward to turning on the radio late at night, when a brave DJ named Kid Jensen used to play the band from a pirate radio ship somewhere in the North Sea. There can be no doubt that Burke Shelley was part of the embryo that became responsible for the creation of Rock, Hard Rock, Heavy Rock and Heavy Metal as we know it today.

Many more Rockfield legends will be created over the coming years and decades. 2023 will see Rockfield hit its 60th anniversary. In those six decades, the world's first-ever residential studio has achieved a status and a success that is astonishing. Rockfield was the right place, at the right time, as rock music was seeking a place of inspiration. It had the driving vision of owner Kingsley Ward who, with his brother Charles, built up this studio and fashioned it, bit by bit and year by year. Starting out as old farm buildings, it became a community where bands could feel at home while writing and creating great music.

Like myself many music fans first stumbled across the name Rockfield on the back of a record cover. Producer Jack Endino was one of them.

> I had first heard of Rockfield in the 70s from looking at the backs of all these great albums I was listening to. It was a dream to go there and record. Kingsley and his wife Anne were lovely people, very nice and full of good stories. I particularly remember Kingsley zooming around the fields on his tractor, wearing a big old floppy straw hat. I wish I had a picture of that.

It's a history that can't fail to impress, as former REM producer Mitch Easter confirms.

> Oh, Rockfield's mighty exciting! It was only when I was there that I realised the full extent of the legendary clientele. We loved being regaled with stories from Kingsley about Queen tapes being stored in a hayloft and accounts of weekly food fights between various titans of Rock. And I have lovely hazy memories from going out drinking with various Rockfield people. What hospitality!

The vast majority of artists who have recorded at Rockfield have fond recollections of their time there, mainly due to its unique charm of being a picturesque farm in the remote countryside. That and its superb studio set-up. Mitch Easter sums it up best:

The combination of first-rate professional audio gear and non-jarring pastoral views out the window is something we never get here in the US!

Mind you, in the countryside you have to be careful with the views. You could see anything, including rock stars indulging in a bit of naked recording!

Some bands take that to greater extremes than others. Finnish band HIM recorded their album *Razorblade Romance* at Rockfield in 1999 lured by the pervading presence of Black Sabbath. But they didn't only get their kicks from singing in the same recording booth as Ozzy Osbourne and Ronnie James Dio.

The band liked to spend plenty of time with no clothes on, both in the studio and in the countryside. The summer sunshine meant they not only recorded naked for much of the time, but would drink beer and run around the fields letting their inhibitions go. They would literally rock and roll around naked! It's enough to make Mitch Easter blush, say to hell with the non-jarring pastoral views and draw his curtains!

As well as being the spiritual home of some great rock records, Rockfield is loved by the music community for its hospitality. Bands would meet and make life-long friendships there. Genesis drummer Phil Collins is one of many who enjoyed the camaraderie of the residential studio and forged enduring friendships. 'What I *am* happy about is that it brought Robert Plant into my life as a friend,' he told me. 'We're still in touch and email each other. I wouldn't have liked to have missed working with him one bit.'

Session guitarist Ray Martinez also revelled in the wide spectrum of people popping into the studio to work.

I could reel off to you dozens and dozens of bands who were there. Robert Plant was down there. My brother Paul was the bass player in his band. Because I was there at the time, I got to sing backing vocals on one of his albums with John David. One of them [the tracks] went into the charts. 'Big Log'. Crazy isn't it?

One day, I remember it was in 1973, Chris Jagger – Mick's brother – was at the studios. He's a good guitarist. He was wearing the first pair of green wellies I'd ever seen, because at the time they were mainly just black. It's amazing what catches your eye!

He brought his band there – an American band – which I believe had worked with John Lennon a year or two earlier. They were called Elephant's Memory. So he turned up with this band, and there was this spaced-out, big guy with a beard and long hair, who sat down at the piano in the studio, played one chord and said, 'This needs tuning, man'. But it had only just been tuned that morning. He was so spaced out. We all burst out laughing.

Record label boss David Howells, who spent time there with Judas Priest and Budgie, has seen nothing like it since. He says

There was a tremendous atmosphere at Rockfield. It was so well thought out. The first of its kind. Many have copied it and not done it so well. There are moments in music that will stay with you. And those times I had at Rockfield are ones which will last with me forever.

That's something former Whitesnake and Black Sabbath bassist Neil Murray agrees with. He sees Rockfield as a place where musicians can, at least, temporarily escape from many of the day-to-day pressures of the music business.

Because Rockfield has been around for so long, it's acquired a mystique that owes a lot to its location. And the fact bands can concentrate on the music, instead of having to cope with friends, hangers-on and record company people dropping in all the time as they would do in London, or any big city. Obviously, the hit albums and singles which have come out of Rockfield are the essential element, which gives it the reputation it so deserves.

Many musicians and rock fans have an idea in their head about what a recording studio should look like. Rockfield does not conform to that.

Its unique homespun charm is difficult to sum up. But I think this tale from former Motörhead guitarist Larry Wallace captures its essence best. Life in a recording studio is not only about drugs, sex and rock and roll (OK, it is mostly!) but it can be homely and twee in a sort of bizarre and surreal way. Rockfield is a legendary recording studio from a parallel universe. And Larry's story sums this up nicely.

The singer Tim Rose had flown from the US to record at Rockfield with our producer Fritz Fryer. He was a huge American star, who'd had a hit with the song 'Morning Dew'. He came over to record an album, because he had heard all about Rockfield through all the stories and legends. One evening Fritz's wife had made a great big trifle. She was so amazingly proud of it. She came to the studio to show it to everyone. But, as she entered the studio control room, she tripped over and threw the entire gallon or so of trifle over the mixing desk. It quickly started to settle in between the slots, faders and switches and began to harden. They couldn't get it off quickly enough. And so it set. Soon they took the front off the mixing desk and for the rest of the session, to get the balance right and the sound right, they had to use a spanner to turn the knobs, because the machinery was clogged up with home-made trifle. Rock and roll!

RECOMMENDED LISTENING

Spring, Spring 1971

Pale Communion, Opeth 2014

Please Remain Seated, Thunder 2019

All The Right Noises, Thunder 2021

ROCKFIELD TIMELINE

1963 Studio opens for business.

1965 First use of accommodation.

1967 Dave Edmunds names the studio 'Rockfield'.

1969 Coach House studio is built.

1971 Black Sabbath rehearse material at Rockfield's Old Mill House facility for their second album *Paranoid*.

1971 Dave Edmunds gives Rockfield its first number one single with 'I Hear You Knocking'.

1971 Welsh rock band Budgie record the first of seven albums.

1972 Hawkwind spend September to October recording the first of many albums. Featuring Lemmy, *Doremi Fasol Latido* would make number 14 in the charts.

1973 Work starts on the Quadrangle studio.

1973 UFO record demos with Scorpions' guitarist Michael Schenker. Some of the tracks would make UFO's 1974 release *Phenomenon*.

1974 July to September sees Queen record their third album *Sheer Heart Attack*. It makes number 2 in the UK album charts and features the hit single 'Killer Queen'.

1974 Ace record their multimillion selling worldwide hit single 'How Long'.

1975 24 August. Queen return to Wales to start recording *A Night at the Opera*, which features the worldwide hit single 'Bohemian Rhapsody'.

1975 November/December. Judas Priest spend three weeks recording their second album *Sad Wings of Destiny*. The record earns a gold disc.

1975 Motörhead are born at Rockfield! The band spend from December through to January recording their debut album. It wouldn't be released until 1979 as *On Parole*.

1976 Former Deep Purple singer Ian Gillan mixes his *Clear Air Turbulence* album at Rockfield.

1977 Mid June. Rush spend three weeks recording the album *A Farewell To Kings*. It features the hit single 'Closer to the Heart' and goes platinum.

1977 October. Lead singer Ozzy Osbourne quits Black Sabbath for the first time while the band rehearse material for their next album *Never Say Die*. He returns to Rockfield, and the band, a few weeks later.

1978 June to July. Rush return to record *Hemispheres*. It's the band's fourth consecutive gold-selling album.

1978 The Stranglers record their third album *Black And White*.

1979 Iggy Pop records his *Soldier* album – produced by David Bowie.

1979 Simple Minds record *Real To Real Cacophony* – their second album.

1980 Echo and The Bunnymen record the first of three albums at Rockfield: *Crocodiles*

1980 Adam and the Ants record *Kings Of The Wild Frontier*, which spawns three hit singles including 'Antmusic'.

1981 Robert Plant records his first solo album since leaving Led Zeppelin. *Pictures at Eleven* is a top 5 hit on both sides of the Atlantic.

1982 Robert Plant and his band record the follow-up *The Principle of Moments*. Like its predecessor the album goes platinum.

1987 Clannad record *Sirius*.

1989 The Stone Roses arrive in January to record their debut album.

1990 Black Sabbath release the album *Tyr*, which was recorded at Rockfield with Tony Martin on vocals and the late Cozy Powell on drums.

1991 November sees XTC enter Rockfield to mix their hit album *Nonsuch*.

1992 In July, Black Sabbath release their second Rockfield-recorded album *Dehumanizer*, with Ronnie James Dio on vocals.

1994 The Stone Roses release their second album, *Second Coming* – recorded at Rockfield five years after their massive selling debut.

1995 September/October. The Boo Radleys score a number 1 hit album with their Rockfield-made *Wake Up*. It also featured the top ten single 'Wake Up Boo'.

1995 Oasis spend a fraught May recording one of the 1990s' biggest selling albums. *(What's the Story) Morning Glory?* sells more than 20 million copies.

1995 Black Grape's *It's Great When You're Straight … Yeah* goes to number 1 in the UK.

1996 January sees Ash put together their hit album *1977* at Rockfield. It includes the single 'Girl from Mars'.

1997 Top 10 hit for The Bluetones and their second album *Return to Last Chance Saloon*.

1998 Julian Lennon records the album *Photograph Smile*.

1998 September. XTC mix their *Apple Venus Vol 1* album at Rockfield.

1999 November. Coldplay start recording their huge-selling debut LP *Parachutes*.

2000 UFO bassist Pete Way records his debut solo album *Amphetamine*.

2000 December. New Order record their first album in seven years: *Get Ready*.

2001 In May, Starsailor spend six weeks recording their debut album *Love Is Here*.

2005 The Darkness arrive to record the follow-up to their hit album *Permission to Land* entitled *One Way Ticket To Hell … And Back*.

2005 Tokyo Dragons record *Give Me the Fear* – their debut CD.

2005 November. Kasabian head to Rockfield to record their second album *Empire* with Arctic Monkeys' producer Jim Abbiss.

2006 July. KT Tunstall arrives to start work on her second album, *Drastic Fantastic*.

2014 August sees the release of Royal Blood's self-titled debut album. It is well-received by critics and the Official UK Charts verify it as the fastest selling British rock debut album in three years in the UK.

2014 Also in August, Opeth release their eleventh studio album called *Pale Communion*.

2015 Thunder release their album *Wonder Days* in February. It becomes the first Thunder album to reach the UK Albums Chart top 10 since 1995's *Behind Closed Doors*.

2016 May. In the build-up to the album release, Opeth post the first *Sorceress: Studio Report* on their YouTube channel. Here it's confirmed that the band has returned to Rockfield Studios, where they previously recorded *Pale Communion*.

2017 Royal Blood release their second album, *How Did We Get So Dark?* on 16 June, preceded by the singles 'Lights Out', 'Hook, Line & Sinker' and 'I Only Lie When I Love You'. It debuts at number 1 in the UK.

2017 February sees Thunder release the follow-up to *Wonder Days*. *Rip It Up* reaches number 3 on the UK Albums Chart, marking the highest position achieved by the band since *Laughing on Judgement Day* made number 2 in 1992.

2019 It's January when Thunder issue *Please Remain Seated*. The album features twelve radically reworked songs from their 30-year career.

2020 October marks the release of *The Rockfield Files*, a four-track EP by English punk band The Damned. The title is a reference to the 1970s American TV series *The Rockford Files*.

2021 Despite the pandemic, March sees the release of new Thunder album *All The Right Noises*. The band promote the album with an online live special broadcast filmed at Rockfield.

2022 April. Thunder release their first-ever double album called *Dopamine*.

ACKNOWLEDGEMENTS

So many people have played important roles in helping me write this book. So many people have been so giving of their time and memories. It's been a pleasure to write and a delight to receive so much help and support.

Thanks to Lemmy for taking time out during Motörhead's 30th anniversary tour to speak to me about his time at Rockfield with both Motörhead and Hawkwind. His was the first interview and set the ball rolling.

Next up, former Rockfield producer John David was very kind in talking to me at his Berry Hill Studios in Gloucestershire. His insights into life at Rockfield form much of the opening chapter, and I could have spent many more hours listening to his humorous and fascinating tales. Dave Brock of Hawkwind has been a legend. He and his partner Kris Tait have been so extremely helpful – and that gave me plenty of encouragement early on. Huw Lloyd Langton was amazing in helping me fill in parts of the Hawkwind story at Rockfield, while bassist Alan Davey gave me one or two great anecdotes during the band's 2006 tour of the UK.

Many thanks also to Burke Shelley and Steve Williams from Budgie and to former Budgie drummer Ray Phillips. Also much appreciated was the helpfulness of the man who signed Budgie and Judas Priest, David Howells, who took time out of his busy day at his record company in London to talk to me and was always quick to answer any query I sent him by email.

Larry Wallis was superb in his humorous recollections of his time at Rockfield with Motörhead, while the band's producer Fritz Fryer was a star with his very funny and eloquent account of life in the studio with the world's loudest band.

Thanks to Peter Hince and Roy Thomas Baker for their help with the Queen and The Darkness sections, while Paul Carrack was another true star with his tales from Ace's time playing football – sorry recording music – at Rockfield and for sending me a wonderful photo of the band in action. Playing football, not recording!!! Talking of photos, Michael Spencer Jones deserves major credit for his excellent photographs from his time with Oasis and his magnificent interview about his time with the band.

Ray Fenwick and Jeffery Calvert also deserve special thanks for their contributions. Ray, in particular, was frequently a great source of help. And thanks to Rush lead singer Geddy Lee for taking time away from recording the band's *Snakes & Arrows* album in Canada to speak to me.

Much special thanks must go to the Robert Plant band. These guys got back together on 15 May 2006 at Rockfield, 25 years after they first worked there. It was a very special day. Robert Plant was a delight to interview, Jezz Woodroffe has been unstintingly helpful (also on the Black Sabbath chapter) as has Robbie Blunt. Phil Collins couldn't be there but answered all my questions from New York and sent an email message to his former bandmates.

Big thanks to Graham Wright for talking to me about his time as a roadie with Black Sabbath. He and fellow roadie, Les Martin, took time out while on tour with The Rolling Stones in Cardiff to regale me with many humorous stories.

Many, many special thanks also to Ray Martinez, Paul Read, John Leckie, Bruce Findlay, Lee Slater, Paul Di'Anno, Tigertailz, Ian McNabb, Jim Abbiss, Steve Osbourne, Pedro Ferreira, Neil Murray, Vinny Appice, Nick Byng, KT Tunstall and her management, Rush's management, Work Hard PR, Ian Gillan's website, *Caramba!* and Paul Cobbold.

From The Darkness, Richie Edwards was fantastic and so generously helpful with an almost never-ending round of great stories.

Top marks also to the Tokyo Dragons, the next people, after Lemmy, to be interviewed. I met with them on a number of occasions during